MENTAL RETARDATION

Mental Retardation

A Phenomenological Approach

Edited by

JERRY JACOBS, Ph.D.

Professor of Sociology
Syracuse University
Syracuse, New York

CHARLES C THOMAS · PUBLISHER
Springfield · Illinois · U.S.A.

Published and Distributed Throughout the World by
CHARLES C THOMAS • PUBLISHER
Bannerstone House

301-327 East Lawrence Avenue, Springfield, Illinois, U.S.A.
This book is protected by copyright. No part of it
may be reproduced in any manner without written
permission from the publisher.

© *1980, by* CHARLES C THOMAS • PUBLISHER
ISBN 0-398-04062-1 cloth
ISBN 0-398-04063-x paper
Library of Congress Catalog Card Number: 80-10988

Library of Congress Cataloging in Publication Data
Main entry under title:

Mental retardation, a phenomenological approach.

Bibliography: p.
Includes index.
1.   Mental deficiency.   2.   Mentally handicapped
—Care and treatment.   3.   Mentally handicapped
children—Care and treatment.   I.   Jacobs, Jerry.
RC570.M393   616.85'88   80-10988
ISBN 0-398-04062-1
ISBN 0-398-04063-X pbk.

Printed in the United States of America
W-2

CONTRIBUTORS

BERCOVICI, SYLVIA MESSINA: Socio-Behavioral Group, Neuro-psychiatric Institute, University of California Medical Center, Los Angeles.

BJANNES, ARNE T.: Center for the Study of Community Perspectives, P.O. Box 66, Patton, CA 92369.

EASTERDAY, LOIS M.: Department of Sociology, Syracuse University, Syracuse, NY 13210.

GALLIMORE, RONALD: Mental Retardation Research Center, Neuropsychiatric Institute, School of Medicine, University of California, Los Angeles.

GOODE, DAVID A.: Department of Sociology, University of California, Los Angeles.

JACOBS, JERRY: Department of Sociology, Syracuse University, Syracuse, NY 13210.

LANGNESS, L. L.: Mental Retardation Research Center, Neuropsychiatric Institute, School of Medicine, University of California, Los Angeles.

LEVINE, HAROLD G.: Graduate School of Education, University of California, Los Angeles.

RYAVE, ALAN L.: Department of Sociology, California State University, Dominguez Hills.

ZETLIN, ANDREA G.: Mental Retardation Research Center, Neuropsychiatric Institute, School of Medicine, University of California, Los Angeles.

INTRODUCTION

T his book is divided into five sections: clinical outlooks on mental retardation; the question of competence among the retarded; the effects of mental retardation upon the family; educating the retarded; and studies of the life of the retarded in institutional settings.

While some of these topics have been dealt with elsewhere in the literature, they have not often been dealt with in the way that they are presented here. For example, one does not often encounter in the literature studies in which the researcher tries to simulate the physical handicaps of those he studies in order to experience the world as they do, studies based upon the conversational analysis of naturally occurring conversations between retarded persons, autobiographical accounts of the retarded themselves, or disruption experiments involving retarded adults.

This work then does not claim to canvass the literature and offer a representative sampling of sociological and/or psychological research on mental retardation. Rather, it offers a select but unique view of the retarded and the problems confronting them and their families. The methodologies vary. The researchers invoke participant observation, experimental design, conversational analysis, simulation studies of various aspects of mental retardation and autobiographical accounts. These studies illustrate a wide range of points and recommend a number of policy changes. Notwithstanding the different methods of data collection and analysis, all fall under the general heading of phenomenological research. Such studies offer the reader not only a different way of seeing, but something different to look at.

CONTENTS

MENTAL RETARDATION

SECTION I

MENTAL RETARDATION:
CLINICAL OUTLOOKS

CHAPTER 1

THE CLINICAL ORGANIZATION OF "SUBNORMALITY": A CASE OF MISTAKEN IDENTITY

JERRY JACOBS

In his essay "Tacit Knowledge of Everyday Activities," Cicourel states that sociologists "seldom concern themselves with the properties of everyday social life" but take them for granted. Furthermore, both the "natural" and "laboratory" events studied "are not established by asking first what a 'natural order' is like, and then what it would take to generate activities members . . . would label 'unnatural' or 'natural.' Instead, the problems taken as points of departure are assumed to be 'obvious' instances of *the* 'real world.'" Any sociologist insisting that such a study should begin with an examination of the properties of routine practical activities in everyday life "is not likely to meet with the approval of colleagues who have already decided what the 'real world' is all about, and they have already been studying 'it' for a long time."[1]

This description of certain key assumptions routinely made by sociologists applies equally well to psychiatrists. Psychiatrists also take as a point of departure the "obvious" instances of the "real world," without being overly concerned about what it would take to generate activities that members of society would label "unnatural." I will be concerned in this paper with psychiatrists who evaluate the possibility of mental retardation in children, and with the ways in which these evaluations generate and preserve certain categories of mental retardation. I will also

From Jerry Jacobs (ed.), *Deviance: Field Studies and Self-Disclosures,* Palo Alto: Mayfield Publishers, 1974. Reprinted by permission.

consider the reasons why these categories do not seem "unnatural" to those who accept and perpetuate them. I will begin by considering one class of "severely retarded" children—nonverbal, nontestable children with no discernible organic pathology —and the general belief among physicians that all children so diagnosed relatively late in childhood have no prospect of ever achieving a normal or above-normal level of intellectual performance. When such children have miraculous recoveries later in life, it is invariably held, in retrospect, that they were wrongly diagnosed to begin with; that is, it is usually assumed that the retardation must have been a case of childhood schizophrenia all along. On the other hand, when children who had been diagnosed as childhood schizophrenics miraculously recover, it is *not* assumed that they might have recovered from severe retardation, or from a combination of schizophrenia and retardation. The evidence seems not to warrant such assumptions, especially when it is so difficult to establish the existence or influence of either schizophrenia or retardation at the time of the diagnosis,[2] let alone several years later. The issue is further complicated by the fact that so many of these cases seem to carry a mixed diagnosis of severe retardation and childhood schizophrenia, with an emphasis on one or the other.[3]

A question then arises. Why, in cases of miraculous recovery (the recovery of children initially diagnosed as severely retarded and later found to possess a normal or above-normal level of intelligence), it is invariably assumed in retrospect that the inconsistency found between the physician's initial prognosis and the child's later performance is best explained by presuming against the original diagnosis? A more convincing hypothesis in many of these cases seems to be that severe mental retardation, at least in the class of children noted above, is sometimes reversible. The reason why this latter position is never entertained, let alone accepted, must be sought in the fact that it is a psychiatrist who is later called upon to rationalize any apparent contradiction found between the anticipated "before" and the resulting "after." This they do by entertaining the possibility of an original faulty diagnosis and then accepting this possibility as "given." The reason for this is to a large extent based upon the psychiatrists' prior "background expectancies,"[4] which in turn rest upon certain assumptions given in the medical model of mental retardation and assimilated by physicians in the course of their professional training. These have been succinctly presented by a popular and influential spokesman as follows: "In the light of present knowledge, mental retardation is essentially irreversible. This does not deny the possibility of prevention or amelioration; but though many therapies and other maneuvers have been hailed, few have survived the test of time. Preventive measures . . . have had some limited success; but *adequately diagnosed mental retardation probably never is reversed to normal* [Emphasis added.]."[5]

Psychiatrists are subject to other constraints in their attempt to rationalize "contradictory" findings. This depends upon their acceptance of some generally held position on mental retardation, which in turn is determined to a large extent by the assumptions and practices of the particular institution or agency they work for. Garfinkel has formulated the general case of this influence as follows: "In short, *recognizable* sense, or fact, or methodic character, or impersonality, or objectivity of accounts are not independent of the socially organized occasions of their use. Their rational features *consist* of what members do with, what they 'make of' the accounts in the socially organized actual occasions of their use. Members' accounts are reflexively and essentially tied for their rational features to the socially organized occasions of their use, for they are *features* of the socially organized occasions of their use."[6]

For example, a psychiatrist—a consultant at several children's services—recently told me of a case where he had occasion to see the same child in five different clinical settings, and in each instance the child received a different diagnosis. In a psychiatrically oriented evaluation center, "nonverbal" "nontestable" children without discernible organic pathologies are likely to be diagnosed as cases of "childhood schizophrenia," whereas in an "organically" oriented center they are likely to be diagnosed as "brain-damaged." One authority has referred to "The diagnostic schizophrenia that exists in many states—in this commonwealth, for example—where certified psychiatrists in one institution claim a patient is primarily retarded, whereas in another they say, with the same conviction, that the person is primarily psychotic or mentally ill, making an individual patient a virtual football between two teams of experts. The commissioner in the state house usually referees these games."[7]

This practice is so routinely accepted that an authority on mental retardation lecturing to an audience of doctors I was attending, got a big laugh by opening with this gambit: "Let's see, I must get oriented. Am I lecturing at X clinic or Y clinic? Oh, yes, this is X clinic; they're all schizophrenic here, aren't they?"

Apart from the inconsistencies in orientation and practice, the confusion of terminology within any one camp can be overwhelming. The use of the terms "functional mental retardation" and "mental deficiency" is a case in point. Functional retardation means that the child is functioning at a subnormal level of intelligence; in addition, it is inferred that the child may possess the potential to operate at a much higher level of intelligence than his current performance would indicate. Autistic children are often given this diagnosis. Whereas those who are "functionally retarded" may improve even to the point of achieving a normal level of intellectual performance, those who are "mentally deficient" are given no hope of recovery. Mental deficiency usually assumes organic pathology for which no known remedy exists. Where it is impossible to isolate the particular organic pathology that a diagnosis of "mental deficiency" implies, such pathologies are not infrequently inferred on the basis of "clinical insight." Then, too, there is considerable disagreement among practitioners regarding the concept of childhood schizophrenia. For example, some consider the terms autism and childhood schizophrenia to be synonymous, while others believe they are distinct entities.[8]

Quite apart from whether or not they are the same, there arises the prior question of what they are: "In planning such corrective remediation, the therapist inevitably assumes a theory of etiology though it is most often more implicit than explicit . . . Indeed, one must not lose sight of the additional fact that the descriptive entity childhood schizophrenia is grossly defined and differences among the children within any schizophrenic sample are as striking as are the similarities. Certainly the notion of a disease in the sense of a single definable pathologic agent remote in time, an inevitable course of development, and a predetermined course of treatment is still a mythical one."[9]

Arbitrary distinctions such as those we have noted need not cause undue confusion here if we keep in mind that among the class of children being discussed, the position of the medical community is that those whose intellectual performance reaches or exceeds the normal level at some later date are by definition not "really" retarded (for example, in the case of childhood schizophrenia), whereas those whose I.Q.'s do not reach a normal level at some later time are considered retarded or retarded and schizophrenic.

The popularity of this medical position notwithstanding an alternative hypothesis can be drawn: severe mental retardation, at least in some instances and for whatever reasons, is reversible. Furthermore, since it is extremely difficult to determine in the above instance whether a child is autistic or retarded or both (or what these terms mean), one cannot help but wonder if some cases of miraculous recovery by "autistic" or "schizophrenic" children were not instances of recovery by retarded children.

I will present in the remainder of this paper well-documented case history material and verbatim accounts which will indicate the difficulty often encountered in establishing the etiology of retardation in cases of nonverbal, nontestable children. This will be followed by a discussion of a case of miraculous recovery diagnosed as childhood schizophrenia, where there was good reason to suppose that retardation was also a factor. Finally, two cases will be cited to show how, when a diagnosis of severe retardation proved "erroneous" because of the individual's complete recovery, it was accepted as given that the error lay in the diagnosis, and not with the commonly held view that the intellectual functioning of *all* "severely retarded" children of the class noted above is somehow permanently impaired.

I will begin by pointing out how difficult it is to establish the "etiology" of mental retardation. Edgerton has noted over one hundred "causes" of retardation in the literature.[10] Another authoritative source gives twice this number.[11] As things currently stand, it is the exceptional case that allows for a causal relationship to be shown. "With present knowledge regarding the causal factors in mental retardation, it is possible to identify precise causes in approximately 15 to 25 percent of cases. In such cases, organic pathology as a result of disease or injuries is often demonstrable, most readily in instances where the degree of retardation is severe and there has been gross brain damage."[12]

The problem of isolating the causal factor or factors in retardation for the group of children being considered here is graphically illustrated by the following case history. What is to be presented below is not an entire case history but only a series of relevant excerpts taken from the case history accounts.[13]

Case No. 1

Paul is a seven-and-a-half year-old Caucasian boy. Both parents are professionals, well-educated, and occupy a high socioeconomic status. Paul is nonverbal, nontestable, and not toilet trained. He seemed to develop normally until about the age of nine months. It first came to the mother's attention at that point that Paul was "slow," and they began to be concerned about his rate of development. In 1961, at the request of their pediatrician, Paul's parents took him for a psychological examination. In March of that year, his I.Q. on the Kuhmann and Cottel scales was 74 and 61 respectively. By August, his I.Q. on the same scales was 55 and 46. In August of 1962 he was tested a third time by the same doctor (one of some eminence in the field of retardation) and his performance had regressed to I.Q. 31 and 28. The diagnosis and prognosis was stated as follows: "There can be no question of this child's retardation, and the failure to make any progress on the tests during a year, all of which were given by me, indicates lack of ability to develop beyond the infantile stage." Paul's parents went to great lengths to establish the reasons for his retardation. Every effort was made to isolate the causal factors. He has undergone psychological testing, observations, chromosome analysis, pneumoencephalogram, EEG, neurological exams, skull films, and more.

All findings were either negative or sufficiently ambiguous to exclude the possibility of any definite conclusions being drawn. The case records note: "Paul's current status is an enigma. No medical person has been able to give a diagnosis of his condition. The Joneses have been to a series of professionals, all apparently quite eminent people."

The professionals' inability to offer a reason for Paul's retardation presented the parents with a series of dilemmas. For example, should they have another child? The case record notes that when Paul's parents put this question to the geneticist, "he could not predict what the chances were of their having another retarded child and made no recommendation as to whether they should have other children." On the other hand, their pediatrician recommended that the Joneses have more children and have Paul put in an institution. Another question was what could they realistically expect of Paul. Whereas the doctor who tested Paul felt he would not progress beyond the infantile level, others were more cautious in their prognosis, since the cause of his retardation could not be established.

The contrary inferences drawn by different professionals regarding the same piece of information has led to much frustration and anxiety for Paul's parents. This account is not intended to reflect upon the competence of practitioners (although this is sometimes an important factor); it is intended only to give some indication of how difficult it can be to establish the cause or causes of retardation, even among the "severely retarded," where it is supposed to be most easily established.

Problems of diagnosis, as previously noted, result from more than the imperfect state of the medical sciences. They are also a function of the orientation of the particular agency for which the clinician works. In this regard, we find that Paul has recently undergone another medical and psychological evaluation at still another agency. There he was diagnosed as both "severely retarded" and "psychotic." The prognosis for his future development is poor. An optimistic prediction at this point would be that he is "trainable." The current evaluation, like the past ones, has left the question of the cause or causes of Paul's retardation unanswered. Furthermore, it has added for the first time to the long-standing diagnosis of "severe retardation" the diagnosis of "psychosis."

The next case presents an example of a diagnosis of childhood schizophrenia being made where the question of mental retardation cannot easily be ruled out. Retardation in this case was deemphasized in much the same manner that childhood schizophrenia was in the preceding case.

Case No. 2

Joanne is a thirteen-year-old Caucasian girl who lives with her mother. The father and mother are divorced. When first seen in 1959 Joanne was five years old and characterized as isolated, "bordering on mutism," and nontestable. All physical, neurological, and laboratory findings were within normal limits. Her diagnosis at the time was "schizophrenic reaction, childhood type." By 1961 the psychologist stated: "In summary, Joanne's functioning is on such a higher, more integrated level than at the previous evaluation that an I.Q. test can be administered to her." Upon testing she was found to be *"in the upper range of borderline defective level."* [Emphasis added].

In 1964 the psychologist's report stated: "Joanne readily understands highly abstract concepts . . . her test responses as well as her behavior indicate many changes during the last one and a half years. Her performance on the Information and Similarities Subtests and Sequin Form Board were adequate, and her spontaneous use of language suggest above average verbal ability."

Currently, Joanne is thirteen and has just completed the sixth grade of normal classes in public school. The case record notes: "She is very verbal and demonstrates an above average intellectual endowment. The reader will, no doubt, be struck by the marked difference in the case summary of 1959 of an autistic child 'bordering on mutism.'"

The first two cases were both instances of mixed diagnosis, the first with an emphasis on retardation, the second with an emphasis on childhood schizophrenia.

The third case, to be presented next, was also one of a mixed diagnosis, in which the diagnosis of retardation in childhood was replaced ex post facto with a diagnosis of childhood schizophrenia; currently neither the retardation nor the schizophrenia is in evidence. In none of these three cases were the clinicians involved able to offer a more or less conclusive statement regarding the etiology of either the retardation or the childhood schizophrenia.

Case No. 3

Johnny is a fifteen year-old Caucasian boy who lives with his mother and two siblings. The father died in 1956. The case record notes: "John's development was slow from the beginning. He sat at nine months and did not start to walk until age two. He had no speech until age 6. He could not yet distinguish colors at the age of six. At age five, mother attempted to enroll him in kindergarten. He sat in the middle of the classroom screaming, soiled and smeared himself and all he could reach. Mother was asked not to bring him back. He was seen by a psychiatrist at that time and diagnosed as mentally retarded . . . and needing special education, to be started at age eight."

For the next three years, Johnny did not attend school and was kept at home. Most of his early years were spent in England. There were a number of moves during this time, and when he was ten his mother enrolled him in a special school in Germany. "He was there evaluated by a German psychiatrist in a residential setting. The conclusion was that John was not retarded, but rather, severely neurotic. John did very well in the special school. In six weeks he learned German and caught up with the class."

Johnny remained in the special school until he was fourteen. By then he had learned to read and write. At the age of fourteen he was no longer eligible to remain at the school because of an age limitation. His mother emigrated to the United States and Johnny, because of his past history of "retardation," was initially enrolled in an "educable" class for the mentally retarded within the public school system. It was soon apparent that he was capable of normal work and he was placed in regular classes. He is now enrolled in junior high school in regular classes and getting A's and B's.

An explanation of John's recovery with respect to the diagnosis of mental retardation is noted in the case records as follows: "In childhood, John was severely retarded and was apparently suffering from a psychosis which is not apparent at all at present."

"Severely retarded" as used here referred to severe "functional retardation," a distinction previously noted. I believe that there is good reason to question this diagnosis imposed by hindsight. John's slow development indicated retardation, his past social and intellectual performance indicated retardation, and he was diagnosed professionally by a psychiatrist at age five as being retarded. To suddenly state in retrospect, in the light of his recovery, that the retardation was in fact a case of childhood schizophrenia (he was diagnosed as "severely neurotic" at age ten) is a position that is not easily tenable. It seems to me more reasonable to suppose that he was in fact severely retarded and for some reason recovered. Such a position was not even entertained by a group of psychiatrists who heard this case. Indeed, they all spontaneously enjoyed a good laugh at the "obvious error" of the original diagnosis. Nor was this case unique. Several others of this kind have been brought to the author's attention within a single clinical setting. A final one is offered for the reader's consideration.

Case No. 4

Joan is a four-year-old Caucasian girl who resides with her foster mother. She was first seen at the age of two and a half, when she was functioning at the six-month level. The case record states: "Diagnostic impression was mental deficiency, severe idiopathic, with severe stress being extreme emotional deprivation and lack of care by parents." Joan was unable to walk or talk and was totally unresponsive to her environment. Her behavior was characterized as "essentially placid and unresponsive." Prior to this, she had received an in-patient medical evaluation elsewhere and was found to be "physically and mentally retarded without specific detectable cause."

A few months after she was first seen, she was taken from the care of her natural mother and placed in the care of a foster mother. Within the period of about a year, Joan had shown striking progress. "She now feeds herself well, is completely toilet-trained, well-groomed, verbal, affectionate and responsive to adults, and engaging in play with obvious pleasure with other children."

It is true that Joan still shows some residual symptoms in terms of her prior emotional disturbance. However, the case record states: "It was clear a striking change in this girl had occurred in response to a change in her mothering relationship. In a few months' time, a girl who had originally been considered to be severely mentally defective at the late age of two and a half years demonstrated capacity for rapid growth and development, physical, mental, and emotional . . . The diagnosis of severe mental deficiency is of course not appropriate at this point and further evaluation is indicated to clarify the nature and extent of her emotional disturbance as well as more definite evaluation of the degree of any remaining functional retardation as indicated perhaps in her play and speech."

There is no way to know for certain whether Joan will eventually reach a normal level of intellectual performance. However, based upon her miraculous rate of development in the past year or so, there are at the very least promising indications. It seems almost certain that she will reach at least a level of "mild retardation" and may well go on to become a normally intelligent child.

How many other cases of this kind can be brought to light is a question that warrants our attention. An attempt at a systematic collection of recorded cases of miraculous recovery among "severely retarded" or "autistic" children and a reevaluation of these and new cases in the light of the above analysis might prove very rewarding, given the serious implications for diagnosis and treatment of accepting per se the widely held set of assumptions described above.

The key question is really whether or not in the case of miraculous recovery of nonverbal, nontestable children (when no organic pathological cause can be established) from a state of severe retardation to one of normal or above-normal intellectual functioning, it needs to be assumed that the potential to realize this new intellectual level had always existed in the individual and that it remained only to liberate it. Case history accounts indicate that the potential necessary to perform at a normal or above-normal level of intelligence may be lost at one point and recovered at some later period. Should this prove to be true, the prognosis for the class of severely retarded children discussed in this paper may not be so hopeless as is now supposed. The author believes that in light of the evidence, this possibility has been too quickly and easily disposed of—or perhaps more accurately, has not yet been entertained.

REFERENCES

1. Aaron V. Cicourel. *The social organization of juvenile justice* (New York: John Wiley and Sons, Inc., 1968), pp. 3-4.
2. S. A. Szurek and I. Philips. "Mental Retardation and Psychotherapy," in *Prevention and treatment of mental retardation,* Ed. I. Philips (New York: Basic Books, 1966), p. 221.
3. Lauretta Bender. "Childhood Schizophrenia: A Review," *Journal of the Hillside Hospital,* 16 (1), January 1967, pp. 10-20.
4. Harold Garfinkel. *Studies in ethnomethodology* (Englewood Cliffs, N.J.: Prentice-Hall, 1967), pp. 35-65.
5. E. A. Doll. Recognition of Mental Retardation in the School-Age Child, in *Prevention and treatment of mental retardation,* Ed. I. Philips (New York: Basic Books, 1966), p. 62.
6. Garfinkel. *Studies in Ethnomethodology,* pp. 3-4.
7. A statement made by Dr. Peter Bowman, Superintendent, Pineland Hospital and Training Center, Maine, in the *PCMR Message,* No. 11, April 1968, p. 1.
8. B. Pasamanick. Etiologic Factors in Early Infantile Autism and Childhood Schizophrenia, *Journal of the Hillside Hospital,* 16 (1), January 1967, pp. 42-52.
9. William Goldfarb. Corrective Socialization: A Rationale for the Treatment of Schizophrenic Children, *Journal of the Hillside Hospital,* 16 (1), January 1967, pp. 58-71.
10. Robert B. Edgerton. *The cloak of competence* (Berkeley: University of California Press, 1967), p. 2.
11. Mental Retardation, reprinted from the *Journal of the American Medical Association,* Vol. 191, No. 3, January 18, 1965, p. 1.
12. President's Panel on Mental Retardation, *A proposed program for national action to combat mental retardation* (Washington, D.C.: U.S. Government Printing Office, 1962), pp. 6-7. Also see "Mental Retardation," p. 1.
13. The following excerpts are taken from the case history accounts of a large metropolitan clinic offering treatment and evaluation services for the mentally ill and mentally retarded. All names, dates, and places have been changed to insure the anonymity of the patients.

CHAPTER 2

PERPLEXITY, CONFUSION AND SUSPICION: A STUDY OF SELECTED FORMS OF DOCTOR-PATIENT INTERACTIONS

JERRY JACOBS

Abstract

This paper is concerned with two popular explanations of three common psychological states—perplexity, confusion and suspicion, as they occur within the context of doctor-patient interactions. It is generally held by practitioners that the above are symptomatic of (1) a failure of personality-maturation or disordered personality-functioning, or (2) an unconscious defense mechanism which functions to allay excessive anxiety which threatens to disrupt interpersonal relations. The author will provide a third explanation of their origins, i.e. the above psychological states are a natural consequence of the ambiguities stemming from the doctor-patient interactions themselves. The author will deal with five forms of doctor-patient interactions in which the doctor's handling of the transfer of information played a key role in establishing feelings of perplexity, confusion and suspicion in the mothers of retarded children.

SEARLES, IN AN article entitled "Concerning a Psychodynamic Function of Perplexity, Confusion and Suspicion and Related Mental States[1]," notes two general orientations towards confusion. The first tends to view confusion ". . . solely as a relative static inert, troublesome product of failure in personality-maturation or, when examined more closely, as the again relatively inert result of various underlying causes having to do with disordered personality-functioning[1]." A second perspective, a minority position, notes that "Nowhere, except in the previously

From Jerry Jacobs, "Perplexity, confusion and suspicion: A study of selected forms of doctor-patient interactions," *Social Science and Medicine*, Vol. 5, pp. 151-157, London: Pergamon Press, 1971. Reprinted by permission.

mentioned paper by Freud have I found presented a viewpoint which regards them (perplexity, confusion and suspicion) as being representative not only of failure in maturation but also of a very active striving on the part of the personality to cope with quantities of anxiety which threaten to disrupt the inter-personal situation[1]." Searles' article deals primarily with a study of the latter position. In a retrospective analysis of a series of psychoanalytic interviews with his patients, Searles discusses the ways in which he and the patient inadvertently contributed to inducing states of perplexity, confusion and suspicion, that either or both felt at one time or another during the course of therapy. The dynamics of these interactions are dealt with from within a psychoanalytic frame of reference.

The author will present another perspective from which to view the perplexity, confusion and suspicion that doctor-patient interactions not infrequently generate. The perspective to be adopted here will be a conscious-rational interactionist analysis of doctor-patient interactions. The source of data will be the transcribed verbatim accounts of a series of interviews the author conducted with mothers of retarded children, which focussed upon the nature and consequences of their interactions with physicians in the course of seeking help for their retarded child.

The general consensus of the parents interviewed was that most of these interactions with physicians resulted in unsatisfactory encounters from the point of view of the child and family. The forms of interactions that parents experienced which left them generally perplexed, confused and/or suspicious of professional opinions and/or practices will be dealt with below. To better understand the process which led to these negative consequences, consider the verbatim accounts of three of the mothers in the author's series.[2]

Mother: Well, do you want to start from the time he was born?
Int.: Yeah. Right.
Mother: All right. He was born premature and at the age of three months he had meningitis. And as far as anyone knows, the meningitis is what has retarded him. It's not fact. It's just theory, that's what they think. They don't know that he wasn't born like this, but they said that meningitis left him with the cerebral palsy condi-

tion. So this is what we work on. And he has progressed very slow up until his 6 years and the nicest thing that ever happened was getting him to come out to the Pre-school, because up until then we just got kind of shuffled back and forth from one place to another. We had ordered a psychological evaluation on Eric and they told me that they had set up a date for it and had ordered it and so I took Eric out and had his evaluation and that was the last I heard of it except when I got the bill for $17.50. I never heard anything from it. Nothing. And that was my biggest complaint about the situation; everytime you ask a question, you're answered with a question. There's no, there's no facts given. And I don't think it's really fair because when you go into this, it's new, it's never happened to you before, you don't know what to expect, you don't know which way to turn, or where to go . . .

Int.: Was one of the things you were worrying about, thinking about then, how much Eric would develop and how far you could expect him to go and what to expect of him?

Mother: Right. We still don't know. We still don't know. We just go from day to day and I assume he will talk eventually because he does have speech. He does say "Ma Ma." He can say "No." His speech is there, but how much he will ever talk is another question too that there's no answer to. But we were also told he wouldn't walk and he walks now. So we just are patient now, and I'm sure he'll say something eventually, when . . . that's another thing. Of course that's something you can't do anything about. You just have to wait for it.

Int.: How did you and your husband feel when you first found out about the retardation and when he got meningitis and so on, those kinds of things?

Mother: Well, the meningitis was a very bad thing because we didn't know if he was going to live or not. There was two weeks there that I didn't know. At the end of two weeks my doctor told me that there was no doubt that Eric would survive. And the thing from then on was to prevent damage to his body, his facilities. So we just . . . he went from then on, my doctor went under the assumption that he was deaf, for the simple reason that in 90 percent of the cases of meningitis that he had been affiliated with, deafness was the handicap that was left. So he assumed that Eric's slowness was because he was deaf. And after Eric was about a year old, we kept insisting that he could hear. We kept insisting that he could hear, he could hear. And finally when he was two, the doctors really understood that Eric could hear. We got a radio out and turned it on and he knew then. So we went for hearing tests. Well of course when he had the hearing tests and the hearing tested out fine, then he told me maybe we weren't quite so lucky. Because it would have been easier if he had been deaf. Because when it wasn't the hearing, it was mental . . .

Int.: How did that take you and your husband when you heard about it?

Mother: Well, you don't know what to think because you really don't know what's wrong with him. And you go into this just like you're blindfolded and nobody says anything. I . . . to this day I don't know whether they actually classify Eric as brain-damaged or mentally retarded, or what.

Int.: Did you try to call them or find out what . . .

Mother: Well, we had consultations and it just seems like it's one big series of questions, questions, questions, questions. And the doctor said that . . . the last time I spoke with her that . . . which was after the evaluation, that Eric would never walk, that he would probably walk with crutches, but that he wouldn't be able to walk and that we would have to be prepared to find permanent care for Eric. And she, at the time, did not elaborate on . . .

Int.: . . . where or how or . . .

Mother: . . . or how much, or anything like that. And of course I have Eric with me most of the time. By the time you get through getting questioned, you're ready to go home. And there's nothing really definite, no. So we just go from one place to the next and from one day to the next. It's just such . . . nothing is down in black and white. I know he's had an EEG, but what that showed— there was never anything done. My own doctor finally told me that if they ever decided to do another one that it wouldn't show anything only that Eric had an abnormal brain pattern. But other than that, it wouldn't show anything. So it's just been more or less a matter of somebody throwing you in the water and you just have to learn to swim, that's what it is. It's an awful, awful thing because it seems like you're just never going to find your way out of it, this maze that you're in.

A second mother had this to say:

Mother: It more or less started out like this. When Norman was born, everything went normal and I had an old-fashioned doctor who didn't believe in telling the parents. When Norman was six months old he came down with bronchial pneumonia and almost died. And we rushed him into the hospital. And they told us he was mongoloid. And I couldn't accept it and neither did he. But ah, so then he was in there for about a week and I took him out and took him in to my own doctor which I had when I was pregnant with Norman and he told me at that time that he was mongoloid, which was six months later. So I was very upset and so was my husband and I didn't want any more kids and then I found out I was already pregnant two months with my last child. So that complicated matters all the more. For about 6 months, I myself think I lived in a nightmare is the way that I felt about it . . . I think it's been the worse . . . when it's come to almost losing him, and in April the doctor told us, it was just that close. And ah, at the time when it happened, I called my husband up and of course, just like he said and just like we had talked about later and like I mentioned a minute ago, with Norman you have to rush and when he's working he just can't drop everything and rush off to be with me, and so I went through that episode by myself. And it was rough. I sat up with him all night before he went into the hospital. Then I called the doctor throughout the night and he was telling me what to do and I kept telling him that nothing was helping, and he wouldn't believe me and we've been on the outs about that for quite a while now. My private physician for my children doesn't really even talk about Norman to me. In fact the first time I ever met this doctor I walked into his office and he says, you know, eventually you'll have to have this boy institutionalized. And I looked at him and I thought: yeah, from your viewpoint, but not from mine. Because I knew right then and there that my husband and I had gone through that experience once before and it was no fun. (The child had been institutionalized for a 6-month period when he was 1½ years old.) I mean I'd rather keep him at home with me and pick up after him 24 hours a day than say: here son you're going over here and have him lose everything that it's taken him seven years to gain. And so at that time, I says, yeah, maybe. He's never brought it up again, and whenever I try to start a conversation about Norman, he's you know . . . hmmmmmmmmmmmmmmm I've got to do this and that—he just has no interest in talking about it.

Int.: Did you ever talk to any other doctors about it?

Mother: I talked to the doctor when we were going in for an evaluation.

Int.: Mmmmmmmm. What did they think there?

Mother: Well, he more or less feels that he hopes and thinks that Norman may talk some day because on the test that he had he was coming along pretty good, his IQ as I remember he said was approximately 4 which he didn't feel was very bad for Norman—it was about half of what it should be. And so that made me feel fairly good. One doctor felt that Norman may not be a mongoloid, that he may just have hyperthyroid, and my hopes went up zoom—straight up in the air, if you know what I mean. And then I started thinking and going back in my mind to all the doctors that I have spoken to, just briefly, and they all said, well he's mongoloid. And I mean for just one doctor to pop up out of the clear blue sky and say well, it might not be, I just couldn't believe it. And so I went back in to see my private physician and took Norman with me and I told him about it. And he says, Norman is mongoloid. He says he has no hyperthyroid condition at all. And I says, OK. So I mean, zoom, . . . right back down again. And, ah, so we just live with the fact that he's mongoloid. Now then my doctor did say something just last week when I took him to see about a cold that Norman's had. And I said, the life expandment on these retarded children is getting longer, isn't it. And he said, yes it is. I mean you try to strike up something and he just answers you with a short comment and turns you right off. So I mean, I can't say: Sit down. We're going to talk about it. Because I mean I just haven't got that in me either. And I feel if he doesn't want to talk about it, I'm not going to force him. . . . But there's really nothing I want to know more about Norman, not at the immediate time. But it just kind of . . . I like to hear the doctor say himself how he feels Norman is coming along. You know, is there progress? Is it getting more worse? Do you think he may learn this? How far will he get with this? And stuff like that. That's what I would like him to tell me."

A third mother gave this account:

Int.: When did you find out officially about it? (the child's retardation).

Mother: Well, I found out after months of this kind of thing day and night; the child not eating and begging my physician to do something, do something. Is there something wrong. And he didn't answer me. Then when she was 5 months old, he gave me phenobarbitol to give her. And I was trying to give it to her and she fought against anything being put in her mouth. Which is a peculiar thing, the easiest thing to do is to eat, to drink. And she gasped when I put the spoon in her mouth and she began to choke and make peculiar sounds and I thought she was choking to death, and she'd inhalated the phenobarb and I knew it was very serious to have fluid in your lungs, you could drown on a teaspoon, a baby could. So I snatched her up and rushed her to the emergency room at the hospital. And they took one look at her and called upstairs for a pediatrician, a resident. A young Chinese woman doctor came down and she said, she asked me things that frightened me, that were more frightening than anybody telling me. She said what does the physician say about this edema. Edema! I thought she just had bad feet and bad hands. And I knew what edema was. Nothing, he hasn't said anything. And she mentioned the child's features and everything, her development; she couldn't shut her hand on anything. Anyway this young doctor said her lungs were clear, but she said a lot of other things by these questions, in just getting the history which she needed, she told me a lot. I went home and I called my doctor and I was crying. He'd never heard me cry before. I'd cried a lot, but never in front of him.

Int.: Was this a private physician?

Mother: Yes. Dr. G. I said that she said some awful things to me about the child's eyes, about the edema, about the features, about her development. And I said, up until now I've been saying, is there something wrong. Now, good God, I know there's something wrong. I've known it all along, why . . . you know, what is wrong—not, is there? And he said, I will come by your house in the morning. Well, he had never done anything like that before. He said, I want to talk to you. And I'll see you at 7:30 before I start my rounds. Well, he couldn't have said . . . it was like the death sentence. I cried and cried and screamed all night long. Because his saying "I'll come" meant it's happening. Everything you feared is true. And he came and he said that she was not up to other babies her age, that he didn't want me to be alarmed but he thought I should take her—he was not an expert on this, or anything else for that matter—for an evaluation. And I was shocked at those words. But I agreed. I didn't resist at all. I didn't say: It can't be true. He's out of his mind. I knew it was true. So I took her very soon after to see the doctor and she took one look at her and said " 'Turner's Syndrome.' You do have a defective child." I was relieved. Because from that first day in the nursery I knew I had trouble. And all of that time I had accused myself, blamed myself, whipped myself. I was up all night and all day. I knew that a child who got what he needed would be contented, would be peaceful, would be happy. That is if I fed her right—I wasn't feeding her right. Do you know that I paid 50 cents a day for goat's milk? I had a special dairy bring me fresh goat's milk every morning. I rocked her in my arms until I ached all over, until I couldn't move. I carried her everywhere. I didn't use an infant seat. I didn't let her cry. I fed her on demand. And I thought what am I doing wrong? Where am I failing? I tried harder and harder and harder until I ended up in the hospital. I mean I just got carted out one night in a raving, screaming, manic fit. And I thought they were taking me to a mental institution which is . . . because I felt that I had lost my mind, that I just tried so hard that I just couldn't think or feel anything. But it turned out to be just a regular hospital.

Int.: How old was Heather then?

Mother: When I went to the hospital she was three months old.

Int.: You were in for how long?

Mother: For about 48 hours. When I came home my husband stayed home for three days and then we went away for about 5 days, up in the mountains someplace just camping. My mother watched the baby. And that did help some.

Int.: But you felt better when you heard about the Turner's . . .

Mother: Yes. Yes. I didn't need a week off. I needed to know what was wrong with my baby. And it was like everyone was deceiving me and it made me . . . I had . . . it only gave me a few choices: I'm insane . . . I'm utterly incompetent . . . you know, I mean if the baby is all right and we're having all this trouble, what choices does it leave? So finally they said, you're right—your baby is a mess. I mean, you know, her chromosomes are screwed up. And it was a tremendous relief. I was very grateful to the doctor, I love her to this day. The doctor told me when Heather was three years old that things were worse than she thought. We went up and down and up and down. At first it was Turner's Syndrome. Children with Turner's Syndrome go to regular school. They're in the slow reading group, they're small. But that means if they are a year behind, it doesn't show. They make it. I mean when you think of what average is, it's not much of a goal. It's pretty easy to make. I mean average is waitress and truck driver. Well why shouldn't my child at least make that with hard work, be what these people are with no effort? Then when she was older, it didn't look so good. It looked like maybe she was trainable, or educable, but really retarded. She couldn't go to regular school. Then when she got older, well we don't see her as educable, but really retarded. She couldn't go to regular school. Then when she got older, well we don't see her as educable, we see her as possibly trainable. And then when she was three years old . . . you see we came down, down, down. . . . They told me it was Turner's Syndrome, but they told me it didn't mean a heck of a lot. That she would be slow, she'd be slow. But it wasn't going to be anything horrible. It wasn't until she was three that the doctor said: it does not look good. She is very severely retarded. She will be lucky to be semi-independent. I don't know whether she will ever make it to "city school" (The one public school for trainable retarded children in San Francisco)—I mean that is bad news. That's bad news. That was a much tougher thing to take. I came home, really, . . . I didn't cry when the doctor told me, I just looked at her. I said, I see. Yes, doctor. I see. I understand. And I went home and I stormed and cried. That I guess was really the announcement for me. And, um, she told me then that she told me I should put Heather's name on the waiting list at the preschool. It's a very long list, it takes over a year, maybe she won't need it, maybe she'll be beyond that stage. But maybe she will need it. Maybe she won't be up to it, at four. But it looks like—you know, they're pretty permissive and tolerant there, and as long as the child is ambulatory they take him. And Heather was already showing signs of trying to walk. Anyhow, somebody on the staff took it upon themselves to do it for me. And they did call me and tell us we were on the waiting list. And it took about 14 months for her name to . . . it is a long list. Thank God I was put on. I'm grateful for . . . to the doctor, if she walked in this room, I'd fall down and kiss her feet. I adore the woman.

A sequel to this account is that six months after this interview, the child was reevaluated at another medical center, where studies revealed she did not have Turner's Syndrome. Indeed it now seems she had no chromosomal abnormalities at all. The mother is now in the process of trying to reorient her past, present and future with respect to this latest professional opinion.

It is clear from these accounts, when they are taken seriously, that notwithstanding the physician's tendency to attribute unsatisfactory encounters between himself and the parents to the parents' unconscious defense mechanisms, e.g. "blocking," "distorting," "resisting," or "projecting," the doctor was responsible for much of the untoward feelings that were generated during these encounters.

The ways in which the doctor contributed to generating these negative outcomes usually took one or more of the following five basic forms.

1. Doctors at one agency disagreed with those at another agency, or there was professional disagreement on a child's diagnosis and prognosis within the same agency.

2. The doctor's diagnosis and prognosis proved in some instances, or in other cases in every instance, to be inaccurate. This led the parents to feel that they could no longer take the professional's evaluation of their child's condition seriously.

3. The parents learned that certain information relevant to the diagnosis or, not infrequently, the diagnosis itself, was withheld from them.

4. A diagnosis was made that was not explained or adequately explained. This left the parents with the task of interpreting the child's ambiguous status and its projected consequences as best they could.

5. The doctor, while certain of the diagnosis of mental retardation, was uncertain of its origin, leaving the parents with an ambiguous situation which provided simultaneously for hope and frustration.

The author does not mean to imply that perplexity, confusion and suspicion never serve as defense mechanisms, but rather that they do not serve in this capacity as often as the doctor would like to suppose. That he is prone to invoke this explanation as often as he does is, in the author's opinion, itself a defense mechanism incorporated by the doctor.

The reader should be cautioned that these accounts of professional practices are in no way peculiar to the parents in the author's series. Others have noted the negative effects upon the retarded child and his family resulting from the doctor's inept handling of the transfer of information[3]. Nor should the prevalence of this complaint come as any surprise. It is not a key feature of medical curriculums to stress procedures dealing with the "nonmedical" problems of information transfer and/or counseling during periods of stress. This is unfortunate, since it is clear that the way in which medical information is related by the doctor to the patient or his family during these periods has a direct bearing upon the patient's health and the family's well-being.

Given the nature of the above encounters between doctors and parents of retarded children and the forms of interactions that they occasioned, the origins of the parents' feelings of perplexity, confusion and suspicion are in no way enigmatic. Such feelings do not require the assumptions of a "failure of personality-maturation," "distorted personality-functioning," or "unconscious defense mechanisms." Rather, these feelings stem from the ambiguity surrounding the patient's diagnosis and prognosis, which in turn resulted from the physician's inaccurate diagnosis, diagnostic disagreement among professionals, withholding of pertinent information from the parents and/or the inept presentation of medical findings. In light of these findings the author believes that medical schools would do well to reevaluate their current priority structure and place greater emphasis upon procedures for handling the "non-medical problem" of information transfer in crisis situations. It is clear that their past neglect in this regard has had dire consequences for both the patient and his family.

REFERENCES

1. Searles, Harold F. Concerning a Psychodynamic Function of Perplexity, Confusion, Suspicion, and Related Mental States. *Psychiatry* 15 (4), 351-352, November 1952.
2. The verbatim accounts cited below were taken from a series of interviews conducted by the author with mothers of retarded children and noted in a previous work, *The search for help: A study of the retarded child in the community.* New York: Brunner-Mazel, 1969, pp. 4-20.
3. See for example:

   Kramm, Elizabeth R. *Families of mongoloid children,* Washington, D.C.: Children's Bureau, U.S. Department of Health, Education and Welfare, p. 8, 1963.

   Waskowitz, Charlotte H. The Parents of Retarded Children Speak for Themselves. *Journal of Pediatrics* 54, 319-329, 1959.

   Tizard, J. and Grad, Jacqueline. *The mentally handicapped and their families: A social survey.* London: Oxford University Press, 1961.

   Ehlers, Walter H. *Mothers of retarded children: How they feel, where they find help.* Springfield, Illinois: Charles C Thomas, 1966.

SECTION II

THE MENTALLY RETARDED: COMPETENCE VERSUS INCOMPETENCE

CHAPTER 3

IMITATION AND COMPETENCE: A STUDY OF RETARDED ADULTS

Arne T. Bjaanes

In the course of making observations of the mentally retarded, one area of behavior, that of imitation, came to interest me considerably. The function of imitation in the coping behavior of the retarded has not been dealt with in the literature. The question posed here is this: Is imitation part of the general process of getting by in the world of the mentally normal, or is it undertaken in order to get along with a particular person? If a "normal" person does some activity differently than a retarded person, does the retarded person imitate the normal person in order to get along with him and reduce conflict? If this is so, he could do this while retaining his own understandings of the activity and how it is properly done. Alternately, does he imitate the normal person as a strategy for correcting his own "faulty" understandings about how to do things in the world? If this were so, the retarded person might adopt the new way of doing the activity with others in the future. Further, he might change his own understandings of how the activity is properly done.

To gain insight into this problem, an experiment was designed, in much the same manner as some of the experiments of Garfinkel and his students.[1] The objective was to take a situation in which a retarded individual was known to have an understanding which is shared and known by others, and to deliberately violate that common knowledge or understanding.

A second goal of this experiment was to see how far the

From Howard Schwartz & Jerry Jacobs, *Qualitative Sociology: A Method to the Madness.* New York: The Free Press, 1979. Reprinted by permission.

retarded person would go in doing imitating behavior. The basic question being approached here was: To what extent will the retardate use another's set of rules and understandings to determine his own behavior? To examine this, the experiment was divided into two sections. In the first part of the experiment I would violate a common practice whose violation does not per se destroy or contradict the situation. In the second part I would violate a rule which is essential to the very doing of the situation. That is, if the rule is violated, the situation can no longer go on without strong contradictions and will in effect become meaningless.

The situation chosen for the experiment was a pool game. Conveniently, there was a pool table in the game room of a residential facility for retarded adults. Several of the residents were proficient at playing pool. From Mrs. Brown, the caretaker, I learned that John was very good at pool. He frequently played with Mike, the caretaker's son, and at times with Sam, the caretaker's husband. He played well enough to win quite frequently. In addition, John and I had developed a friendly relationship in the course of the observations. It can be assumed that I had come to be, at least to some extent, a significant other to John, in that there frequently was behavior designed to show affection and friendship.

I initiated a conversation with John with the objective of getting him to ask me to play pool with him.

> Arne: Hi, John. I hear you like to play pool.
> John: Yeah. I sure like it. I win. I win. I win over Sam some time.
> Arne: How long have you been playing pool?
> John: I play pool a lot. A lot.
> Arne: How long?
> John: Oh, I don't know. Don't know that. No, I don't know that. Maybe six month.

According to Mrs. Brown, John had been in the home over four years and had played pool ever since they got the pool table, shortly after John came.

> Arne: I would like to see you play pool some time.
> John: Yeah, I play pretty good. Pretty good. I play Sam Brown.

I win over him. He don't like that. He sure don't like that. He sure don't. He pretty good too. You wanna see me play pool? I play you. Yeah, I play you. You wanna play me?

With that we went into the pool room.

The following points can be made at this time:

1. John knows how to play pool.
2. He has a working knowledge of the rules of the game.
3. He has established a friendly relationship with me, the observer.

The strategy for the experiment was as follows. During the first part of the game I would follow the rules, but I would shoot with the blunt end of the stick. This is a violation of a common practice, but it does not destroy the game. In the middle of the game, while continuing to shoot with the blunt end, I would immediately replace all balls shot into the pockets back onto the table. If I missed, I would push the ball I missed by hand into the pocket. Furthermore, I would do the same to the balls hit and missed by John. This is not only a violation of common practice, but it also destroys the game as such. The first violation is labeled A and the second, B.

We went to the game room; all the while John was talking about his prowess in pool. John got the balls out, arranged them properly on the table, and positioned the white ball. He then went to the rack and selected a cue stick.

JOHN: This mine. Sam Brown gave it to me.

I also selected a cue stick. John chalked his tip, and I proceeded to do the same. He then asked me if I wanted to break. I suggested that he should do that. After breaking and shooting two balls into the pockets, he missed and it became my turn. I chalked my stick again and proceeded to prepare to shoot with the blunt end. John noticed this immediately. He stood for a moment with a very perplexed look on his face, rubbing the cue stick against his chin.

JOHN: Hey . . . you holding the stick the wrong way. That's wrong. That's wrong. You suppos'ta shoot this way. [He demonstrates the correct way.] That's wrong.

When I missed, John smiled and got ready to shoot. He chalked his stick and shot in the conventional way. He missed and it became my turn. Again I chalked the tip and shot with the blunt end. This time I succeeded in getting a couple of balls in the pockets. Again John stood with a very perplexed and worried look on his face but did not say anything. When his turn came up, he chalked his stick, shot in the conventional way, and missed. Again I shot with the blunt end. A couple of pockets were made. This time it appeared that John was really worried. He was scratching his head, his brow knitted up, and his mouth hung open. Clearly something was amiss. When his turn came, he chalked the tip of his stick and proceeded to shoot *using the blunt end.* He missed and then stood up shaking his head and looking at me.

JOHN: That's not right. You like to play pool?

I did not give an answer and proceeded to shoot using the blunt end. After getting one ball down, I missed. John chalked his stick and proceeded to shoot with the *blunt end.* Again he missed.

JOHN: Shiieet!

At this point I decided to include violation B in the experiment. I shot, using the blunt end, made a pocket, and immediately put the ball back on the table. On the next shot I missed and proceeded to roll the ball into the pocket by hand. John appeared to be very surprised. He did not say anything, but his mouth was wide open. I then told him it was his turn. He chalked his stick and shot with the blunt end. He missed and I proceeded to push the ball into the pocket. Again nothing was said, so I proceeded to shoot, again with the blunt end. One ball went into a pocket, and I immediately replaced it on the table. The next shot missed, and I pushed the ball into the pocket. This apparently was too much.

JOHN: You like to play pool?
ARNE: Yes, I sure do.
JOHN: That's the wrong way. You not suppos'ta push the ball. You like to play football?
ARNE: Yes, I like to play football.

Note that John made no mention of the way in which I had been playing, but he was obviously irritated.

JOHN: Let's play football.
ARNE: Why don't we play pool?
JOHN: No, let's play football. It's too hot in here.

The reference to heat was obviously a ruse to get out of playing pool; the game room was air conditioned.

I left the home shortly after this. I returned three days later. Mrs. Brown told me that John had been talking about the pool game.

MRS. BROWN: Do you really know how to play pool?
ARNE: Yes, I do.
MRS. BROWN: Well, I guess John really got confused then, because he didn't think you knew how to play. You know how confused they get about simple things sometimes.

In the hope that further feedback might be forthcoming, I decided not to tell her about the experiment at this point. After a while, John came in, and after the usual greetings he started talking about his bowling ball.

JOHN: You want to see my bowling ball? I got a new bowling ball.
ARNE: How would you like to play some pool?
JOHN: You want to go fishin' with us next week? Sam is taking me fishin'. Yeah, Sam is goin' ta take us fishin'. Good. Good. [He rubs his hands together as he talks.]
ARNE: You want to shoot some pool?
JOHN: Did ya see the patio, Brown? Is it clean enough?
MRS. BROWN: Yes, you did a real fine job today, John. It looks real good.
JOHN: O.K., Mrs. Brown.

It appeared that the idea of playing pool with me was not a very comfortable one, and it was quite clear that John was trying to avoid it. The behavior going on was typical of what I have labeled "keeping safe."

ARNE: Come on and let's go shoot some pool.
JOHN: O.K., we play pool.

He seemed quite unhappy about this. He motioned to me to come along, and we went to his room. He started to take out his "family pictures" but then changed his mind. He kept searching for something in his duffel bag. Finally he gave up.

JOHN: O.K., we shoot pool.

With that we went out to the game room. John set up the balls and selected his cue stick.

JOHN: This my stick. Sam Brown give to me. Sam and I go fishin' soon.

He spent some time chalking his stick and then looked over the table for about two minutes. It appeared that he was trying to postpone the game. Finally he started the game shooting with the conventional end of the stick. As he aimed, he looked at me and then shot. He pocketed four balls before he missed. He stood up with a big, proud smile on his face. He was obviously very pleased with the results.

JOHN: Hey, I was lucky. Yup. Good shots.

As I started chalking my stick, he watched me very intently. When I looked at him, he quickly looked away. I got ready to shoot, using the conventional end of the stick. I shot and made a couple of balls. While this was going on, John started smiling.

JOHN: You shoot pretty good now. That's much better, much better.

After I missed, I did not immediately move away from the table. John stood watching my hands. When I moved from the table without pushing any balls into the pockets, he was visibly relieved.

JOHN: That's good. You play pretty good.

At this point Mrs. Brown came into the room with a couple of glasses of lemonade.

JOHN: It's O.K., Mrs. Brown. He know how to play pool pretty good. Pretty good.
MRS. BROWN: Well, that's what I told you, John.

In the middle of the game, I decided to see if suggesting another game would have any effect.

ARNE: You want to go out and play football?
JOHN: No, it's too hot. Pool is more fun. You like to play pool?

. It is interesting to note that John used the same excuse for pool. At the beginning of the game, John was quite tense, but as the game proceeded, he became more relaxed. This gives some indication of the tensions that had build up during the experiment.

DISCUSSION OF THE EXPERIMENT

It is clear that one experiment cannot be the basis for any clear-cut conclusions, but it does indicate some tendencies. It was hypothesized that imitation which would become a permanent part of the behavior vocabulary of the subject would be an indicator of the use of imitation to structure behavior. Conversely, if the behavior imitated was used for a short period, then imitation can be seen as a means of coping with an unknown and non-understood set of rules, and thus as a means of getting along in that particular set of behaviors. If this is the case, then it is clear that John was in part trying to cope with my ignorance of his understood and known set of rules. Once we had established a friendly relationship, getting along with me was a desired objective for him. A further confirmation of this notion is that when the game was played subsequent to the experiment, John chose to use the conventional way of shooting, that is, to abide by the rules of the game as he understood them. Two other types of behavior were also involved at this point. The first was an attempt at "keeping safe" by avoiding playing the game at all. The second type was "acceptance testing." When he shot in the conventional manner, he was keeping a close eye on me to gauge my reactions to his violation of my rules.

The second notion that was central to the experiment was the extent to which a retardate was willing to violate rules with which he was comfortable in the process of imitation, or, as we have tentatively interpreted it, coping with a difficult situation. Imitation ensued after a minor rule had been violated a number of times. However, when a major rule—a rule central to the game—was violated, there was no imitation at all. Instead there was considerable tension and irritation. Rather than go along with a major violation, he sought to abort the whole activity and suggest an alternative. The process of aborting the activity and suggesting an alternative can be seen in terms of "playing safe." That is, the current activity had become non-understandable, not in terms of John's knowledge of the game, but in terms of my behavior relative to the commonly understood and taken-for-granted rules of the game. A switch of roles had thus, in effect, taken place. John was in the position of being competent, and he was confident in his competence to the point of telling Mrs. Brown that I did not know how to play pool, while I was in the position of being incompetent. One can thus speculate as to the motive for imitating. Could it be that John, seeing my obvious incompetence, was merely humoring me lest perhaps I become violent? Doing humoring would certainly have had precedents in the Brown home, and thus could have conceivably been a part of John's behavioral vocabulary.

Of interest here also is the fact that the relationship between John and myself was strained during the experiment but reverted to being a friendly relationship once I started complying with the rules of the game as John understood and knew them.

The last idea brings into focus the set of relationships between the residents and Mrs. Brown. In the case of John and myself, it is clear that the relationship was friendlier when there was a convergence between the rules and behavior as experienced by both. It could be posited that a similar process operates between Mrs. Brown and her residents. Mrs. Brown's notions of what mental retardation is centers on her perception of the retarded as children or childlike. As a consequence, she tends to play the mother role. If friendly relations are to occur, a compatible set of behaviors must be done by the residents. This clearly is the case when there is face-to-face contact. The residents frequently adopt childlike gestures and mannerisms. Mrs. Brown reacts to this like a mother, and a friendly relationship goes on. On the other hand, while some of this carries over—for example, references to Mrs. Brown as "Mamma Brown"—there are clear differences. There tend to be small and brief revolts, at times demonstrated to visitors. An example of this is John's use of "damn" and "shieet" after Mrs. Brown has made clear that she gets angry when such language is used.

CONCLUSIONS

This study has been largely exploratory, and the findings are at best sketchy. Very little has been written about how the mentally retarded act, since the majority of the studies relevant to mental retardation have been medically and biologically oriented. Others have dealt with I.Q.'s and adaptive behavior. A notable exception to these studies is Edgerton's *The Cloak of Competence*.[2]

The notion of "passing behavior" has been defined as that type of behavior which the retardate engages in so as to appear normal and thus hide evidence of mental retardation. That this type of behavior is frequent has been demonstrated by Edgerton and was observed in the course of this study. The fact that passing behavior does take place has some implications which stand contrary to popular notions of how the mentally retarded see themselves. In order for passing types of behavior to take place, the individuals engaged in such behavior must have some notion of their subnormality. It could be argued that they do, in that the retarded have been told that they are retarded, and in all likelihood they have also, at one time or another, been institutionalized.

What is significant here is that not all behavior is passing behavior. That is, some acts are chosen to be used as passing acts, while others are not. If the labeling process is to be assumed to be the major factor in determining passing behavior, then the specific areas of incompetence must have been labeled, thus providing the retardate with a guide as to which areas he needs to do passing in. There is little information as to whether such act-specific labeling takes place. On the other hand, if the labeling process is not assumed to be act-specific, then it must be considered possible that the retarded, in some areas at least, have reasonably well-developed competencies. Cases of the "idiot savant" provide some reason to believe that this is the case. Certainly the data in this study show limited areas of well-developed competence that is resistant to manipulation.

This line of reasoning suggests a somewhat different conceptualization of what mental retardation is. Laws and Ryave have suggested that mental retardation be viewed in terms of competence rather than incompetence, claiming that the latter point of reference tends to blind one to areas of competence.[3] In line with these notions, mental retardation can be regarded as a segmented set of competencies, in which some sets are relatively well developed and others are relatively poorly developed. That is to say, competence is not uniform for a given person, and one may be equipped with areas of competence, as well as with areas of incompetence.

If mental retardation is viewed in this fashion, then the fact that the retarded show remarkable competence in some areas, while at the same time showing little or no competence in others, is not surprising. The observations in this study tend to support this view of retardation.

REFERENCES

1. Garfinkel, Harold. *Studies in ethnomethodolgy,* Englewood Cliffs: Prentice-Hall, 1967.
2. Edgerton, Robert. *The cloak of competence,* Berkeley: University of California Press, 1967.
3. Laws, Donald F., and A. Lincoln Ryave. "Toward a Sociology of Experience: The Abandonment of Concepts of Defectiveness," unpublished paper, California State College, Dominguez Hills.

CHAPTER 4

ON THE ART OF TALKING ABOUT THE WORLD

ALAN L. RYAVE

A RATHER COMMONPLACE conversational activity is telling and hearing stories about the world.[1] Frequently such stories appear in a conversation in clusters of two or more.

In the data to be focused upon here, in each case presented, there occurs a cluster of two stories and related story commentary, told at separate times by two conversationalists. In the second instance presented below, Peter tells a story about a dangerously close call he experiences at a fairgrounds, and then Gordon follows with a story dealing with the possible prevention of trouble in amusement park rides in Long Beach. In the first instance, Blanch presents a story dealing with the fact that an accident was witnessed which evidently was not subsequently reported on by the media, whereupon Beth tells a story of a witnessed event that received the same fate. These instances are presented immediately below, and the reader is encouraged to examine them carefully before proceeding to the ensuing analysis.[2] In my analysis, particular attention will be given to instance 2.

Instance 1

BLANCH: Say did you see anything in the paper last night or hear anything on the local radio?—Ruth Henderson and I drove down to Ventura yesterday.

BETH: Mh hm.

BLANCH: And on the way home we saw the:: most gosh-awful wreck.

From Howard Schwartz & Jerry Jacobs, *Qualitative Sociology: A Method to the Madness,* New York: The Free Press, 1979. Reprinted by permission.

BETH: Oh::::

BLANCH: —we have ev—I've ever seen. I've never seen a car smashed into sm— such a small space.

BETH: Oh::::

BLANCH: It was smashed from the front and the back both it must've been in—caught in between two cars.

BETH: Mh hm uh huh.

BLANCH: Must've run into a car and then another car smashed into it and there were people laid out and covered over on the pavement.

BETH: Mh.

BLANCH: We were s—parked there for quite a while but I was going to listen to the r—news and haven't done it.

BETH: No, I haven't had my radio on, either.

BLANCH: Well I had my television on, but I was listening to uh the blastoff, you know.

BETH: Mh hm.

BLANCH: The uh ah— // astronauts.

BETH: Yeah.

BETH: Yeah.

BLANCH: And I-I didn't ever get any *local* news.

BETH: Uh huh.

BLANCH: And I wondered.

BETH: Uh huh.

BETH: No, I haven't had it on, and I don't uh get the paper, and uhm.

BLANCH: It wasn't in the paper last night, I looked.

BETH: Uh huh.

BETH: Probably didn't make it.

BLANCH: No, no you see this was about three o'clock in the afternoon.

BETH: Uh huh.

BLANCH: Paper was already off the press.

BETH: Uh huh.

BLANCH: Boy, it was a bad one, though.

BETH: Well that's too bad.

BLANCH: Kinda // (freak)—

BETH: You know, I looked and looked in the paper—I think I told you f-for that uh f-fall over at the Bowl that night. And I never saw a thing about it, and I // looked in the next couple of evenings.

BLANCH: Mh hm.

(1.0)

BETH: Never saw a th— a mention of it.

BLANCH: I didn't see that, either.
BETH: Uh huh.
BETH: Maybe they kept it out.
BLANCH: Mh hm, I expect.
BETH: Uh huh, deli//berately.
BLANCH: Well I'll see you at— at—
BETH: Tomorrow // night.
BLANCH: —at six at— hehhehh.

Instance 2

HAL: They're-uh-they::'re uhm, they're easy.
PETER: Boy, don't go at the fairgrounds through.
    ((whistles "wow"))
STAN: Oh(hh)o Go(hh)d'   OO'.
HAL: Why?
PETER: C'z uh, —(2.0)— have one a' them things, they break loose up there.
GORDON: Oh wuhnyuh buildin that yeah I know about that. — They're prob'bly—there's cables wasn' uh strong enough tuh, —pull'm *back*.
PETER: Uh-no those big cable cars. Y'nuh the ones up on the, track.
GORDON: Mm.
STAN: Wih A one Boat YUH::: UHLON DOHLENKO, — ETCHEruh WOOOOOPS.
    (1.7)
HAL: I wouldn' ride on them (cars.)
STAN: Gah' No *me*.
    (1.7)
GORDON: Aw me I'd ride onna *bumper* car.
PETER: An ah know who almos' got hit bah one a' them things.
STAN: YOU?
HAL: (((You?)
    ( )
(STAN): *Go::d.*
GORDON: Mm hm.
GORDON: Not me.
PETER: ((with mouth full)) If I didn' stop bout; —
GORDON: ((with mouth full)) Eh w'z this— ((chewing))
(GORDON): ( )
PETER: (The cable car jus' went past me'n:: dropped. —dat, close to me.
HAL: Jeez.
GORDON: ( ).

PETER: That's how far ah was 'way f'm that cable car.
STAN: ((whispered))   Go::d.
HAL: *Wow.*
STAN: (*Yeah.*)
PETER: I woulda been pinned under it.
      (4.0)
GORDON: They should check those things out—When they rent'm (they should check'm out.)
STAN: Yea::h.
      (3.0)
HAL: W'sometimez they don't—
      (1.7)
GORDON: Th-they should—they (should
HAL: —check'm.
      (5.0)
GORDON: If they're gonna rent'm (through the day), the:n, they should sheck'm out. —(2.0—or the boss should—sorra, "Got this thing checked up?" "No," "What's duh mar:: wih you."— "Y' be'r check it out." —(4.0)—Cuz down here in Long Beach idjuh —anh-an bumped inna the bass'n I say "Hey. (one a'yuh rides goin out over here"— "Well, which izzit.")— "Yerruh:: merry g'round ennuh::: dee–deh d'bump'm cars." — "What? I'll go to um *now.*" Boy did he *go.* ('E really *told'*m though.)
      (3.0)
PETER: One time I w'z pinned in the bump'r car one time.
GORDON: Boy he check dem out 'e finally tol'm you guys better check the equipment out. hh(an' *now.*)
STAN: En hyou know(a' jing go ups go down eh duh—de(awduh)
GORDON: (check'm out.)
      Better check'm out.
GORDON: ((He) did:d too.
      (2.0)

THE SERIES-OF-STORIES PROBLEM

By using the term *cluster*, I mean to point out that the stories being referred to occur in close proximity to one another. However, it is clear that the relationships that exist between them extend well beyond the fact that the second is told immediately after the first.[3] For example, in instance 2 each story is devoted to a similar topic, amusement park rides, also suggesting that each event being related occurs in a similar setting. More refined, each story focuses, in some manner, on the faulty operation of these amusement park rides and not, for example, on how much fun they are or which ones are too expensive. Second, in each story the storyteller is somehow implicated as a principal character in the story he is reporting. In fact, all character portrayal is built in and around the issue of the operations of the amusement park rides. And each story has a course of action that either leads up to or out of the faulty operation of amusement park rides. Finally, each storyteller constructs his story in such a manner as to make a moral point or illustrate a maxim. The storytellers do not leave this matter to be understood from the specifics of the events they relate. Peter and Gordon both describe the moral point independently of the actual relating of the story. And both moral points are so constructed as to relate to the issue of faulty amusement park rides. The reader is encouraged to make the previous observations for himself so that he will be better acquainted with the data and the phenomenon to be addressed in this paper.

Although these observations by no means exhaust the number of relationships that exist between the two tales told in instance 2, they do suggest the following possibility: The relations between these stories are not capricious and happenstance, but are instead the product of the careful attention and management of the conversationalists. They may have reasons for producing and exhibiting these relationships within a conversation; indeed, they may be obligated to do so. In this sense "talking about the world" is a markedly different activity within conversation than it is on a news show or in a classroom. For who says what about the world, and when, will all be highly contingent on the unfolding sequences of talk within the conversation itself.

When two adjacent stories are *designed* by their tellers to be related in these (or other) ways, I wish to speak of them as a "series of stories" rather than a mere "cluster." How could this be done? One procedure would be for each "next" storyteller to construct his own tale so that it had definite observable relationships to the previous one. This would require him to listen to the story before his own, in very special ways. Thus the occurrence of a "series of stories" would not be a preordained, pregiven matter, but would reside in each succeeding storyteller's *decision and achievement.* But if this is so, the question arises: Why would conversationalists want to do such a thing?

Having stated this preliminary but primary problem, we can turn our attention to a more detailed consideration of the particular data under investigation.

REFINING THE PROBLEM

Implied in the above problem is a way to search for a solution. Since the resources for Gordon's succeeding story are presumably in Peter's preceding one, the researcher should begin by carefully comparing the contents of the two sequentially adjacent stories. However, closer inspection of instance 2 calls this approach into question. The origin of Gordon's succeeding story seems to be more directly traceable to one of *his own prior utterances*—"They should check those things out—When they rent'm (they should check'm out")—than to Peter's story itself. Further, when I speak of Gordon's story being *derived* from his previous utterance, I am not only pointing to something Gordon might have actually done; I am pointing to something that the conversationalists can *see* he has done. That is, I am raising the possibility that Gordon constructs his story so as to deliberately show that it was motivated by his own preceding utterance. Before attending to the implications of this observation, I would like to provide substantiating evidence for it.

It is not unusual to find instances in conversation where a story is being told so that it can be seen as occasioned by, or derived from, some preceding or succeeding utterance. For example, one might state a maxim, proverb, rule, or assertion and design a story so it can be seen as an illustration, proof, explication, or demonstration of such an assertion. In such cases the very design of the story displays the motive for telling it, that is, to substantiate some asserted state of affairs. For a story to be heard in this way by others, it cannot be produced in just any manner, but has to be worked up with an attention to this state of affairs.

Gordon's story illustrates one way of doing this. It is organized so that its *developing conclusion* ends up being an utterance —"Boy he check dem out 'e finally tol'm you guys better check the equipment out. hh(an' *now*"–that markedly resembles the preceding utterance that motivated the story in the first place: "They should check those things out–When they rent'm (they should check'm out.") What I am pointing to here is not some concluding remark which is tacked onto the story as an afterthought. Instead we have a series of events, related to us in succession so as to properly and reasonably culminate with the presentation of Gordon's preceding utterance as the story's conclusion.

The import of these observations is that they challenge our earlier definition of a "series of stories." Recall that we wanted to discover the process that spewed out a particular product– two or more adjacent stories which possessed many common elements. We assumed that such a product was produced by each next person designing his tale so it was similar to the one told by the person before him. Now, it is proposed that Gordon's "next" story was not designed to be similar to Peter's but was instead designed to be an instance of Gordon's own maxim, "They should check those things out." How then do we get what clearly looks like a series of stories when Gordon was not designing his story to be one in a series?

THE SIGNIFICANCE AND RECOUNTING ASPECTS OF STORYTELLING

Two major concepts can be introduced here in order to solve this problem. There are two separate, but deeply related concerns which people frequently have in telling stories. I refer to these concerns as the *significance aspect* and the *recounting aspect* of storytelling. Conversationalists not only involve themselves in the relating or recounting of some event(s) but are also concerned with expressing the import, relevance, or significance of those events and/or indicating just how this significance can be appreciated in and through the way these events are recounted. The "and/or" was not an incidental usage, but was meant to indicate that these two concerns of storytellers are intimately interrelated and, together, dictate just how to present the tale in question.

In general, recounting events is done by reciting a number of separate utterances which are tied together by some developing course of action. Showing the significance of these events takes the form of an abstract assertion, accomplishable within a single utterance.[4] In Peter's case, for example, both of these aspects of story organization are exemplified. There is a recounting of a particular event that once occurred at a fairground, which is prefaced by a general statement admonishing and warning the other participants about visiting such places. The admonition seems to show the relevance of recounting the dangerous event which occurred at the fairground. The recounting, in and through its presentation, serves as a source of evidence and support for producing the admonition in the first place.

What happens next is critical. I want to propose that Gordon produces an utterance whose function is the same as Peter's original admonition. That is, Gordon's "They should check those things out—When they rent'm" is designed to describe the significance of Peter's story. Support for this contention can be obtained by a few observations. First, Gordon makes this comment after Peter completes his entire story. Second, it is a response to the story as a whole. In this it contrasts to the utterances produced by Gordon, Hal, and Stan that appear within the confines of Peter's unfolding story and which are directed to concrete elements of what is being recounted. Third, it is "reflexively" fitted to what Peter has said. That is, what Peter recounted stands as a source of testimony for what Gordon said and, at the same time, what Gordon said suggests one conclusion that can be drawn from what Peter has recounted. Fourth, notice that one can actually remove Peter's opening significance statement (his admonition) and substitute Gordon's statement "They should check those things out—," and Peter's entire story and all intervening commentary still make perfect sense.

Of course, it is no news that a given story can have two different significances. What might be news is that, within conversation, a listener can give a story a second significance which is different from the one announced for it by the teller of the story, and that this second significance need not be derived from, or commensurate with, the first. Apparently this is morally permitted in conversation, and there are ways to do it. In particular, notice that Gordon places his "second significance statement" in a certain "slot"—he says it right after Peter completes his story. These observations will give us a "road home" in terms of solving the problem which started this article. They will suggest one reason why conversationalists deliberately design their "talk about the world" so that it takes the form of a series of stories—a consecutive set of tales which are visibly tied to one another like the links of a chain. We will also see why the views of the world expressed in a conversation may be as much the result of the unfolding talk in the conversation itself as it is the product of the beliefs of those who express them.

THE SAME-SIGNIFICANCE PROCEDURE: TYPE 1

We can now state a general procedure for constructing a succeeding story which others can see to be related to the first—i.e., to be "one in a series." One can use the significance statement for the first story as a "blueprint" for remembering, inventing and organizing a tale which has the same significance. One way to do this has already been described. One can use a "developing conclusion methodology" in organizing one's own tale. That is, one can "recount" a succession of events, which naturally culminate in the preceding storyteller's significance statement as their conclusion. Alternately (as additional data demonstrate), one can restate (or paraphrase) the preceding significance statement, and use it as a "story preface" to one's own tale.[5]

However, one need not be as blatant as this. Merely recounting events in a manner that *can be heard* as having the same significance as the first recounting, will allow others to hear it that way.[6] In fact, this third procedure is apparently employed in instance 1. First the issue of the media failing to report a newsworthy event is introduced by Blanch, and an instance of this given. Beth achieves a clear connection and series of stories relationship by recounting her events in strict conformance with this significance. Support for the contention that this procedure is often used (and that it works) can be obtained by noting the following: It is common to find the first story in some series containing both a significance statement and an appropriately organized recounting, while succeeding stories may lack any explicit indication of their significance. Yet they are heard by all parties as a "series of stories."

Additionally, it should be noted that all the similarities between adjacent stories which we discussed initially may be an *indirect* consequence of the same-significance procedure. That is, in recounting events in such a way as to exhibit that they have a particular significance, one may have (or be able) to include in them similar characters, similar settings in which they occur, and so on. Yet, importantly, events with a visibly similar significance need not be similar in other ways.[7]

Finally, one of the benefits of using the same-significance procedure is that it allows one, in the very way he tells his story, to show that and how he understands, supports, sympathizes, or agrees with the preceding story.

SAME-SIGNIFICANCE PROCEDURE: TYPE 2

As already indicated, Gordon does not use the procedure we have just discussed. He uses another kind of same-significance procedure by making his intervening utterance function as a significance statement for both the story he later tells and for Peter's last story. Why does he do this? Why does he not employ the significance statement introduced by Peter? Relatedly, if the type 1 procedure allows one to show support, sympathy, or agreement with a preceding story, what does the type 2 procedure do?

Recalling our earlier discussion, we can see that being the "first" person to tell what will be a series of stories gives one strong control over the subsequent conversation. It is the first storyteller who not only provides a maiden recounting (with all its implications of topic, setting, characters, and so on) but also gets first crack at indicating the significance of that recounting. Any succeeding storyteller must pay close attention to what the first one did, or risk the possibility that his own tale will not be heard as one in a series, that is, it may seem irrelevant, off the topic, and so forth.

One way to deal with this is to provide new material (as Gordon did) for connecting two stories in a manner that might not be in any way apparent. This supplies the listener with a new sense of what the preceding story was actually about. Further, if the new significance statement is quite different from the first, it will be the second that becomes the only one that can meaningfully interrelate the two independent recountings. Recalling that "telling a story" includes both recounting events and displaying significance, we can now see that the second significance statement is, potentially, "competitive" with the first, for it can challenge, question, or correct what the first recounting is taken to mean.[8] Finally, the type 2 procedure provides a way to recount something that might otherwise be heard as quite out of line with what was said before and yet have it heard as commensurate with, and similar to, the first tale that was told. One might thus give a series of events a particular significance, merely to exhibit their connection to what was previously related. But such a significance statement will, in turn, affect how the events themselves must be described.

We see, then, that when one talks about the world within conversation, one does not merely report information; one undercuts or agrees with the view of another, talks on, or tries to change the topic, and so on. Because of these contingencies, talk about the world, in conversation, frequently takes the form of a series of deliberately interrelated stories. Both the events related and the significance attributed to them are as much the result of conversational dynamics as they are of the personalities and attitudes of the conversationalists. In fact, we can venture further. If a person's general "point of view" is, in part, the product of the proverbs and stories he relates to others in daily life, then he may end up with a particular viewpoint on, say, sex or politics because of the conversational sequences he happened to get into!

THE IMPORT OF THE ANALYSIS

At this point there may still be some readers who are waiting for a "punch line." After all, while the preceding may be interesting and plausible, what does it have to do with sociology? We have uncovered some methods by which competent, socialized adults "talk about the world." It is now time to point out that the data we analyzed from instance 2 were not produced by adults who were "competent" and "socialized"—at least from the standpoint of our society. It represented a conversation between two males who resided in an institution for the mentally retarded. Insofar as what they do and understand when they talk is structurally similar to what the rest of us do and understand when we talk (as evidenced by instance 1), perhaps we had better reexamine our conception of the retarded. Perhaps the initial intuitive feeling that their communication is somehow "defective" is superficial. Before deciding what about their behavior is defective and what is normal, we had better learn explicitly what the "normal" consists of and how what they are doing might be different. This article represents a partial effort in that direction.

NOTES

1. The study of storytelling in conversation, as a topic of research, was established by Harvey Sacks. For a number of uniformities and regularities uncovered in his researches, see Harvey Sacks, unpublished lecture notes, University of California at Irvine, Spring, 1970. The basic thrust of this report is deeply indebted to features of this work, although I accept full responsibility for uses made of these materials.

    A couple of additional clarifying remarks follow. First, by the notion of "story," I mean, for now, the telling of some event in more than one utterance. Second, when I speak of the "telling of a story in conversation," I have in mind not only the utterances of the storyteller but also the comments made in the course of a story presentation by those who are the recipients of the story. The fact that recipients make these comments can affect the in-progress unfolding of some relating of an event, and consequently the very meaning that a series of utterances might obtain. This is a distinguishing characteristic of stories told in conversation as opposed to, for example, stories told in performance situations. This characteristic not only differentiates our concerns and interests in storytelling from those of, say, students of folklore, who show an abiding interest in this phenomenon, but it also affirms the sense in which storytelling in conversation is an interactionally collaborative achievement.

2. Instance 2 is part of a larger corpus of tape-recorded conversations made at a Los Angeles County Board and Care Home for the mentally retarded. Instance 1 was supplied by Harvey Sacks and consists of a telephone conversation between two adult females. Any interested reader can obtain additional instances of the conversational phenomenon

discussed in this article by writing to Alan Ryave, Department of Sociology, California State University at Dominguez Hills, California.

3. The present line of discussion should not be construed as undercutting the fundamental importance of proximity to the general phenomenon of telling "another" story. For example, on occasion, a prospective story-teller is unable, for whatever reason, to adequately present a succeeding story in the sequential place they deem relevant. When this occurs, there are special conversational devices for indicating the slot in which the story should have appeared. Thus, in the conversation from which instance 2 was taken Peter attempted to start up a story, following Gordon's, with the utterance "One time I w'z pinned in the bump'r car one time." He was interrupted. When the opportunity came to start up again, he began his story again, but in a slightly different manner: " 'N' like I w'z goan say about bumping cars . . ." With a preface like " 'N like I w'z goan say . . .," Peter is able to link the present unfolding story with his prior effort and thereby indicate where his story should have been told.

4. By "utterance" I mean a complete turn at talk in conversation.

5. As articulated by Sacks, "story prefaces," often framed in the form of a question, serve to "clear floor room" for a prospective storyteller. That is, they announce his intention to tell a story, give listeners some idea of what is coming, and allow them to give him the floor for a certain amount of conversational time, in order to accomplish his task.

6. One import of this hearer's maxim is that a previous story does not have to be an immediately preceding one in order for the series-of-stories phenomenon to be obtained. That this is the case can be appreciated by the way in which this maxim is invoked by lawyers in locating and determining a precedent for some story they are presently involved in constructing. For further articulation of this point, see Michael Moerman, "The Use of Precedent in Natural Conversation," *Semiotica* 7 (1973). There are numerous other analytical disciplines that require practitioners to know and work with intricacies of this procedure, e.g. historians, psychological counselors and therapists, analytical interpretation of open-ended interviews, doctors, etc.

7. When the same-significance device is employed, it is not uncommon to obtain two related stories whose story elements (such as characters, setting, time, and topic) do not display any sense of strict commonality. Therefore, searching for common story elements as a means of substantiating their status as a series of stories will not necessarily yield valid results.

8. There is a sense in which Peter's and Gordon's significance statements stand as alternatives to Peter's recounting. It can be observed that Peter's significance statement, which prefaces his impending recounting, takes the form of a "warning." It uses a conventional frame for doing

"warnings"—"Don't do X" (that is, don't go to the fairgrounds). Where his succeeding recounting stands as an evidential instance of a dangerous thing that can happen to you if you choose to do X. In contrast, Gordon's appended significance statement locates specific blame and explanation for the fairground's catastrophe, thereby providing potential resolution to the troubles, and dangers described in Peter's story. That is, the danger as developed by Peter in and through his story is presented as embedded in the setting, whereas Gordon, by assessing specific blame, shifts the attention from the setting to certain individuals; the danger is not irremedial. If "they" would check those things out, then presumably the sort of danger incurred by Peter could be avoided—and, along with it, the propriety of Peter's warning.

SECTION III

THE MENTALLY RETARDED: EFFECTS UPON THE FAMILY

CHAPTER 5

THE RETARDED CHILD:
FAMILY MODES OF ADAPTATION

JERRY JACOBS

T HE FOLLOWING IS A study of parents of retarded children at a cooperative preschool in San Francisco. The work is based upon a year-long participant observation study of the preschool's activities and the friendships that developed between myself and the mothers of the retarded children. Toward the end of the study, I conducted a series of tape-recorded interviews with the parents. The following is an analysis of these transcribed verbatum accounts, as they relate to the retarded child's effect upon the family.

Before beginning the discussion proper, we will open with a brief description of the parents and children to give the reader some idea of their backgrounds.

THE PARENTS

Age: Mothers' ages ranged from 31 to 51, with a mean of 38. Six mothers were over the age of 40 at the time of their retarded child's birth. Fathers' ages ranged from 26 to 67 with a mean of 43.

Race: Of the 14 mothers interviewed, 12 were white and two were Negro.

Religion: Religious affiliations were given as follows: Eleven mothers were Catholic, two were Protestant, and one, Russian

Edited and abridged from: Jerry Jacobs, *The Search for Help: A Study of the Retarded Child in the Community*, New York: Brunner/Mazel, 1969. Reprinted by permission.

Orthodox. In three cases, the husband and wife held different religious affiliations.

Income: Net family incomes ranged from $327 to $1,000 per month. The average net family income was $650 per month.

Marital status: Thirteen of the 14 families in this series were intact. There was only one instance of a "broken home," i.e. an absent father. Eleven mothers had been married only once; three had been married twice. Of the fathers, eleven had married only once; two had been married twice.

Number of children: The number of children in the family unit ranged from one to ten, with an average of four. Nine of the 14 families had three or fewer children. All families had only one retarded child.

Residential mobility: All the families in this series showed considerable residential stability. All fourteen had lived in the San Francisco area since the birth of their retarded child, i.e. for the past four to eight years, often in the same house.

Employment: Eleven of the fourteen mothers in this series were "housewives." At the time of the interview, only three mothers were employed. Two of these were the only Negro parents interviewed, and the third mother reported the only case of a "broken home." One of the Negro mothers was employed with the telephone company; the other worked in a laundry. The third and only white working mother managed an apartment house. The fathers worked at a wide variety of jobs. These occupations are listed as follows: auto mechanic, house painter, longshoreman, pharmacist, army colonel, public school teacher, shipping clerk supervisor, retired limousine driver, mechanic's helper, lawyer, city fireman, lather and state investigator.

Education: One mother had not graduated from high school, six were high school graduates, and three had some college or were college graduates. In four cases the level of mothers' education remains unknown. Of the fathers, three had not graduated from high school, one graduated high school, and five had some college or were college graduates. In four cases the level of fathers' education was not given. In two cases, mothers claimed they had never known the level of their husbands' education. It seems it was a topic that never came up.

THE CHILDREN

Of the 14 children in the author's series, there were six males and eight females ranging in age from 4 to 8, i.e. within the age range accepted by the preschool. In terms of diagnostic categories, there were 10 cases of Down's syndrome, one case of Turner's syndrome, one schizophrenic child, and one case of cerebral palsy resulting from meningitis. While all the children at the preschool were by definition "retarded," the prognosis was for many ambiguous at best. In some cases even the diagnosis of mental retardation itself, as it is commonly understood within the medical model, was questionable. Perhaps a more meaningful description than diagnostic categories is obtained by considering the physical, mental and social flexibility and adaptability of these children. In this regard, their abilities were widely distributed. Six of the 14 children were not toilet trained. Toilet training was an area of considerable stress for the parents, not only because of the frustration and the unpleasant task it routinely entailed, but because one criterion for acceptance into the only public school facility in the area for trainable retarded children was that the child be toilet trained. (This was not an official criterion for acceptance as given by state law. However, it was an acknowledged unofficial school policy.) Most of the children were nonverbal. In fact only four of the 14 children in this series had a limited but conversational use of language. Four had "simple speech," i.e. used simple words or sentence fragments. Six were nonverbal.

INFANTICIDE

One mode of adaptation parents of retarded children entertained early in the child's career was infanticide. This option was always viewed by the parents within the framework of an altruistic gesture. The parents' contemplation of infanticide as a means of sparing the child and the family future problems that they felt were sure to develop as a result of the child's retardation is, of course, of great import. Its greater significance, however, lies in the fact that it is a specific instance of the general case of "what will it all (the extended effort and suffering on the part of parents, sibs, and retarded child) come to anyway?".

Entertaining the notion of infanticide was in no way peculiar to the parents in the author's series.[1] For example, a parent in the study by Brice and Bartelme states the following:

> I never really planned to kill my child, but I have thought of how much easier it would be if he died; my religion is the only thing that keeps me from killing my child.[2]

If religion kept some parents from murdering their retarded child, it may have served for others as a means of constructing the moral justification of infanticide.

> The Reverend Mr. Sholin . . . said his son, Edward Allen, suffered brain damage when his oxygen supply was curtailed just before birth. The minister said after being told the infant would be 'something close to an inanimate object,' he decided to take his pediatrician's advice and remove his son from an oxygen tent. The infant died three days later.

The Reverend went on to say:

> *Tragic decisions like this one are made every day.* I believe that the people who have to make them, under the proper circumstances, should no longer be lawbreakers. (Emphasis added.)

The article also noted that:

> . . . while still 'burdened' by his decision (to let his son die), he (the minister) would do the same thing today.[3]

The altruistic murder of the mentally retarded is noted elsewhere.[4] D. J. West cites four cases of murder-suicide involving a parent's murder of a retarded child, followed by the suicide of the parent.[5] Forty-seven percent of a total of 148 cases of murder-suicide studied by West were instances of parents killing their own children.[6]

One mother in the author's series recounted her contemplation of murder-suicide as follows:

> A year ago, we (the mother and child) reached a crisis. When her behavior went so haywire, when things were so bad, you mentioned Sonoma, that I was on the verge of committing the child and because that was so intolerable, I thought that perhaps suicide and homicide together would be a better solution for her and for me. And it sounds awful, but it is an alternative. And it is one way. If you can't do what's necessary and you can't buy it, you can't ask it, you can't beg it, it's like if there's nothing on TV, simply nothing. Even people who are completely hung up on TV will sometimes turn the damn set off. And I just considered, you know, that turning her off

and turning myself off because I couldn't bear to live after that, might be the, you know, best thing. That's how bad things were.

Conditions have improved markedly and unexpectedly for this family within the last year, and the mother no longer entertains murder-suicide as a possible solution to her and the child's problems. In fact, things are so much better that the mother now states she is able "to live with it."

Another mother had this to say about the prospect of her son surviving her and her husband. Here, as in all the verbatim accounts, much is lost in transcription. To have heard the inflection in the mother's voice and seen the sheepish expression on her face as she spoke the words would have left the listener with little room for ambiguity when she said:

> . . . I wouldn't want Norman to live until he's forty without John (her husband) and I being there to go through it with him. I don't know what he would do. I feel this way—if Norman outlives us, please God take him with us when we go. Because I mean that's the way I want things. I don't want him . . . I don't want him . . . If John and I can't keep him with us all through life, until it goes one way or the other, if we're taken before he is, like I said, I want him to go with us. If he's taken before us, then we are ready to accept it. Because if he goes through life with us, if all of a sudden we're not here tomorrow, he's going to be in a terrible state of shock. And of course if they throw him in a colony again, or a state hospital, then that might even be worse than anything else. So it might actually be better if Norman were taken with us if we go before he does. I mean that's the way I feel about it. Many other people might not agree with me. But I do. I believe that a retarded child has just as much right to live as a normal child, but I don't want to see them living in a miserable way.

A third parent who felt at one point that it would be a "blessing" to let her retarded child die gave this account:

> . . . sometimes my husband will call me during the day and we talk on the phone and I tell him, you know, a lot of things that were upsetting me and I wouldn't tell anyone else, the things that I tell him, you know, we wouldn't share with other people, the kinds of things we share with each other, feelings about Paul, and for a long time we wished he would die, because well, we would have regarded it a blessing. Of course this comes kind of naturally because a good section of our society regards the death of a retarded child as a blessing. It is a common reaction . . . I mean there was

. . . one time I was giving him food and he wasn't eating it or taking food, he was about two; he had a respiratory infection—he was very ill for days and I was giving him fluid by rectum and I found myself thinking at the time, gee I wish he'd just die—but I couldn't do that, you know, I could not make that last effort.

INSTITUTIONAL CARE

A key factor in the benevolent view that parents of retarded children took toward infanticide revolved around the prospect of their ultimately having to institutionalize their child. This sentiment was clearly expressed in the above accounts. The general feeling was, why let the child live and the family suffer if all that results is that the child is finally "put away"? The despair that was felt by parents of retarded children at this prospect was based upon their low opinion of institutional care, i.e. parents tended to see an institutional setting for their retarded child as a "dead end." Once the child was institutionalized, parents felt there was no hope for his future development. In fact, it was generally believed that his condition was likely to deteriorate. One parent, the only one in the author's series who had her child institutionalized at one point and removed him from "residence care" after a period of six months, had this to say about her experience:

So when Lucy, my third child, was born, it was a few months later in January when Norman was a year and a half that we took him to X Children's Colony, and he was there for six months. It's something like X State Hospital. He couldn't adjust and he was getting sick and was sick for the six months he was there. And so it was on our last visit that we seen just how bad he was doing. He wasn't improving at all and was getting worse. He had lost weight. He forgot how to walk. He couldn't hardly crawl. I mean what color he had when he was put in there was all gone. And so we thought that by having him there, it was more or less killing him.

In this case, the process of having their child institutionalized was seen by the parents as tantamount to murder. Had the child died while in the "colony" the parents would have felt responsible for his death. Nor in one sense was this an unrealistic appraisal. The fact is that since his removal from the institution five and a half years ago, the child has shown constant developmental improvement in all areas—physical, psychological and social.

The parents' concern for their retarded child's welfare in institutional settings was not without good grounds. One expert in the field drew this parallel.

> Literally, more money is publicly expended on the care of animals in our zoos than in the care of human beings in our state institutions. I have studied five of our largest zoos and find that they average $7.15 per capita daily cost for the care and feeding of animals of human size. The most recent survey of the United States Department of Health, Education, and Welfare this past August (1967) reports a per capita daily expenditure of $6.71 per patient under treatment in public institutions for the mentally retarded.[7]

An article reporting on a recent "confidential" study of state mental retardation facilities conducted by a team of experts from the California Medical Association and "pried" loose for public consumption revealed the following:

> SONOMA—Drastically overcrowded . . . Built for 2,400 patients, it now houses over 3,400. The understaffed maintenance department is facing a crisis. Building and interior repair work is at least five years behind current needs. Few teachers are available for the mentally retarded children. Their schooling is neglected. Staff standards are low. The only dental care made available is emergency extractions.
>
> NAPA—Patients receive less staff time than before (before current administrative cutbacks). The staff shortage is most noticeable in the children's wards. The size of the group therapy sessions has been increased 50 percent. The food is drab and sometimes served cold. Many patients spend time looking after other patients. It is incongruous that many of these patients have all or part of their costs paid by their families, insurance policies, estates, etc., but they receive no remuneration for this alleged work therapy . . .[8]

The article is too long to include in its entirety. Suffice it to say that the above was not unrepresentative of the conditions found in most of the other state institutions for the retarded considered in the study.

Some statistical indication of current inadequacies in public institutions for the mentally retarded on a national level is found in the 1968 report of the President's Committee on Mental Retardation. It is indicated that residents reported overcrowding in 75 percent of all the larger institutions. With respect to staffing, the report indicates that there are half or less than half the number of staff required in the following occupational categories: attendants, registered nurses, social workers and psychologists. In addition, there is a shortage of 2,300 occupational therapists, 2,900 physical therapists, and 5,100 medical social workers. The salaries of many attendants at institutions for the retarded were below poverty levels. These were only a few of the areas of crucial shortages noted in the report.[9]

Some idea of what former adult institutionalized retardates thought of their institutionalization can be had from the following accounts:

Martha recalls her stay at Pacific as one of unrelieved misery. In the first place, she felt exploited: "Nobody paid me anything. I did all that work every day and never got one cent. They just kept us smarter patients there because if it wasn't for us who'd do the work? The employees wouldn't do it. They just stand around and make the patients work."

But she also felt fear and the loss of freedom. "I was just like an animal in a cage. Bars and all. And anytime you did something they didn't like they'd threaten you with punishment like being locked up in a side room all alone. That's what they'd do, you know. They'd drug me with narcotics, like amdol (amytal), then put me in a room all alone. How is a person going to live right when they're full of narcotics? . . . The problem is that when you have been locked away in there for a long time you get nervous and also you don't learn about how to live outside, so when you get outside you can't act like a normal person—even when you're smarter than outside people. I was in there so long I thought I was going to rot. It's not right. I never belonged there and then they kept me so long that now I'm confused and nervous and can't get a job. All my troubles come from being in that place."[10]

Another former patient felt this way about it:

Mary went to school at Pacific for about a year and was able to improve her reading and writing considerably. Moreover, her IQ score increased in this period from 44 to 56. She was given jobs in the hospital and learned to care for children and to perform simple housekeeping tasks. She was never a troublemaker and got along quite well with the employees. She also lived fairly happily with the other patients in her 'cottage,' where she made many friends among the girls of her age.

Despite such generally pleasant experiences, Mary was usually unhappy in the hospital and was always anxious to leave it . . . She resented her loss of freedom, privacy and individuality; she disliked some of the girls in the institution, especially the homosexuals; she felt that the food was not fit to eat; she was disappointed to discover that there was no swimming pool or riding stable as she had been led to believe. She wanted to leave Pacific as soon as possible.[11]

Edgerton had this to say about the mortification of patients during their initial period of hospitalization:

> . . . entry into Pacific State Hospital presents the retarded person with a new dilemma. Although he is by now thoroughly familiar with mortification and has probably developed means of self-defense against suggestions of mental deficit, he is surely not prepared for the experiences that the hospital will inflict upon him. The cumulative impact of the initial period of hospitalization (at the time of the research) was greatly mortifying, leaving the patient without privacy, without clear identity, without autonomy of action, without relatives, friends, or family in a regimented and impersonal institution where everything combines to inform him that he is, in fact, mentally inadequate. A typical patient reaction is seen in the following words of a teenage boy who was newly admitted to the institution: "Why do I got to be here with these people? I'd rather be dead than here."[12]

Edgerton goes on to note that even after the initial adjustment period,

> the patients seldom appreciated either the hospital confinement or its regulations. As a result, *freedom from institutional confinement was a primary goal for every patient in the cohort*.[13] (Emphasis added.)

Keeping in mind all of the above, it is perhaps not surprising to find that parents placed their retarded children in institutions only as a last resort and usually with the understanding that it was more for the family's benefit than the child's.[14] Whether or not the press of necessity was felt early in the child's life or later depended upon a great many circumstances, e.g. the availability of outside help, family size, the parents' financial resources, the psychological makeup of the parents, etc. However, at whatever point the parents filed an application and got on a waiting list to have their child institutionalized, it was usually done only as a backup measure "just in case" or, in the final analysis, as a last resort. Kramm had this to say about the attitude of parents of mongoloid children toward the prospect of institutionalizing their children:

Not until they felt convinced within themselves that it was necessary for their child's future security could they even consider the idea of placing him.[15]

The reader is asked to note the distinction between "future security" and future development. In the above regard, Kramm reports the following findings:

When the parents were asked what they thought an institution could do for a retarded child, only fifteen of the one hundred mentioned special benefits; some of these thought he might receive better training and supervised recreation; others, that he would have round-the-clock supervision, good medical care, and the companionship of "his own kind." Fifty parents said that an institution had no advantage except to give shelter to the child after the parents were dead. Twenty-two others stated flatly that the institution could do nothing at all for the retarded child. Thirteen had no opinion; they had never thought about an institution in connection with their child.

But regardless of what the parents thought the institution could or could not do for the retarded child, twenty-three families had filed their first application for placement. In thirteen of these families, neither parent had ever visited an institution for retarded children. This was also the case in nineteen of the twenty-seven families that had not filed an application. Among those who had applied were ten families in which the parents could not agree about placement. Only two of these twenty parents had ever gone to see the place where their child might be sent.[16]

Given the nature of care in institutions for the retarded and the parents' early recognition of these inadequacies, most parents were under considerable strain waiting to see if their child's future development would ultimately necessitate placement. Since the children at the preschool were between the ages of four and eight, and the usual cautious predictions of doctors and other experts regarding the child's potential for future development was "wait and see" (in fact, wait until the child was about twelve), the parents usually became anxious early in the child's life about what to expect of him as an adolescent.

Well ... it's hard to tell (how far the child will develop). I've been waiting for that. In fact, every ah, ah, he sees the doctor two and three times a year unless an emergency, but ah, Doctor Jones has been seeing him on the average of two and three times a year. And that's a question I'd always ask him. Could you tell us now how far will Louis go—cause he does different things with Louis. And he sees a difference in him. I says well now, and he says Mrs. S. he says it's hard to tell. He says really he says I'll tell you maybe when he's ah eight years old. Well maybe I can't tell you anything till he's ten or eleven twelve. That's as far as he went. Twelve was the furtherest. So, my husband and I have in mind we're going to wait until Louis is twelve. They should tell us by then if he's going to go any further or he'll be lower or what.

"LEARNING TO LIVE WITH IT"

The question arises—what did parents do while awaiting future clues to their child's development? For the most part, parents in the author's series adopted a policy of "not thinking too far ahead" or "going day to day" as a strategy for "learning to live with it." One preschool mother put it this way:

You, you don't know what it's going to be like in the future. You, you have to think about it a little bit but it can get a little frightening at times . . . thinking about the future. So John (her retarded child) has taught me one other lesson of how to take things as they come and live from day to day. And that you really can't plan that far in advance.

Another added:

No. See I go day by day and month by month. But I'm not going to sit—like when they interviewed me before, (they asked) what are you going to do when you have to tell her she's going to become a woman? I'll worry about that at the time. When the time comes, then we'll take care of that situation. I'm not going to sit down and . . . she's only seven now. Am I going to sit down for the next nine years and think, what am I going to do and all that stuff? Let nature take its course in time. Time heals everything, and I figure work day for day, month for month. Take care of things as it comes.

A third parent, in summing up her primary concern with the concrete everyday problems of the here and now, had this to say:

They used to say things to me like—do you feel guilty, (about having a retarded child)? Are you disappointed? Disappointed? Guilty? Christ if I could just get a bottle down her. It's much more real, Dr. Jacobs. It's not all this theory. It's really not as psychological. It's . . . it's solid. It's something, you have to deal with it like you have to deal with this table. Are you going to sit on it, under it, beside it . . . (you deal with it) day by day, it isn't . . . you don't look so much, especially in the first few years, to the future. You can't imagine your child five feet tall, weighing 130 pounds and punching boys in the nose. You don't think of that.

It's a tiny thing. It's five, seven, eight, ten pounds, thirteen pounds in one year. Many of these children are undersized. It's even harder to imagine them growing up. They don't grow up. So why should you think of their growing up? No, it was the effort of lifting her over and over and over again out of the crib. And putting her down and praying she would sleep, and begging to any god that existed, even Satan, if she would only sleep.

The notion that retarded children fail to grow up leads the author to a consideration of how this tends to further restrict parents of retarded children to a present-oriented time perspective. We have already noted that the child's future career was defined by professionals as ambiguous, e.g. "he might not develop beyond the six-year-old level," and that the acceptance of this assessment by the parents led to the further prospect that the child might ultimately have to be institutionalized, or that the parents might die and leave the child stranded, helpless in a hostile world. The accumulation of such prospects was for the parents overwhelming. As such, they were avoided in self-defense and helped to minimize—for the parents—any consideration of the child's future and to orient them instead toward the here and now.

Another factor working to orient the parents toward the present was the idea that retarded children fail to grow up. This notion is so pervasive that it is difficult even for professionals to overcome. The author, during a number of field trips to various homes and workshops for adult retardates and state facilities with adult wards, was struck by the fact that dedicated and well-meaning nurses, technicians, teachers, social workers and vocational rehabilitation counselors, all consistently referred to thirty- or forty-year old retarded adults as "the kids." With the professional as with the parent, such an orientation probably tends to leave the helping agent with the feeling that the child "does not have much of a future." One preschool mother expressed it this way:

> . . . It is a blessing in a lot of ways (having a retarded child). You have a child who is, you have a child who is home longer, who is a baby longer. Everybody always says oh I wish they could stay babies a little longer. . . . It is nice to have one who will be home longer than the rest of the children. And particularly being that we're growing older.

ADOLESCENCE AND ADULTHOOD

However, the tendency of all of the above forces to negate the child's future were only partially successful. Two main areas of future concern always managed to assert themselves, i.e. the child's future development as an adolescent or adult and the well-being of the child after the death of the parent. The latter was particularly important in generating parental anxiety. The following are some of the parents' accounts regarding their hopes and fears for their child in adolescence and adulthood:

Well, it's like little wisecracks have been said to me, about some day he's going to be pulling you instead of you pulling him. And it's going to be true, too . . . And if and when Jeffrey does get to the point that he controls us, then he will be put away. I mean, there's a drawer at home that's very handy that's full of butcher knives. Jeffrey never touched it. The first time he does, he's going to wind up very sorry for it. And if and when he learns that he feels like he wants to go around to stab at the kids, and I can't control it, he will be put away. Like I say—when he controls us, I've had it. I won't take no more. It won't be because I don't love him, and it won't be because my husband and I very seriously feel that we've done wrong; it will just be that he's uncontrollable now and that we've done the very best that we could.

I haven't been able to bring myself to consider that quite yet (the prospect of institutionalizing her son). I think the chances are that he will need to be placed in some kind of residential situation, and we've kind of accepted that, when he gets to be a teenager and difficult to manage, assuming he doesn't change too much from what he is now since he hasn't changed much in the last five years; I don't expect him to change a lot, you know. I would expect that he probably will need a residential type of situation . . . unless we can control his behavior considerably more than we really can now. I don't think I could manage him.

If he continues at his present rate of development, we have every intention of keeping him at home . . . unless, as I say, I can't foresee the future. If he got to the point where we couldn't control him or something, you know, that might lead to it (having him institutionalized) but other than that we wouldn't consider it. And I don't think it's necessary; he does fine in a family situation.

Oh yes I've thought about it (what her child will be like as an adolescent). Well I hope mentally she develops much better. Cause

I thought of her going through the menstrual period with diapers. Now I don't know how that would be. How much she would understand. And how come, you know, it would be a problem too, well, I guess it would be a problem anyway, but with a young lady that doesn't understand. . . . But like I say, it's a long way off.

Well, that was the first trip we made to X school. They had a PTA luncheon, a fund raiser that they have around Christmas time, and they sell things that the children made. . . . So we made a date with them to where we went the following May, and she the principal took us to the different classrooms from the little guys up to the big ones. And then your eyes are opened; you feel the real light. I did, and I'm just hoping that Roy (her retarded son) will be able to do that. . . . And when I told him (her husband) that this 18-year-old boy that reminded me of Roy so much . . . well this little guy, even his coloring reminded me of Roy. I says I picture Roy that old already. Oh, he says, you're sending him off to work already. And this little boy was in the cafeteria, and getting lunch. We stayed there until lunch because we purposely did that because we wanted to see the children. They helped prepare the lunch for, in the cafeteria with the mothers, and it makes you feel a little better, especially when you see a child that's the same as yours that's doing it.

Well, you know, I've learned that . . . you don't think about that (the child as an adult). You know, I often think that the bubble is going to burst, and everyone is going to say that there was never anything really wrong with the child to begin with and everything's going to be perfect. I think we all kind of wish that. And then I think well maybe I'll have him home with me for the rest of my life. He'll be able to do things, but he wouldn't be able to . . . wouldn't like well get married if there's something the matter, depending what it would be. And then I just think I shouldn't think at all, because none of us, none of us can plan . . . I mean there are things that you sort of wait until the time comes. Yeah, well, . . . well sure I used to think well, will he be able to get married, you know, when they said he needs a special school. What, what have I got here? You know, and all that type of thing. And you learn from many of the other mothers who have children with problems that . . . you just don't even think about these things. I think if you think too much (you'll be overwhelmed).

So I guess it's natural that he (the husband) would be (overprotective) because he figures that she (the retarded child) can't defend herself as well as . . . Of course he's always, even with the older girls with dating, he is always very very strict because you know, he felt that there was so much harm could come. Well, God knows it happens all the time. You see the terrible things that happen, you've just got to pick up the newspaper. But he worries all the time about her, very much so. And in fact we had an interview with Dr. Jones (who) invited us to go up to Stockton last summer to be interviewed by a group of public health nurses. And some of these women brought up, such as we hadn't thought of before—at least I hadn't thought of before—marriage. . . . I just took it for granted that she wouldn't, . . . well, I know retarded children who are in their thirties, and they're still living at home, and they're perfectly content. So I just kind of figured that this was the pattern that most retarded people followed, well unless they were institutionalized. And one of the people, I don't remember if it was Dr. Jones or one of the nurses, said—and just what do you see for Joanne in the future? And he says, well he says, I think she'll probably get married. And gee, I, you know, we've never talked about it. We've never talked about this kind of thing. . . . Well, I've done a great deal of thinking about that since that time. And in fact, I've talked with other people about it, Mrs. H. in particular (the preschool director) . . . and she told me of a young couple that she heard of that were both of them retarded, and they wanted to get married, but they felt it was inadvisable to have children and the girl was sterilized. So under those circumstances, why I guess this would, you know, like my husband was saying, well with birth control pills, you know who needs to worry about having children. But of course we're Catholic, which kind of . . . right now we're kind of under a cloud as far as this is concerned, as far as birth control pills and as far as sterilization is concerned, because the church does not allow sterilization even for people who are mentally retarded . . . I had never thought of her getting married, although I think that Joanne might be a very good housewife, she loves to help around the house, set the table, and do things . . . and she loves babies—oh she dearly loves babies.

THE CARE OF THE CHILD UPON THE DEATH OF THE PARENTS

We have already given some indication of the problems that face parents of retarded children. Would their child become unmanageable in adolescence or adulthood and have to be institutionalized? Would they be able to find future educational facilities? Would they marry and/or have children or be partially self-sufficient? These were all future problems that parents of retarded children struggled with. However, perhaps more important than these with respect to the ability of future concerns to generate current anxiety, was the question of what would become of the child upon the death of the parents. This problem was one that parents often considered but rarely discussed with others. Then, too, they found small solace in such discussions on the rare occasions that the topic arose. The parents' expression of this problem and their inability to resolve it is illustrated below in a sampling from the transcribed verbatim accounts:

Ooooh! Oh yes. Heavens, Yes. (She had thought about what would become of her child in the event of her death). Boy, one day something happened to me and I can remember the block in which I was walking, you know, and it occurred to me then I must have had a very sharp pain, I can't really tell you what happened to me, because I don't remember. But it gave rise to certain emotions, you know, and that was the first thing I thought about. And I didn't give one thought to my other two children. That was the first thing I thought about. If I am not around and . . . and I still tell myself that, you know. These two (her normal children) can take care of themselves. . . . But Patricia, if something happens to me, what about Patricia? Who's going to take care of Patricia? Oh . . . I used to, oh boy, I'll tell you, that really was always uppermost in my mind and it still bothers me. But as I think about that right now, I don't think about that nearly as much as I used to. And I think it's because I see evidence of the progress that she's making. But that used to bother me—oh that particular day I actually started praying that nothing would—and I pray that prayer all the time, that I might live to see her grown, because I really don't know, I have every hope that she's going to be all right, but if she isn't, I want to be the one to take care of her you know. I always think about that. That more than anything else. And when I think about that, I never involve my other two kids in that thought. I wonder about that all the time you know. I figure that they've got it made, I guess; I don't know. Which is maybe not the way to feel, but it's always Patricia that I'm thinking about when I think maybe the day will come when I won't be around and then what. I say no don't let that happen, you know, anything but that.

As I say, I intend as long as I am able to keep him at home. And we wrestled this around—whether it's better for our other children. You know, to grow up and take on responsibility for Sam. And I don't think they would have to unless they wanted to as they grew older. So at that point we might have to, possibly we might have to institutionalize him. If something happened to my husband and I. And as I say we wrestled this over whether we should bring up our children with the idea that one of them is going to take over Sam if something ever happened to either of us. But I don't know if it's fair to them. Because they're entitled to a life of their own. It's not their fault they have a retarded brother. That's why my husband felt we should at least put in an application in the event that it ever becomes necessary (to have him institutionalized). And this is kind of like saying—what are you gonna have for dinner next Wednesday? Who knows where I'll be next Wednesday? You know, this is sort of a far-fetched thing, but I think it's one of our biggest worries.

Yeah, what do we do with Mike? How far do you go with him? Of course, the big thing we take everything and just kind of go along with it. But the big thing is if something happens to my husband and I, then what is there for Mike? That's the big big problem, because the brothers and sisters won't be able to take him. Because he's mine and he's my husband's, and we take care of him—they're a lot of care. And there are a lot of people who just can't cope with them.

I sort of dread it, but well the only time I was real frustrated about Janet going to Sonoma, I talked to Dr. Black and Dr. Smith, and Mrs. H. was the only one who I think sort of knocked me to my senses that day. Cause I was really considering it, because I thought if it was best for Janet then this was what I wanted. But I wasn't sure that this was best for Janet. I wanted to go see what Sonoma was like . . . and I said well what would happen to her if we died? And she (Mrs. H.) said well, she would automatically go to Sonoma. And I didn't know this. She said there is something called an emergency something or other. But I couldn't ask her godmother to take her. But the more I think about it she might change. But I believe she would take her. Although I never really discussed it with her. But it would be, I don't know, now that I think about it, it starts me to feeling that way again. . . . But then you wonder—okay, as things stand now, they say they're understaffed and overcrowded and oh there are so many things, nightmares you can have about somebody beating your child. Or a bad mental case, maybe vicious who'll maybe grab her and hurt her, oh a lot of things you think about that are frustrating. And at the same time you're hoping that it doesn't happen but you really don't know.

And I immediately thought well, what's going to become of her? This was the first thing that entered my mind. I don't know whether it's because I'm older, and I suppose if it were my first child or even my second I might have gotten more upset, but having four for myself, I wasn't shocked (to learn that she had a retarded child). I thought well, those things happen, why should it be any different for me? We'd had a good life and all the breaks up till that time. That didn't upset me. But what did upset me was the fact that she had had elderly parents, or they would be elderly in no time at all. And this still bothers me. This is my big concern.

Yeah, we've thought about this quite a lot. In fact, we've thought about it from the standpoint of both the children; my husband has been talking for years about making a will and setting up some sort of guardian procedure for David. We would like to set it up in such a way that if anything happened to us, we're going to make reciprocal wills with my sister, and that if anything happens to them, we would take the children, and if anything happened to us, they would take the children, but we wanted to make provision for David to be admitted immediately to say Sonoma, so they wouldn't have to worry about that, you know. . . . Where Mary could be absorbed easily with my sister's two-year-olds, David would be considerably more of a problem. . . . So anyway, we've been going to do this for a number of years. I don't know why we didn't get around to doing it. It's a funny thing—this business of making a will. I guess you, it's sort of the thing you don't really think about *really* needing, and although we've talked about it a lot, we just haven't done it yet.

But like I say our problem is what's going to become of Charlotte, if something happens to us? Where will she end up? And nobody's given me an answer. . . . You never know. You can be healthy today and . . . I've given it a lot of thought; like I say we both think but we don't know what to do. We just don't know what to do or who to turn to.

Here again, the above concern was in no way peculiar to the parents in the author's study. The following are a few illustrations from the verbatim accounts of the parents in Kramm's series:

The only thing that worries his father and me is what will happen to Alex if anything happens to us. This is more recent thinking because the mister and I are getting along. His dad has always thought of his future. I'm sure that is the reason why, just as soon as we knew about Alex, he took out a 20-year policy for him. And we've never tried to put him away. We want to keep him home.

He's not a bad child. I'm strong. I don't mind doing for him. Still, we can't expect his brothers and sisters to take care of him.

We want to see what we can do for Bob—if we can manage. All the relatives say keep him—don't let him be taken away. We have all learned to love him. We'll keep him as long as we can. We applied for care to give Bob security only because we hate the thought of his being left out if we die.

. . . Earlier, I thought he would grow up to be a comfort to me. Now, we have to coax him so long it's hardly worthwhile. I hope we'll outlive him or all go together. I wish he could be placed in a happy individualized atmosphere, near home, before I die. . . . We'd never dump him on our other children or suggest they take care of him. If they suggested it, that would be different, but they have their own life to live and we keep out of it. The thing now is to find a place for Malcolm. If there's money, that's possible. But we'd miss him if he were gone.[17]

The practitioner's awareness of the serious and ubiquitous nature of this problem and his free and open discussion of it with the parents, would go a long way toward providing a much needed and sought after relief.

The anxiety generated by the uncertainty of what would become of the child upon the death of the parents was only one of a series of effects that the retarded child had upon the family. The following discussion will consider some additional ones in two sections: the effects upon the parents and the effects upon the sibs.

EFFECTS UPON THE PARENTS

The literature relating to the effects of the child's retardation upon the parents is divided into essentially two camps. One group of researchers feels that fathers make a faster and/or better adjustment to the child's retardation than mothers do.[18] Another group believes the opposite.[19] The author's data very definitely favors the latter view. Most fathers in the author's series (according to the mothers' accounts) were less able to accept the diagnosis, tried to hide from the public the fact that they had a retarded child, and/or were more often overprotective. The following are a series of relevant excerpts from the verbatim accounts as they relate to the effects of the child's retardation upon the father, and their consequences for the father, mother and child.

> I don't think he's (the husband) accepted it (the child's retardation) yet. My husband is a very deep man, and he keeps most of his thoughts to himself. He doesn't believe in showing any emotion. And this has hit him harder than he realizes. And his behavior has changed a great deal, and this is quite (clear)—to other people, not only me, but many people have seen it in him. My husband doesn't see it in himself. He's just been the way he is, (he thinks) but there's been a drastic change in him. . . . He used to be quite easygoing, and nothing seemed to get to him too much, and he was much happier and much more relaxed. And I mean I don't think he's over Paul yet. He's the type that may never get over it. He's closer to Paul than to any of the other children. Spends all of his time with Paul. And this got to be a problem, because he was spoiling him so much that the pediatrician said—if you ever hope to accomplish anything, he'll have to learn discipline. So the pediatrician wrote a letter to my husband, you know, that he would have to crack down and not let him get away with murder. . . . I don't feel he (the husband) has recouped. He won't even go to a doctor. And I say he's just one of these people who has to hold everything in and thinks emotions are reserved for other people, and he has no real release. . . . And he cannot talk about it very readily. I don't think I've ever heard him say that he has a retarded child. I'm sure the people he works with have no idea that we have a handicapped child.

> . . . he (her husband) tries not to see the bad side of it (the child's retardation). He would more or less like to think that there wasn't anything really wrong with John. But as each day went by, we could see it more and more. Not so much the days, but when the months go by, and he makes no improvement, and then we have little nieces and nephews, well we have one niece that was born three weeks before John. And when you put the two of them together, it hits you in the face like a ton of bricks. . . . But that's when it really, uh, you know, you really get the cold facts. There's no ands or buts; it's right there. But my husband didn't say too much. He'll hold more inside than he would let out.

> . . . I told Sam, (her husband) I says—I've got to tell the people I'm close to (that she has a retarded child) because I just can't keep that to myself. . . . That's not solving anything. Well, Sam didn't want to talk about it, so I would tell them. But myself, I

think I'm the luckier of the two because I can talk about it. . . . Oh sure, yeah, because if it helps (talking to someone else about it) I hope that it will help my husband. This is what I'm hoping more than for myself. Because like I said I probably need a lot of help, but I'm able to talk about it more. If they say—how's Herbert (her retarded son), I don't clam up. Sam doesn't do that as much any more. At first, people were almost afraid to ask him—how's Herbert. Because they could just see the tension in him; that's not good. You can't, you know, live that way. . . . I guess it bothers me in different ways than it bothers him or something. I just feel that you kind of have to take it as it comes.

Well, it's rather interesting (what her husband thought about the child's retardation). I don't think he felt there was anything wrong with him at all. . . . When I first mentioned to him that there might be something wrong, I wasn't quite sure how to put it, because this baby meant everything in the world to him. I mean, you know, like he felt like the king of the road. This was the culmination of all his hopes and dreams—to have a son. And I suggested to him that I hoped he wouldn't be too disappointed if it turned out that Robert was maybe not able to go to med school. And he was quite upset when I mentioned that. He was really angry. He said—well, I never said I wanted him to be a doctor. He really reacted to that. And I, you know, actually I didn't think Robert was really terribly impaired at that point. I was just wondering if maybe he might not be quite as bright as we thought. Maybe he would never make it to college. . . . But I had a hunch he (the husband) would have had some kind of special goals for him.

And my husband is the kind that likes the voice of authority . . . and this was authority (the doctor's advice to the parents not to say anything to others upon first bringing their retarded child home from the hospital). And so we said nothing. We didn't tell the children either. . . . My older daughter was still in training (to become a nurse) so she wasn't there to tell, and finally around the end of October, around Christmas time, I just couldn't stand it any longer, and when we called our folks and our daughter, it was just before Christmas, she was with her grandparents. . . . I called and told them then. They took it very well. . . . And I called and told his (her husband's) sister, who I think is almost my best friend, a sister-in-law and one of the most nicest people around. But my husband still didn't want me to tell anybody else. In fact, he was quite angry when I told them.

Well, it broke him up. He tried not to show it, but I felt it because at that time he was shipping out. He was a merchant seaman. And

Simon (her retarded child) was about six weeks old and he had to get a ship to leave, and I could see it all over him. He hated to leave us. And uh, he says he doesn't believe the doctor. You know that's when I, well, I sensed it, that he still doesn't. Where I could see, you know, that Simon is (retarded), but him, I guess it was this way and that way—not having any children you might as well say. And it broke him up I think quite a bit, because there was a difference in him to where we couldn't get along for a while together. I mean, I felt that was what was causing it. But then, after Simon was a couple of years old, there was a difference to where, well, it's something you've got to live with and things have changed. But I think now for instance, when he sees the granddaughters and Simon tries to keep up with them, you could see in his face, in fact Sunday he says—if Simon was a normal child, he'd be eight years old; now look what he'd be doing. So that's why I feel I guess, well, I have my four normal ones (from a former marriage), and he couldn't have one.

And my husband was very good (upon first hearing his child was retarded), although he was very, the fact is the night that we found out, I don't know, I called him or he called me, and I told him there was something wrong. And my husband is the type that really goes to pieces, and then I have to feel like I'm the strong one and have to kind of buck up and keep him from going to pieces. Fact is, seems to me, the doctor gave him a sedative that night. . . . Yeah, well of course my husband is very overprotective. And, uh, very overprotective with Joan, which is why his first reaction about sending her to school (the preschool) was rather on the negative side. He sees now that I was right about a lot of things, but he's still holding back on a lot of things. . . . I felt that he should have gone along with me more on trying to advance Joan. Because he can see now so much where it really has, the schooling and all, has meant so much to her. . . . What would she be like today (if he had kept her at home)? She's a bright child in her own way, but she needs someone to bring her out, and I don't think parents are the people to do it. Parents are not trained for that sort of thing.

Well, what can I say? How do you feel when you know that your child is, you know, . . . (the mother failed at this point to say the word herself) . . . This is a word that people used to shy away from. That was a kind of undercover thing, a well-guarded secret. And I know it's more open and above-board now, but I don't know, you certainly have some reservations or some feelings of anxiety. And I'm sure both of us (she and her husband) did. I think we could have helped Susan, had he not catered to her whims when she was small . . . my husband used to have a very bad habit when we first found out that she had a retardation problem. I have two other children. . . . He would say to them—now if Susan were doing something she wasn't supposed to be doing, and they knew that they weren't supposed to do it either, and they would tell her— don't do that, he would say—well now don't yell at her like that, you know Susan is not normal and . . . so we kind of got away from that. We had a little talk about that. . . . We used to try to make her say things (the child didn't start to talk until she was three), just anything, and she wouldn't. Because she used to suck her pacifier. And that was always in her mouth, and everybody was handing her things on a platter, you know, everything. So why take that out to talk? There was just no need to talk. And she wouldn't. She was really just about three years old before this happened. Then she started talking. She kept that pacifier until I guess she was about four years old. She was still walking around with it in her mouth. And I thought, oh, she would just have such awful tantrums when I would take it away from her. My husband would say . . . let her have it. Give it to her; let her go to bed and go to sleep, because I have to get up in the morning and go to work. A cousin of mine moved into the house with us for a very short period of time, . . . and everytime she saw it (the pacifier) she would put it in her overcoat pocket and take it with her. And she would say— now Susan you're too big for that. Keep it out of your mouth. And I'm gonna take it away. And Susan never cried when she spoke to her like that. She was very firm with her. And that is what stopped it. And every time my husband would go out and buy another one, this cousin would take it and hide it, and she wouldn't have it, so she stopped then. And you could see evidence of words coming out after that. She had nothing in the way, so she started to talk.

And sometimes it gets pretty frustrating. He feels like . . . you know, it made me feel like I was the hired hand, that whatever he (the husband) did was fine and whatever the child did was fine (their retarded child), but I couldn't chastise her. I said— now if you're gonna raise her, you do it; if she dirties her pants, you clean em. You be her mother and her father. You put her to bed; you comb her hair; and you take her to school. You do all these things. I said—now if I'm gonna play some role here, when I figure she's wrong, she's gonna get spanked. . . . But I think like I say, little by little, where it takes people about a year to adjust, it's taken us almost ten years. But I think we're finally gonna make it; we just might.

I have presented above some of the mothers' accounts of the ways in which the child's retardation affected the father and some of the consequences for the mother and child. With respect to the child, fathers were more overprotective and solicitous. Because the child was waited upon "hand and foot," it required little initiative or inventiveness on his part to get what he wanted and/or do as he pleased. This in turn tended to retard the child's development in two ways, firstly by encouraging a lack of initiative based upon necessity and secondly by assuming (as in the case of insanity) that the child is neither responsible nor accountable for his actions. The latter position resulted in excluding the child from a key feature of any normal socialization process, i.e. he was rarely subject to "limits" or to disciplinary action stemming from a breach of limits. In short the tendency was to view the child as either blameless (ultra-moral in a Rousseau sense in that he was incapable of being corrupted) or amoral, in that if he did wrong it was in no way by design.

Overprotection also led to the child's isolation. For example, fathers tended to feel that no one could or would care for the child as well as he and his wife and that the child should be kept from the "corrupting" influence of either outside helping agents or other retarded children, e.g. at the preschool. Add to this the father's initial desire to keep the child's retardation a secret and we can readily see some of the ways in which this isolation was extended.

The author wishes to emphasize at this point that the influence of the child's retardation upon the father and the consequences for the mother and child were not all negative. The net result of the child's retardation upon the parents varied from family to family. While nearly all families experienced a serious disruptive influence resulting from the child's retardation, this was for most parents associated with the initial shock of discovery and a period of adjustment. Granting that the adjustment period was sometimes a lengthy one (in a few cases, a satisfactory adjustment from the point of view of the parents' interaction has not yet been accomplished, even after five or six years), in most cases the parents succeeded in accommodating to their new situation, and in the final analysis found that having a retarded child had "all worked out for the best" or proved to be "a blessing in disguise."

> Neal, you know, you talk about a child being very sensitive, he is. Whenever he sees my husband and I had an argument, and I mean a serious one where we're screaming and hollering, and he (the husband) is trying to run in the closet for his clothes (packing to leave), and I'm begging on my hands and knees, Neal gets very upset. And he cries. He tries to pull us apart. . . . I mean Neal sees that and he gets right in there between us and he stands down there just crying his heart out. And I mean he's enough to make you want to come closer together. So I can actually say that if sometime we didn't have Neal, we might not be together now. So we can be very thankful to Neal for a lot of different things. And especially with keeping us together too.

> And, uh, you can't fool them (retarded children); you may think that they don't know what's going on. I felt that way. Now I learned you can't, uh, he knows (her retarded child) what's going on. Even if my husband and I have a little misunderstanding, he knows there is . . . he'll come in between us and look at the both of us as if to say—well, make up, forget it—you know. You can't fool them in any way.

> But as far as Stanley changing anything in our lives, if anything he's brought us closer together. And he's taught us a love I'm sure we wouldn't learn from ten normal children. As a matter of fact, my best description of Stanley is love. I mean he is . . . sweetness personified. I can be in a rage about something and turn around and see Stanley and his smiling little face, and he'll really kind of calm me down . . . Ken (her husband) is pretty easy-going and pretty level-headed. Some days I don't like him too well, and I'm sure he doesn't like me too well, but on the whole, we really have a closeness to start with. But with Stanley, it has grown a much closer feeling, and I think a deeper love between the two of us. . . . And also it has taught us to be more and more understanding of other people, a lot more tolerant of things, you know. Well I thought I was tolerant before, but I'm much more tolerant now. And cause sometimes you listen to somebody else and you wish they'd shut up; they're really bugging me. But since I've lived with Stanley and been out here at the preschool, I can take much more time at listening to somebody else's little problems. . . . Once you've been through I think a real big emotional upset and a real big hurt, you can understand all these other emotions in yourself and other people. To me, I think Stanley has been a wonderful experience.

> . . . At the time I took her home (her retarded child) the doctor had suggested leaving her in the hospital. I think maybe he felt it might have been too much of a crisis for me to handle or something. And of course I couldn't see that. But I realize that if she'd been left in the hospital, she'd have slept her life away. She'd have never lived through it. And we'd have missed a beautiful experience.

However, a few parents who had not been able to satisfactorily adapt to the situation felt that their child had exerted a disruptive, or in two cases, a disintegrative influence upon the family.

> My mother came occasionally. She would come if we were leaving. We went away for several weekends. I wouldn't say we took this (the child's retardation) lying down. We didn't just succumb and say—it's the end of our lives. And we'll do everything for her, and no one else will ever touch her. We didn't do that. And a lot of parents do. I know many parents of handicapped children who didn't leave their children; I mean for a minute or the father is there. We did struggle to stay together, to be a unit, you know, outside and beyond her (the retarded child). We did retain and maintain some kind of adult exchange, but it was a losing battle.

But even in these cases, the mothers expressed a warmth and love for their retarded child and indicated that the interaction between them (if not between the mother and father or mother and other children) had grown closer and stronger with time. In short, notwithstanding the family conflict the child was seen to have generated, or the mother's feeling that "she had to live with *it*," or the mother's homicidal feelings toward the child from time to time, there developed between the mother and her retarded child a state of strong ambivalence and frustration that somehow resolved itself in the child's favor. Even when infanticide was entertained, it was (from the parent's point of view) "for the child's own good." One mother expressed it this way:

> And I am sure that probably every parent that has talked to you has told you somewhat in the same manner that when you have more children, you know, the handicapped one is really the one you love the most. I don't know why it is, but it just exists; I don't know why. I had friends who had a deaf child, and this was the only one I had ever closely encountered with a handicapped child, and I could see they always felt sort of special toward her. And then, after I had Billy (her retarded child), I could see why. The idea

because they're less than perfect, you know, that you don't care about them is not true.

Most mothers indicated, directly or indirectly from what they said, that their child's retardation had a strong influence upon their social life. Parents went out only rarely, and when they did, it was usually one at a time. One went while the other stayed at home with the child. If both parents and the retarded child went out at the same time, there were certain restrictions placed upon where they could go. It usually excluded them from public places and restricted social outings to taking car rides, a trip to the park, or socializing briefly with a few close friends or relatives. This pattern was perpetuated in part by choice and in part by necessity. In the first instance, it was true that parents often felt that no one could meet their child's needs quite as well as they could, since only they really understood them. However, with time and notwithstanding the father's tendency to be overprotective, both parents would have liked to go out and socialize the way they used to, i.e. as other parents with normal children do, and leave their child with a babysitter. Babysitting services or other forms of respite care for retarded children were practically nonexistent. In most instances, the sitters were the child's grandparents or an older sib. This arrangement often proved a mixed blessing. Many parents stated that their retarded child had little influence upon their social life, because "we take him with us everywhere." This was generally true, since not taking the child often meant they could not leave. What was frequently understated was how infrequently they managed to socialize at all. This was especially true during the first few years. The following excerpts are illustrative of the constraining influence the child's retardation had upon the parents' social life:

> We try not to do anything that would involve having anybody come in to sit. If my husband goes some place, like a ball game or something like that, he takes my son; that's their affair. Then other places where I can take all of them I will do that. Or, if I want to go out alone, I leave them (her children) with him (her husband). Or he does the same. Between the two of us, or we will do something where all of us can go out together. Other than that, we don't—our social life is really very limited, so we don't really get to do anything else that doesn't involve the children or where we can't

have them actively participate with us. So I can't say that I do call
on anybody. . . . Oh heavens, yes, sometimes I would dearly love to
(get out and socialize more). I haven't really thought about that
since I've been working the way I am now. But when I was working
days, I don't know, my activities are much more now than they
were when I was working days, of course, because this part of our
life, this school here (the preschool) wasn't taken into account.
We didn't have this to deal with. I was far less active, but I seem
to be much more tired than I was, and when I would get home,
that wasn't the place I wanted to go, because I knew my kids were
there, and I wanted to go and relax, and you just can't, you know.
But I don't have that feeling now. I'm much busier now than I
was then (before entering the preschool). Maybe underneath there
was that frustration of not knowing where to go next with Anne
(her retarded child), or what to do . . . that probably had something to do with it. But all of that's settled in my mind now, and
I just don't feel the tension that I felt before; I'm much more at
ease with myself than I was then.

You know, we really haven't had too much in the way of vacation
trips. That's the only one we've taken (in six years). And we did
take him (her retarded child) along; it was a two-week trip. And
other than that, we . . . now we've gone away for a weekend and
left him with relatives. We've left him with my husband's parents
or with an aunt and uncle of his. They have been very good to us
and to John. His grandparents won't take John anymore. It's mainly
because he's not trained (toilet-trained). Because they were very
upset about my not training John. But I just never found a way to
master it. . . . Yes, partly they (the grandparents) feel (that her
failure to train him was some shortcoming on her part), and they
took him when Joan (her second child) was born, and he was 3½.
And they feel they had him trained. And you see when they
brought him back, they said—he's all trained. All you have to do is
put him on the potty after every meal. And, uh, it just didn't work
out . . . it got to be . . . we had a very unpleasant experience
centered around this whole business of toilet-training. . . . My husband stayed home for the first week after the baby. And he'd call
them (the grandparents) and ask them how long did you . . . say
you kept John on the potty? And then he'd say—well, he's been on
45 minutes; how much longer do you think we should keep him on?
So we thought maybe this would get across to them that it just isn't
working. . . . So finally after he got the infected rash which was
all over his body (as a result of their toilet training effort) . . . we
just decided that that was it. We weren't going to do it anymore.
We were just going to let it go for a while. And once we did

that, why then we could never get him back on the potty chair. He would never sit down on it. He just cried.

But now (of late as opposed to the first few years) I mean he (the retarded child) goes out with his daddy on Saturdays. On his day off, they're buddies, especially since he's been able to go to the bathroom. Frank (the husband) didn't take him a lot of places, not because he was ashamed of him that he couldn't go to the bathroom, but you don't take a child to a game and bring their pants and this and that along with them; he, you know, he made a mess because he was older.

. . . both of them (her mother and her sister) used to always be talking about how mean I am to Fred (her retarded son) and this and that. And I said—have you ever raised a boy? They said no. I said—well boys are different than girls, and you don't mollycoddle little boys and you don't sweet-talk little boys, cause they don't even hear you; they don't. And then my sister got involved working with groups in school, and she was working with little boys, and she found what little boys were like then. And she found out that you don't just say—now sweetheart, you don't do that; you might be able to say that to a little girl, but you don't talk like that to a little boy. . . . My mother's fairly young; she's only in her early fifties. But my mother, uh, well she makes me very angry sometimes. . . . You get so you're talking to her, and you no sooner get through than she has you repeating it three times. And by this time you're getting so mad, you say—mother, I just told you that. And then she gets mad at you because you're hollering at her. . . . And then a lot of times she'll tell other people—oh she wishes she could help poor Evelyn (the mother) more with poor Fred, and you know, this and that, but . . . she is not about to stay home and take time to take Fred to school or go pick him up or anything, you know. She's not about to get stuck with anything like that. So there are times when I just grit my teeth and I would like to say to her— mother, if you want to help, you could, but you don't.

She (the retarded child) gets into everything . . . everything . . . busy busy all the time. So that you always have her in your mind. You never have one minute that you can, you know, kind of blank out. So this four hours (spent daily at the preschool) is good for both her and for me.

We have seen how being confined a good deal to the home isolated not only the child but the parents. For the most part, the only persons that mothers could discuss their problems with were the grandparents, a close friend if they had one, and—on occasion—an older son or daughter. Unfortunately, attempted dialogue with the above persons often proved frustrating and/or unrewarding. Add to this the fact that many mothers felt (at least during the first few years) that they could not discuss their child's problems with their husbands, either because they were "quiet hard-working men who didn't talk much," or because the husband would not admit to the child's retardation, or because the husband spent so little time at home (compared with the time the mother spent in constant contact with the child) that there was little time to discuss the child's problems in any case, and one gets some notion of the extent of the frustration and isolation the mothers faced.

The mothers' discovery of the preschool changed all this in a very significant way. It ended their isolation as well as the child's and opened an avenue of meaningful discussion with others in similar circumstances who could understand and empathize with the mother's day-to-day problems. It also provided both mother and child with a respite from one another and afforded to each new and meaningful forms of interaction that neither had previously enjoyed. Not only were these forms of interaction new but they were in many instances the most meaningful either had managed to establish of late and at a point when the need was strongest.

Notwithstanding the parents' desire to be able to socialize more, or have more free time, or witness the miraculous recovery of their child, had any or all of the above occurred they would have been viewed by many parents as mixed blessings. Some key reasons why parents felt this way are given in the following account:

> Doctor Jones asked me a question one day, and it goes like this: 'If you could have John turn normal right now, would you want it that way?' And I came out and I said—No. I said it so fast that I wanted to pull the words back in right after I said it, cause I feel like this, and some day I'm going to tell Dr. Jones this. I'm going to answer him in this way, and that is that I wouldn't want John to turn normal just like that, right now, because there are so many things that I enjoy out of John the way he is that I would miss actually, and besides that to just all of a sudden have so much time to yourself, it's kind of a shock to you too. I mean I'm going all the time

after John; now if all of a sudden I've just got the time to sit and relax, that's going to bother me—just drive me crazy. And so, now I should have really answered, that is I would have liked to see John turn to be normal, but to do it just gradually. Even if it takes five years.

Had the child miraculously recovered or the diagnosis proved false or the child died or been institutionalized, it would have meant for the parents, and especially the mothers, two things. On the one hand, they would have had more free time (which was something mothers both wanted and were no longer accustomed to), and they and their husbands could have, in time, taken up a more active social life. On the other hand, it would have destroyed in one fell swoop a way of life that the parents had established since the birth of their child, i.e. for the last four to eight years.

> He (*the retarded child*) *was the one* child who was not expected to grow up; who was disciplined, praised, teased, humored, coddled, was expected to have no will of his own, but *around whom family members, especially the parents, rotated.*[20] (Emphasis added.)

As a result, while the child's significant improvement or complete recovery was something all parents hoped for, they did not do so without some feelings of ambivalence. The above was especially true for the mothers, only two of whom were employed outside of the home. The fathers' days were occupied at work. For the mothers, the allocation and distribution of time revolved almost exclusively around their retarded child. Even when there were other children in the family, they were usually at school or in the case of older children, married, in the army, or away at college.

The above discussion has outlined for the reader some of the reasons why and the ways in which parents of retarded children had managed to redefine the effects of their child's retardation so as to convince themselves that it was, in fact, "a blessing in disguise."

EFFECTS UPON THE SIBS

Eleven of the fourteen cases in the author's series involved the presence of one or more sibs. We have already discussed the retarded child's effects upon the parents. What were his effects upon the sibs? The author's findings tend to support those of Kramm that ". . . most of the normal brothers and sisters were sympathetic and helpful. Only a few were not."[21] Mothers reported that sibs loved the retarded child, got along very well with him, and were understanding and helpful.

Notwithstanding the mothers' tendency to preface their accounts of interactions between their retarded child and other children with this cheerful and optimistic note, it soon became clear that things were in many respects something less than ideal. The following excerpts are illustrative of the general tone:

> Joan (her retarded child) is nowhere near as much a handicap as some children, but still it's kind of a growing experience. For a family, it's a real testing experience; it was hard on the others, on the children who were younger. Not younger than her, but we have two teenage boys . . . I think Len (one of the two boys) took it harder than anybody at first . . . Len is . . . well, there are two boys at home. Len is 15 and John is 13. And Len was, I'm sure that Len was particularly affected because of the fact that he couldn't say anything to her (the retarded daughter), but he called John a retard. Every time he got mad at him, John was a retard see. Well this, if you understand anything at all about this, you realize what it was. You know, it's his way of reacting. And John in turn, John of course being the youngest of six boys, was in a particularly bad spot, because everybody picked on him you know. He had to battle before he could stand up . . . and he has had problems . . . John does tease Joan in his own way; see he's got subtle ways, and of course she has learned, like all children learn, that if she screeches when somebody looks cross-eyed at her they'll get into trouble. . . . So it's meant problems in the family.

> Fine. Fine. (how the sibs relate to retarded child) The older one gets annoyed with me, mostly because she thinks I'm spoiling her, but she's an R.N. so she thinks she knows all the answers. And she's very good with her; if she had more time. . . . I think she could discipline her better than I can. The 19-year-old is in the army, but he's sending a small amount every month to put in the bank for her. And he was real good when he came home on leave, took her for walks and watched her for me and played with her. The 16-year-old she likes best of all. And he can take her or leave her. When he plays with her, she knows he really wants to play with her. He's taking time out to play, and when he doesn't want to be bothered, he just doesn't want to be bothered and she knows it, but she seems to like him best of all. Anne (a younger daughter)

plays with her and then after a while Anne gets tired because she can't keep up with her, and she gets lonesome for other playmates. We don't have, as I said, we don't have any children in our neighborhood. . . . There has never been any sign of animosity at all. They've done marvelously well. . . . Once in a while, little Anne feels she'd like to have a little more attention, and she really doesn't get enough. I'd like to give her more, but she's a very happy child, and I can't see that there's any lasting effect. . . . I think she should have a little more attention than she does get. But the others you see (the older sibs), one is already gone, and the other keeps threatening to leave cause the family is so noisy and all.

The one that Evan (the retarded child) has hurt the most has been Ruth (her 5-year-old daughter) because Ruth being a baby, whenever something happened to Evan, she was pushed aside. Where I can actually say that it grows on the youngster's mind, why is he getting it when he's older and I'm still a baby and I'm not getting it? Things just don't go that way, now do they? And I feel that she will always have that in the back of her mind, because even now she gets a little resentful at times when Evan does something that he's got to have my attention for quicker than hers. And it's just like with potty training. Ruth feels, well he's older; why isn't he (potty trained)? Why do I have to be when he's still older than I am? Why am I getting pushed above Evan? Why do I have to do everything before he does when it comes to learning things? But then on the other hand, why does he come before I do? So I mean it's quite confusing to her and I feel that Ruth feels it more than anyone else. If I could start all over again, I really don't know what changes I could make, but I could only hope that Ruth could come before Evan. Because I feel that she . . . would have come along a lot faster. I mean Ruth still has some accidents at night; she gets up the next morning, and it doesn't bother her at all because she comes out and what am I doing but taking diapers off of Evan. Why should it bother her? I mean she's still the baby and feels why can't I wet the bed. And I mean it was the same way with walking; she was slow at walking, very hard to take the bottle away from and everything else because Evan still had all these things and she was getting away from it. . . .

She (her seven-year-old daughter) gets along good with Evan. . . . She slaps him down whenever he needs it. But she won't let him get by with nothing. Well, just like I've told her with this here pushing habit that Evan gets into, I said whenever Evan pushes you, turn around and push him right back, just make sure he doesn't get hurt. I says don't push him into the wall or onto the bookcase or bang his head into a cabinet or something. I says just push him.

Let him sit down in the middle of the floor but let him know that you don't approve of it.

And it is a little hard for his (the retarded child's sister) because, you know, he destroys her things—eating her crayons and tearing up her books, carting off her doll furniture and breaking it, . . . he doesn't deliberately break it, but he treats it so rough that it breaks. You know, he bounces it along, scratches up the walls. . . .

Yeah, fine (how the sibs get along with retarded child). In fact, they tend to overprotect him. And of course like I say they still get stuck with the duty of taking him out. I can't trust him out by himself, so it's kind of six of one half dozen of the other, but on the whole they're very very good to him. And even our 13-year-old, we've been having a great deal of problems right now; he's the one that's closest to Peter (the retarded child), and he's very good with him. And it's funny. When I first told the three of them (that their brother was retarded), they reacted very differently. The oldest boy cried, ran into his room and cried. My daughter took Peter into her room and she was reading a book to him, trying to teach him the alphabet—A, B, C. And then the third one, I just kind of felt the whole thing kind of went over his head, I'm not sure how much he got out of it. So every once in a while, I have to remind him that Peter is a little slower and we need to treat him a little differently. But he's the one that's got . . . he was the baby until Peter came along, so I think there's a little jealousy there.

But . . . it seemed like the day that I was coming home from the hospital, my son-in-law was bringing us home from the hospital, and I also wondered what my children would think (of the retarded child). And . . . it took me a week (to tell them), and here they said there was nothing wrong with him. And here it's hard! And I just feel for the ones whose children never show a difference (no visual signs of retardation) and it's harder even for them (the parents and sibs to accept the retardation).

It was generally true that sibs were understanding and helpful toward the retarded child. However, younger sibs seemed to have felt more of a disruptive influence. They were jealous of the greater amount of time and attention shown by parents to the retarded child and his exemption from the demands and expectations associated with normal children. Younger children tended to view this differential treatment as parental favoritism, especially when the normal child was so young that he could not grasp what the retardation meant and/or if he was the only other child in the family. In general then, the older the sibs, the more helpful and accepting they were.

With sibs, as with adults (and outside helping agents), the general attitude towards the retarded child was paternal. The notion that the retarded child would remain "retarded" and "a child" into adulthood was a key determinant of the sib-retarded child interaction. In the author's series, the age range of the retarded children was from four to eight. Even at this young age, a younger sib would refer to an older retarded brother or sister as "the kid." This outlook perpetuated itself into adulthood.

> Although in life age a few of the mongoloid young people in this study were adults, they were retarded as children. One sister of a 32-year-old mongoloid brother coaxed, 'come, honey, eat your dinner like a good boy.' The younger brother of a 16-year-old mongoloid sister inquired, 'have you been a good girl today?'. Still other children referred to their mongoloid brother or sister as 'Little Jack' or 'Little Jane,' irrespective of age. If the retarded child was the first born, his brothers and sisters grew up past him and looked back on him as the last born and as the 'baby' of the family.[22]

In short, the nature of the retarded child-sib relationship from childhood to adulthood was, depending upon age differences and family size, essentially one of "play" and/or jealousy and rivalry. Much less emphasis was placed upon the role of the sib as teacher. This is unfortunate, since sibs often spent, in the aggregate, a considerable amount of time with the retarded child. If both parents and sibs adopted the perspective that the retarded child was both responsible and accountable for his actions (as indeed most are), i.e. if they treated him seriously, these forms of interaction might have progressed from "play" to more advanced educational and social forms of exchange. The beneficial effects of home educational and training programs upon the child's future level of competence has been noted elsewhere.[23] That retarded children are denied the benefit of such programs and/or access to some outside educational programs, needlessly results for many in their ultimate institutionalization.

REFERENCES

1. See for example:
   Elizabeth R. Kramm, *The families of mongoloid children,* Washington, D.C.: Children's Bureau, U.S. Department of Health, Education and Welfare, 1963, p. 6.
   S. Olshonsky, Chronic sorrow: a response to having a mentally defective child, *Children,* 1962, 43, pp. 191-194.
   E. Smith. "Emotional factors as revealed in the intake process with parents of defective children," *American Journal of Mental Deficiency,* 1952, 56, pp. 806-811.
2. Roy De Verl Willey and Kathleen Barnette Waite. *The mentally retarded child,* Springfield, Illinois: Charles C Thomas, Publisher, 1964, p. 197.
3. *San Francisco Chronicle,* September 26, 1968, p. 7. For an interesting parallel, see a previous essay by the author entitled "The Use of Religion in Constructing the Moral Justification of Suicide," in *Deviance and Respectability: The social construction of moral meanings,* edited by Jack D. Douglas (In press, Basic Books).
4. D. J. West. *Murder followed by suicide,* Cambridge, Massachusetts: Harvard University Press, 1966, p. 48.
5. *Ibid.,* pp. 49 and 82.
6. *Ibid.,* p. 48.
7. *PCMR Message.* April 1968, p. 3.
8. *San Francisco Chronicle.* October 13, 1968, p. 21.
9. *The edge of change: A report to the President on mental retardation program trends and innovations, with recommendations on residential care, manpower and deprivation,* President's Committee on Mental Retardation, Washington, D.C., Government Printing Office, 1968, pp. 12, 16.
10. Robert B. Edgerton. *The cloak of competence: Stigma in the lives of the retarded,* Berkeley: University of California Press, 1967, pp. 59, 71.
11. *Ibid.,* pp. 76-77.
12. *Ibid.,* p. 146.
13. *Ibid.,* p. 147.
14. Kramm, *op. cit.,* p. 35.
15. *Ibid.,* p. 43.
16. *Ibid.,* p. 28.
17. *Ibid.,* p. 33, 31, and 34 respectively.
18. See for example:
   Alice V. Anderson. Orienting Parents to a Clinic for the Retarded, *Children,* 1962, 9, pp. 178-182.
   A. Hersh. Case Work with Parents of Retarded Children, *Social Work,* 1961, 6, pp. 61-66.

19. See for example:

Fanny Stang. Parents' Guidance and the Mentally Retarded Child, *Public Health* (London), 1957, 71, pp. 220, 234-236.

Mary L. Yates and Ruth Lederer. Small, Short-Term Group Meetings with Parents of Children with Mongolism, *American Journal of Mental Deficiency*, 1961, 65, pp. 467-472.

M. J. Begab. *The mentally retarded child: A guide to services of social agencies*, Washington, D.C.: U.S. Government Printing Office, 1963.

J. W. Oberman. The Physician and Parents of the Retarded Child, *Children*, 1963, 10, pp. 109-113.

20. Kramm, *op. cit.*, p. 18.
21. *Ibid.*, p. 18.
22. *Ibid.*, pp. 20-21.
23. See for example:

Nigel Hunt's *The world of Nigel Hunt: The diary of a mongoloid youth*, New York: Garrett Publications, 1967. It notes how a mother of a retarded child, having been told by ". . . the senior officer concerned with mental affairs . . . 'oh, yes, a little mongoloid. Quite ineducable. Do you want him put away?'," proceeded to educate him. The child in question grew up to author the book.

Ray R. Battin and Olaf C. Haug. *Speech and language delay: A home training program*. Springfield, Illinois: Charles C Thomas, Publisher, 1964.

W. M. Cruickshank. *The brain-injured child in home, school, and community*, Syracuse, New York: Syracuse University Press, 1967.

Ruth Mallison. *Education as therapy*, Seattle: Special Child Publications, 1968.

Edward L. French and Clifford J. Scott. *How you can help your retarded child*, Philadelphia: J. B. Lippincott Co., 1967.

CHAPTER 6

BEHAVIORAL SCULPTING: PARENT-CHILD INTERACTIONS IN FAMILIES WITH RETARDED CHILDREN

DAVID A. GOODE

A SEARCH OF THE literature reveals that previous studies of families with retarded members have focused upon the social background of the family (social class, religion, ethnicity), response patterns of the family (stress, emotional reaction, institutionalization, changes in family life-cycle, marital problems, role negotiation), characteristics of the retarded member (age, sex, birth order, degree of retardation), and characteristics of parents and/or siblings (personality traits, reactions to stress, changes in role enactment).[1]

While such studies provided interesting information to clinicians, public health officials, social scientists and parents, they are characterized by a complete lack of naturalistic data. They tell us a good deal about "factors" or "variables" (social class, ethnicity, religion, birth order, etc.) which were reasoned to contribute to "typical" adjustment patterns (institutionalization, acceptance, high stress, marital problems, personality alteration and so forth), but very little about the way members of such families experienced their lives.[2] In our pursuit of typical patterns we have "lost" the family.[3] In a very literal sense I could not find a single family in those writings if one means by "family" the kind of social organization we know so intimately as a fact of our own lives.

It is to rectify this shortcoming that the following case study of a family with a deaf-blind retarded "Rubella Syndrome" daughter is offered. The data presented is based on the author's participant-observation with the family within their home and with the retarded child at school. Methods employed included the overt use of a cassette tape recorder whose presence was explained in each setting as a way for me to avoid the distractions inherent in taking copious notes. A large amount of the data was taken from these tapes or from notes made while listening to them.

It might seem that the presence of a tape recorder in the home would prove to be a highly "reactive" method of data collection. Quite the reverse was the case. The family accepted my explanation for and quickly normalized to its presence. In fact the whole idea of using the recorder grew out of prospective considerations of how note taking might prove an even more reactive method of data collection in a context such as a "home" where informal and open interaction is common. The idea of constantly turning away to write notes seemed unwise in terms of the quality of field relations with family members as well as with regard to the completeness with which I would be able to attend to observation *per se*. On both these counts the tape recorder proved highly successful.

FAMILY BACKGROUND

The Maxey's are a middle income family of four. The father, Jim Maxey, a forty-two year old high school educated machinist from a small town in Georgia, came to California in the early 1960s. He was married, had a son and divorced within a short time and proceeded to "live the life of a sponge" till he met his present wife Betty. From the time of their marriage Jim worked in a machine shop six days a week for usually sixty hours per week. At the time of this study he was earning about $20,000 per year and owned his own four-bedroom house in a blue collar district in Los Angeles County. Betty, four years Jim's junior, was California raised. Her parents had come to the state in the 1950s. She was a secretary when Jim met her and they married in 1966. When Breta was born Betty became a full-time mother and housewife till Breta was old enough to go to school. During the study she was doing "day care" (care of other people's children in the home) because she wanted to supplement Jim's income and because she likes kids and gets lonely while hers are in school.

When Breta, their Rubella Syndrome daughter, was born she brought extreme collective troubles and personal suffering. Breta herself was in medical difficulty from the moment of birth and, as one story has it, actually almost died a short while before heart surgery became an indicated procedure. While that procedure did allow her to live and return home with her parents, that return made Betty a full-time mother, custodian, nurse and teacher—an almost martyr-like existence because Breta needed special training to accomplish even the most basic developmental stages. Perhaps it is testament to the parents' strength and adaptability that their marriage survived and that they were able to parent a normal female named Tara some six years after Breta was born.

Breta was functionally deaf and blind but used her eyes and, with the assistance of hearing aides, her ears. She could see persons walk across a room but would have to "study" them to identify who they were. Her hearing was likewise degraded although she could rock to music on a radio near her or respond to changes in inflection or volume in human voice. Breta had significant brain damage to the motor areas of the brain and this profoundly affected her walking. At the time of the study, after a major orthopedic surgery, she was barely able to walk independently with the aid of a walkette.[4]

The "last" member of this four-person family was Tara—a very pretty and precocious seven-year-old. Her behavior and activities within the home so interested me in my initial visits that in a way it was she who convinced me that the family as a unit deserved my analytic attention. At the time of the study she was going to first grade. She was usually home by the time I arrived and would generally "be around" while I was in the home. I had many opportunities to observe and talk with her. In her behavior I found many clues to interpreting Breta's.

SCULPTING BRETA'S PRESENCE

In dealing with the term "sculpting" we will examine in "naturalistic" or "emic"[5] terms what would be considered clinically "pathological" or "abnormal" normal parent/retarded child interaction. The clinical professions, which in many ways influence the lives of persons like Betty and Breta, employ non-naturalistic, "objective" procedures whose consistent application is supposed to yield reliable information about them. Very often these procedures and their concomitant forms of observation and analysis allow parent/child interaction to be examined with respect to "scientifically" produced standards of "normality." Clinicians then speak of the family in terms of its continuities and/or deviations from "normality." In the case of the family with a retarded member, families are spoken of almost exclusively in terms of their deficiencies—as they are deficient from the usual or typical case or abnormal.

Such forms of reasoning completely dominate professional assessments of developmentally disabled children and their parents. Ironically, as much as they dominate professional thought they are equally as extrinsic and irrelevant to understanding such persons' behavior together. They are, to borrow a phrase from Garfinkel, "specifically indifferent" to the familial context of action.[6] They decompose meaningful familial interaction into clinically locatable problems with regard to—in fact sometimes in direct contradiction with—the lived realities of everyday family life. To some degree I am also guilty of transforming family life, though, into "analytic" problems, not "clinical" ones. However, my being sensitive to the imposition of extrinsic categories onto family life does differentiate this work from all previous studies.

LOCATING THE PHENOMENON OF BEHAVIORAL SCULPTING

In my presentation of background materials I briefly discussed Betty's biography with Breta. I indicated that when Breta was brought home the basic responsibility of child care fell exclusively to Betty. Recall that Jim spent twelve hours per day, six days per week at the machine shop. At first it was all Betty could do to help keep the child alive and even months later a "hopeful" sign was Breta's ability to defecate without the aid of suppositories. Later medical custodial duties widened to include pedagogic ones—pedagogies designed to teach what is normally learned without specifically arranging for their being taught—for example, to be able to crawl from one point to another. Even these learning sessions were extremely labored and difficult for Betty. Betty's efforts in this regard were, however, rewarded as Breta did learn to do many of the things about which the doctors had not been hopeful. Her success should not distract us from an overall view of these early years for Breta and Betty as extremely difficult years for both of them. The infantile phase of total dependence of the infant on the mother was prolongated in Breta's case and, because of Breta's weak constitution and frequent bouts with illness, school was only irregularly a relief. Betty ended up spending an incredible amount of her time with Breta and, considering the way she was medically, custodially and pedagogically working with her, she became unusually intimate with her—from the perspective of normal mother-daughter relationships perhaps even "hyper-intimate." Under such conditions each became well practiced in the routines of life with each other and this feature was evident in the look of their mutual work when I entered the household. In some sense Betty had a tremendous investment in her daughter and since the household was more or less her "show" (strict division of marital labor according to sex-role typifications) I focused a lot of my observations on them. There was another sense in which they recommended themselves to be studied as a dyadic unit.

During the course of observation it was quite common that the identities of and authorship of action by family members were not always clearly discernable from the look of things. This lack of clarity was most evident in Betty and Breta's relationship and relatively early in my work in the household I characterized their relationship by the terms "alter-ego confusion."[7] The term's usage was motivated by the observation that it was often difficult for me to unequivocally separate who was an author of some action. Many of their activities involved such an exquisitely delicate, complicated, detailed and mutually coordinated work as to make one consider that mother and child were part of some identifiably distinct behavioral unit with *sui generis* characteristics. A description of some of the practices that constitute this work is one goal of this chapter and will be attempted through the explication of field notes. Let us begin our discussion by presenting some characterizations of Betty and Breta's work. In so doing, we will further define our phenomenon and analytical problem.

Listening back to the tapes of my sixth visit to the home I came across an interesting though troublesome section of tape. During a guitar session (see below) Betty was insisting that I make Breta do the deaf-sign for "more" without making any allowances for her lack of muscular control in her hands. Practically this meant I had to reinstruct Breta since she had already learned my modified sign for more. After showing her the proper sign a few times I addressed a question to her, "OK," meaning (intending) to formulate whether or not she had got the message about the called-for modification (while addressing conversational terms to a deaf-blind, alingual person is not a particularly efficacious procedure, it is typical of persons who regularly interact with them). In this case the question was taken by Betty as a question directed to her and answered it *on her own behalf,* "Yeah," i.e. that the new sign met with her approval.

The talk sounded "funny" to me and when I sought to draw out its anomalous character I came up with the following: Usually Betty would be able to distinguish when I talked to Breta and her next utterance would be one which would be an answer on *Breta's behalf;* for example, David: Hi Breta. N how r you feeling today? Betty: She's doing alright. David: You been eatin up all your food? huh. You been eatin all your food. Betty: She's been real hungry today . . . I don't know why.

In such talk Betty would linguistically provide the information which Breta could not supply directly. Sometimes Betty would talk on Breta's behalf *as if she were Breta.* That is, she would answer a question posed to Breta in the first person using a child-like voice.[8] With respect to the normal everyday regularities of family life Betty's failure to answer my question on *Breta's behalf* was hearable by me as an instance of trouble on the tape. The anomalous character of the incident provided me with powerful access to a feature of family life previously only tacitly recognized by me—that is, as a way for me to comprehend Breta's presence to Betty as a "to be spoken for" speaker. *That* was most interesting.

Through discussing this and other observations in a similar

vein, Mel Pollner and I came to speak of a "family average of mentality." By this we meant that in many cases (this being one) where one finds a family with four members, they will do the work (or they will do their best to do the work) of producing four members.[9] Another way to put this would be to say that the family is "allotted" the work of producing four full persons and that, in the case of a family with a child like Breta, (a severely retarded, deaf-blind, alingual, nonambulatory child), other members may have to "make up for" persons who do not fulfill their share of this work. Consider that most middle Americans (such as Jim and Betty) have a loose and useful conception of what a "normal" family looks, feels and acts like. Our preconceptions in this regard run the gamut from sexual taboos to eating habits, dress to sleeping arrangements, diet to religion and many of us employ this stock of practical knowledge in hand as a way to manage and understand our own and other families.[10] For Jim and Betty, as for most of us, this interest in having a normal, good family life is not idle. They deeply desired this and toward this end devoted a good deal of their thought, time and feelings. They, especially Betty, even had aspirations and dreams in this regard. Now even if we grant the wide diversity of interpretation as to what "good" or "normal" means, a child such as Breta is bound to create severe difficulties in achieving such aspirations. I propose that much of Betty's work with Breta can be understood if we construe it as a way to display to herself and others that her family was a "normal" one—i.e. an accountable normal, inspectably normal family with a retarded daughter.[11] We can further refine this analytical formulation.

The family's enterprises, and in this case primarily Betty's work, were intended to provide a manageable, mutually satisfactory and inspectable quality of life—inspectable to family members *and* to outsiders. While my initial entry into the household (as an outsider) provided me with a particular form of these "normalizing" practics—i.e. those which I call below "presentational practices" and which are designed specifically for to understand that the ways Betty made up for Breta's various outsiders—through prolonged contact with the Maxeys I came deficiencies were not *just* presentations intended for me. They were also ways to normalize the look and feel of the family *for themselves*. In the following cases, the ways Betty can be seen to be "making up" for Breta's deficiencies will be explicated in these senses of the work.

The following examples are exemplary.

(a) *During the course of interaction*—(This was the first visit and I had just met Breta for the first time). I am sitting at the table with Breta playing with her wrists and hands (Betty had showed me this form of bodily play which Breta thoroughly enjoys). Breta starts to peer at me apparently working to try and see who I am. The mother does a formulation of Breta's action and asks *as if she were Breta* in a child-like voice with high inflection and a baby-talk character "Who's that?" Breta pushes my hand away and I say, "I guess that's that." The mother informs me that she will "tell me" if she wanted me to do it anymore. Breta does so by grabbing my arm—Betty notes this to Jim.

(b) *During interaction*—This example most clearly illustrates the kind of behavioral sculpting which initially led me to call this phenomenon by the term ego-alter confusion. Breta is in the standing table and has another half hour to go. Mother goes into the playroom and attracts Breta's attention. (I already have a sneaky suspicion of what's about to happen so I start to tell her to leave Breta in the standing table.)[12] As Betty passes by the rear of the standing table she begins to fidget around with the wooden pieces which hold Breta's back erect. She jiggles them out of their slots almost teasing Breta with the possibility of her getting out of the table. Then Breta turns and reaches at the wooden pieces herself. The mother then turns to me and interprets this behavior as Breta indicating that she can't take the standing table anymore and that she should let her out. There is something funny here. The mother seems to use "props" to stir up motives in Breta and then takes these interactionally produced motives as Breta's motives.

(c) *After the fact*—I am upstairs with Breta and Betty is downstairs making dinner. Breta crawls out of her playroom towards the steps. I pick her up and start her to the bathroom thinking that she wants the "next" in her routine. She pushes me away, falls to the floor and "runs" away (crawls quickly) into Tara's room. There she throws off the pillows and lies on the bed. Unsure as to what this was all about I go downstairs to ask Betty.

B: She's been doing that . . . is the shade open?

D: Yeah.

B: She'll close it . . . you didn't turn the light on?

D: No, I didn't.

B: She doesn't want the lights on. I been pulling the shade up and she's been pullin it down. She wants it dark in there. She's been doin that lately. I don't know why she goes to Tara's room. She knows it's not hers.

D: She's been doin that lately?

B: Yeah. She goes into all of our rooms. Like at night. She knows where her room is. She knows its her bed. For awhile she was wanting to get in bed with Tara. Just wanting to be in bed with Tara. She's be laying there and all covered up. Just laughin'. Like it was neat or sumpthin' . . . She used to get in our bed too. She plays in every room in the house. She knows where every room is and what's in there and whose it is. I'm positive.

D: I wonder why she came out then?

B: She came out to play.

D: And she crawled out into the hall.

B: She'll go into her room and play too.

D: I mean she crawled out into the hall to get somebody's attention right?

B: No. She just crawled out. She jus' starts to play when it gets kinda dark in there. She just likes to play with the lights out . . . or she'll turn the hall light on and she'll go into her bedroom and lay down on the floor and play with the door and the light. You know, like peek-a-boo. She'll open the door this much (indicates an inch distance with fingers) . . . she has her own little games, you know what I mean? (I go upstairs and find Breta playing exactly the peek-a-boo game the mother had described).

(d) *During interaction*—We are walking Breta from the school bus to the door of the house. She appears tired. She collapses a few times before we reach the house. Each time she falls on the floor she first begins to laugh. All the while the mother is telling me that she really isn't tired but she's just being a brat. Finally we get inside the house and Breta just crumbles to the floor in a fit of laughter.

B: She knows I'm mad.

D: She's laughing cause she knows you're mad at her?

B: Cause she knows I'm gonna give her a spanking (taps Breta in rear).

B: She just sort of teases you . . . she's a big tease.

(e) *During intereaction*—Both parents are present. Breta is sitting at the table and waiting for dinner. She is impatient and begins stomping her foot. Jim goes up from behind her and tries to pick her up and put her on his lap. She resists and seems to want to go back to the table to await her food. She tries to hit him and then to bite him but he knowingly avoids these attempts and maneuvers her so that she can't get at him.

D: Gonna bite huh?

J: No, she's just gonna get mad . . . she likes to set down and eat.

D: (Turns to Breta) Breta, don't you know you can't have everything the way you want it when you want it?

J: Pretty soon she gets mad and comin' after me (laughs). She's gettin strong. Hard to hold.

Betty adds that when her food isn't ready she get real angry.

BEHAVIORAL SCULPTING

When I first reviewed these cases the term "behavioral sculpting" suggested itself to describe Betty's work. For the most part this work consisted of the mother's physically supplying "missing" pieces or aspects or interaction (supplying a question in case (a) or narrating the meaning of Breta's behaviors (cases c, d, e). Sculpting could also consist of a more literal molding of behavior wherein actual displays of Breta's behavior were managed through using, for example, "props," knowledge of likes and dislikes or routines. The most general form of "sculpting" was displayed in almost all instances of copresence and consisted of direct manipulation of Breta's body to literally put her into various positions. The import of these forms of work, its rational or directed character, seems to be towards: (1) the accomplishment of creating a desired course of action with Breta or avoiding ones which were not desired. (For example, cases (a, b) are "positive"; a negative case was once when Breta was stomping her feet at the table, and I saw Betty run over to her and pour her a glass of milk. She then told me she had just got there in time to prevent her from "blowing it") and (2) constituting non-ordinary or non-understandable behaviors as normal and interpretable (cases c, d, e). Through this kind of work I became acutely aware of how Breta's social identity was fused materially with her mother's behavior. Also, since Betty was for others visibly engaged in the work of sculpting, her identity was intimately bound up with that of her daughter.

The artistic metaphor is instructive in that the form and meaning of a sculpted object is accomplished through the work of sculpting, just as the form, meaning, look and feel of a sculptor's life is made available through that same work. Part of the metaphor's resonance with the work I observed Betty and Breta do consisted of this mutually defining character inhering in sculpting and parenting. The sculpting metaphor, as we shall see below also leads us to a feature of Betty and Breta's relationship in the way in which a sculptress is held strictly accountable to the detailed features of the medium or object upon which he works. Detailing and describing some of the practices which constitute behavioral sculpting will be the focus of the remainder of this paper.

A last point before proceeding with analysis of the cases: while sculpting constituted a set of practices through which Betty tried to "normalize" Breta's actions for herself and others I prefer calling what Betty did "sculpting" rather than "normalizing."[13] The former term provides one with the sense of embodied work in creating real objects in a real world—it says little about why the work was done or to what ends. The latter term sets up specific relationships between the craft of sculpting and certain societally defined, typical ends. As such I saw normalizing as a subset of sculpting practices and chose to use the more general name. We shall see (below) that sculpting could also be used for purposes other than simply making Breta appear more normal [see cases (b) and (d)].

THE WORK OF BEHAVIORAL SCULPTING

Cases (a) and (b) were taken from field notes recorded early in the work. Case (a) displays nicely the way mother and daughter would act in concert and how Betty's work accomplished the "filling in" of a missing piece of interpersonal work which might ordinarily be present—i.e. the child's question, "who's that?" Note that Betty, through voice inflection and aliteration does a *child's question.* Breta provides a bodily gesture which provides Betty with the visual cue which makes her utterance sensible and relevant—i.e. Breta leans towards me and begins to "study" me. The gesture even looked like (perhaps even a stronger word than "like" is in order here) the question's semantic referent. For Betty observing her daughter trying to see what I looked like, peering up and down at my face and body with a somewhat puzzled look, Breta's work was nothing else but "who's that?" Moreover she knew Breta's asking of the question in the kind of detailed way she could. Through years of knowledge mutually built Betty could not only recognize the question but even the different ways Breta put and answered it. Breta could look to see who someone was with the object in mind, for example, that if the person were anyone other than a family member he or she should leave. Or she could simply be interested in whether the person in her daddy's chair was in fact her daddy (that is, a simple matching procedure with no proposed action on its basis). Betty would understand these gestures as they occurred and in their look could find their detailed meaning. Cotemporaneous with a looking gesture then, I would find such statements as "she's lookin to see if you're her daddy cause he usually sits there—but it's too early for him to be home and she's confused" or "I think she wants you to get out," etc.[14]

Betty also understood in a detailed intimate way the various "answers" Breta would provide to her own question. Typically she would do the question and follow it by the following work: rejecting gestures and signs of displeasure; an accepting gesture—either returning to her activity or solicitation to the observed person; or, a puzzled expression displayed during a prolonged form of doing her looking.

Example (a) also displays another way Betty achieved a sculpting of her daughter's actions. In the above instance Breta's action is given its character through Betty's more or less cotemporaneous verbalization as if she herself were doing the action. Another craft is evident in the way I am told that my interpretation of Breta pulling her hand away ("that's that") was premature and that Breta would "tell me" if she wanted me to shake her wrist again (this is exactly what occurs). This kind of craft was an extremely common form of sculpting which was accomplished through (what I have labelled) "prospective narration." I was being told how to interpret what Breta might do in the future and in many cases the mother's narratives proved themselves to be extremely accurate.

I want to argue about Betty's explanation that it was grounded upon not only her knowledge of what Breta's typical or usual gestures meant—i.e. as lexical items in a gestural vocabulary—but also *who* Breta is and *how* Breta might react to specific situations. Gestures were understood as occasional—as growing out of some specific context and were interpreted via a diffuse body of knowledge about not only the gestures themselves but the way they were part of that setting. On any occasion of interpretation her diffuse body of knowledge involved not only a gesture's typical meaning but also Breta's likes and dislikes, motives for gesturing, how she felt that day, what happened last week and so forth. Breta's communications were "indexical expressions" and were so treated by the mother.[15] In the case under consideration, I do not think that Betty said to herself "she might want Dave to shake her wrist again." Instead, that prospect was evident to her in the very look and feel of our behavior and thus the faulted character of my utterance, i.e. my perception that she was through with me was available to her in the hearing of my words. Betty "knew" that our play activity would not end just then and that I would be "told" so by Breta. Summarily then in our examination of cases (a) we have named and briefly described two kinds of forms of sculpting work—to supply during the course of interaction, elements which "normally" would be present, or to "narrate" the meaning of some prospectively available behaviors.

Through case (b) we are able to see just how complex sculpting could become. The sculptress is strictly accountable to the character and features of the medium in and through which she works. Better sculptresses take advantage of their medium and this is no less a feature of the competent behavioral sculptress. Consider the way Betty takes advantage, in this scene, of working with an object which has a will of its own—a will expressed in terms of likes and dislikes, goals, motivations, projects and so on. The idea is that Betty knows the properties of her material well— she knows what jiggling the wooden slats in the standing table will mean to Breta and in so knowing, uses this in order to accomplish her creation.

The sculpting metaphor is not intended to lead us away from the concrete features of the relationship under study—nor to embellish it or make it sound more interesting, but rather to direct our attention to the sense of the work, its "feel," as it was observed. I could have alternatively said that Betty was interactionally accomplishing a way to get Breta out of the standing table without appearing that *she* (Betty) was the author of the action to some degree. The jiggling of the wood then would be the mother's way to produce a behavior display which would look like it was Breta who wanted to get out of the chair. This description would also, in some sense, be accurate and yet does not contain the notion of sculpting. The idea of sculpting is offered to the reader because it points to the way Betty accomplishes interaction through "shaping," "manipulating" or "molding" (all good words for sculpting's work) her daughter's behavior. In a way I find the metaphor a clearer explication than, for example, purely behavioristic or ethno-graphic accounts.

There are two other features of cases I wish to briefly discuss. First, I notice that the sculpting of Breta's behavior was intended or designed primarily as a way to get *me* to see *Betty's* work with Breta in a certain way—i.e. that she was being a good parent in acceeding to Breta's "demands" to be let out. In many ways her work was a presentation designed for me and was less designed to "normalize" Breta's presence to herself. It is of interest however that Betty's management of her own presence to the scene is so intimately bound up with the behavior of her daughter that she sculpts her daughter's actions in order to give a certain look to her own. That sculpting work could be in service to such a goal leads me to think of the work's import for family life as somewhat diffuse—as a way to handle not only the problems of the look and feel of Breta's behavior but also their own.

This leads us to a second less obvious feature of the work in this case—Betty's motivation for getting Breta out of the standing table. This whole scene was more or less staged because getting Breta out of the standing table at that time allowed Betty to accomplish her normal daily routine while still providing me with time to play guitar for Breta (also see "guitar activity" below). Footnote 10 explains why Breta was supposed to stay in the standing table and also alluded to some sources of dis-content on Betty's part as a result of this change. The activity was thus problematic before my entry into the home (in fact the week before my first visit Breta's teacher had visited the home to talk with Betty about this very subject), and, given that a full hour and a half in the table would have meant that I would have to wait till seven thirty or eight o'clock (approxi-mately three hours) till I could play for her and hence cut into normal post-dinner family routines, Betty's problem was how to get her out of the chair without appearing to me to be irrespon-sible and without interrupting too much her normal routines. The kind of sculpting I note above is a fairly elegant solution to the problem. This type of sculpting work may have been used when I was not present, i.e. the use of molding techniques to present displays for other family members, or when other persons were in the home.

Thus far we have seen three separate crafts involved in sculpting or molding Breta's presence to interaction: (1) supplying seeably missing parts of interaction on Breta's behalf; (2) prospectively framing her behavior and; (3) actually manipulating behavior through knowledge of the person and use of "props."

Case (c) exhibits yet another craft and I would like to examine it and its features. Note that I go downstairs and request Betty to talk about the meaning of the behaviors I had just witnessed—that is, I involved the work of retrospective sculpting through narrative. That I initiate Betty's talk attests to the vulgar way a Betty-Breta behavioral unit was vulgarly available to me and used by me as an ethnographic resource.[16] I did not hesitate or reflect upon how I would find out what Breta's behavior "meant." I did not consider the methodological implications of asking Betty to speak about the semantic content of Breta's behavior. I simply went downstairs and asked her. In some sense I want to argue that the Breta-Betty "unit" was a natural one and presented itself as a resource through which the family could be explicated.

Another interesting feature emerges through this case. While actually observing Breta's behavior I was aware that its semantic character (its meaning to her) was not available to me *but* that it was unavailable in a way which would soon be remedied—i.e. by asking Betty. While the syntactics of her behavior rested upon the progressive, undirectional flow of time (actual behavior displays in "standard time" never to be done or seen again) the semantics of her behavior—its meaning to her—was not similarly locked into a progressive time flow. Meaning was a feature of behavior which could await clarification or, alternatively, meaning was a feature of behavior which could await clarification or, alternatively, meaning was a feature of Breta's behavior which could be in some sense, done again (retrospectively, meaning was a feature of Breta's behavior which could be in some sense, done again (retrospectively finding meaning) or done before (prospectively narrating meaning). It was precisely this openness to semantic interpretation which Betty used in accomplishing narrative forms of behavioral sculpting—any behavior past, present or future was a candidate for the narrative device and this is precisely what made it such a powerful and so often used form of sculpting.

Note also that Betty completed her narration by telling me what Breta would typically do next in the sequence. The retrospective narrative smoothly becomes prospective and the accuracy of the prospection became available to me when I went upstairs and actually found Breta playing as described. As in case (a) Betty's prospection was very accurate and I was often struck by this feature. "Accuracy" was a natural indicator of just how well Betty knew Breta and in the use of prospective narration there was even a natural "test" of accuracy since the claimed events either would or would not actually occur. Thus in prospective narration it was not only the semantics of behavior which were at issue but also its morphology or syntactics, i.e. whether the bodily work would actually be manifest.

Another thing which impresses me about Betty's narrative is the way it points to an exquisitely detailed knowledge on Betty's part. It is so detailed and so matter-of-factly presented that one is tempted to think of the description as authoritative —that everything Betty said was exactly or concretely the case. The detail of her account displayed not only what she knew so well about Breta's behavior but also what she did not understand about it, i.e. that she enjoys lying on Tara's bed at night because she thinks "it was neat or sumpthin'" or "I don't know why she goes to Tara's room." Thus an aspect of Betty's display of familiarity involved the recognition of the ways her authoritative descriptions were not adequate for every occasion. In the face of such detailed, intimate knowledge I could only come upon my own knowledge of Breta as a deficient, less coherent, less detailed, less familiar version of Betty's. Within the household at least Betty was *the* expert on Breta-related matters. Not only was she the expert but she was so in a way which I could never achieve. Even as I write about her work with Breta and subject my field notes to a kind of scrutiny probably never employed by her I still feel that anything I might say about her arts must be an extremely simplified, "chunked" or glossed version of what

Betty displayed praktognosically.[17] Even Betty's narration or account in example (c), while in its own way an impressive display of intimate knowledge, itself chunks and glosses the kind of detail which *she would have to be able to recognize in her work with the child.* In some sense this is as it should be since the account was not designed to present this detail for my analysis but is rather meant as a way or an instruction as to how to render my observations meaningful. In fact the inclusion of such detail, of "deglossing" talk, or talk designed to provide another access to the technical character of her work, would have, as some of Garfinkel's demonstrations have revealed,[18] proved a distraction or even troublesome to the talk. Within the context of family life and its tasks there was no locally available reason for pursuing that kind of de-glossing talk. But consider that I cannot even achieve the kind of intimate glossed knowledge Betty has about Breta—as for example, as evidenced in case (c)—*let alone* gain access to the concrete audiovisual somatic detail of it and one can see why in terms of the actual production of family life, my knowledge of Breta would have proved inadequate.

Case (d) was included primarily because it shows that interpretative work was a form of sculpting used cotemporaneous with or in coordination with on-going action. I did not ask Betty why Breta was laughing but, instead, she volunteered the observation of her own accord. The nonsolicited work was an outgrowth of her growing intolerance of Breta's laughter *and how this was making the mutual work of ambulation more difficult* (note here that Betty's remarks are formulations of her work with Breta and how I am to understand it—that is, as a way to frame the upcoming "spanking"). She does not say to me "I'm mad" or "Boy am I getting mad" but rather *"she knows* I'm mad." In so saying she lays a certain culpability on Breta—that is, Breta was laughing *even though* (or even *because*) she "knew" so doing would make her mommy angry. She was teasing her mommy or, in Betty's language, "bein' a brat." I am being told that her laughing is being brattish and, while I presently wish to defer any judgment about the truth value of the proposal, this is certainly a strong claim, in some sense violating the ordinary or plain "look" of the behavior, about what is intersubjectively the case. It is only insofar as I "buy" Betty's proposal that the ensuing spanking is "justified" that I therein find Betty's motive for saying out loud and in so many words how she was interpreting the state of affairs. I also find that her perspective displays the kind of fault-finding procedures common on the ward (within the institution)—that is, faulting on the basis of whether behavior augments or hinders the accomplishment of routine tasks of a day's work.

Finally, we come to case (e) which shows that Jim also utilized these arts. We see both cotemporaneous (Jim's first utterance) and prospective (Jim's second utterance) interpretative narration. Notice that his effort seems to be to get me to see Breta's efforts at biting as *not* biting. This straight denial was somewhat transparent as nothing can "really" (or reasonably given the look of things) be offered as an alternative explanation. As stated above, someone aggressively trying to bite someone is simply not available to renaming or "mystification" by calling it something else. Thus, there were accounts offered of Breta's behavior by her parents which despite their detailed knowledge of Breta did not "hold water" and success in any attempt to narrate what she was doing was contingent upon how their words stood over against the audiovisual character of locally available events. Note also that this sculpting is an attempt to give form to the meaning of Breta's actions and is not an attempt to "make up" for Breta's actions through supplying missing interactional work or even a reasonable narration of it. I was being instructed to ignore the import of the look of things and this itself was an effective and fairly general device used by Betty or Jim to create a more normal social presence for Breta.

The most concrete, direct and general way of sculpting Breta's behavior was not specifically discussed through the cases cited and consisted of physical manipulation of her body. Such manipulation was a massively available feature of Betty and Breta's interactional work, and, while it was part of almost all the examples presented so far, for our present purposes will not be explicated through examining particular incidents of it in detail. Physical manipulation was omnipresent—*anytime* Breta wanted to walk, go to the bathroom, eat, wash, go to bed; or had to be given medication, taken to the doctor's, dressed and so on, I was guaranteed to find another family member (usually Betty) physically manipulating Breta's body in order to accomplish the work. Its details are less important than realizing that almost all normal daily activities were social enterprises for Breta and her mother. This being true, the physical maneuvering of her body was a *sine qua non* of family life just as it would be for the lives of persons living on a nonambulatory ward in a hospital. For Breta especially and for other nonambulatory persons, one may speak of the "socialization" of commonplace personal activity—i.e. the necessary involvement of others in accomplishing the most ordinary routine tasks of daily life. In this case of a motor-damaged deaf-blind retardate this socialization was extreme and was diffusely a part of almost all interactions. Whether at home or at school Breta usually had to be helped to get into her chair, go to the bathroom, to drink her milk and so on. Many of these forms of sculpting had a character to them so that it was difficult to imagine how Breta's work could be accomplished in any other way. While persons could develop minor variations in their technique to help her, *that physical aid of a certain type had to be used was unquestionable.*

SUMMARY

I have briefly examined practices used by Betty in sculpting Breta's behaviors. In this regard I named and characterized three major kinds of crafts: (1) physical aid and manipulation; (2) various forms of narrative, the use of "props," and; (3) denial. Through a consideration of these forms of work we can see an asymmetry in the ways Breta could bring forth interactional technologies designed to deal with how she is not fully in the world. While Breta clearly participated in many of these forms as work, she had access to the intentionality of Betty's work only when that intentionality was resonant with Breta's practical involvement in the situation—for example, that she had to get to the table or to the bathroom or to "love" and so on. Many other intentions displayed in Betty's work were lost to Breta—for example, to "save face," make custodial care easier, or "normalize" Breta's presence to the scene. I think it is interesting to note that mutually satisfactory routines could have been built by Breta and Betty even though they did not share the same motives for work, or definitions of how it was situated in either person's daily life.

It has been my purpose to present naturalistic descriptions of parent-child interaction. While the behavior which I called "sculpting" might be seen as clinically pathological (overprotective, overinvolved, thus inhibiting the growth of Breta's abilities), from the perspective of family members sculpting was life as normal. An understanding of life as normal has been missing from our studies of these families. This paper represents a step toward remedying this.

FOOTNOTES

1. The following is an abbreviated summary of some of those findings: Lower socioeconomic status families tend to make better adjustments to the presence of a retarded member (Tizard & Grad, 1961; Farber, 1960; Mercer, 1966; Holt, 1958; Wolfensberger, 1967). This has been partially explained through the use of a social expectancy model—i.e. the higher the expectations for the child, the more severe the parental reaction (Edgerton & Sabagh, 1962). It has also been suggested that the presence of the retardate in the lower class home interrupts living patterns to a lesser degree than in high SES homes. Catholic families show fewer signs of stress than those families of other religious backgrounds (Ehlers, 1966; Saenger, 1960; Begab, 1956; Zuk, 1959, 1961; Barsch, 1963). These authors propose a general ideological influence of Catholicism which allows believers to more easily adapt to this type of situation. They specifically point to the beliefs in the sacredness of life and to those which construe life's burdens as punishment from God for real and/or imagined sins. In an effort to evaluate the impact of the retardate on family patterns, a number of kinds of studies have been employed. Their findings are ambivalent. Normal/retarded matched studies (Davis & McAllister et al., 1973) show almost no differences in intra- and interfamilial socializing patterns. The one exception to this is the lower rate of neighboring activities noted in families with retarded members (McAllister et al., 1973). Studies of families who institutionalized vs. those who do not (Farber, 1960; Tizard & Grad, 1961; Saenger, 1960; Mercer, 1966; Barsch, 1963; Jacobs, 1974) have claimed only minor differences between these. The major exception to this finding concerns the various types of "secondary stress" (decrease in sociability, increased isolation, custodial burdens) (Wikler, 1976) which arise due to the continued presence of the retardate in the family. On the major indices of family

problems (marital difficulties, divorce or separation, psychological illness, role stress) the two kinds of families are not distinguishable. This is somewhat surprising in that we might expect that the presence of the retardate would increase family stress and with the increase of stress one might expect, for example, an increased incidence of divorce (Tizard & Grad, 1961).

With respect to the characteristics of the retarded child it has been suggested that the sex of the child can be associated with different patterns of parental reaction (Tallman, 1965; Gorelick & Sandy, 1967). It has also been suggested that the response patterns to the child change with age (Begab, 1960), and with regard to sibling response patterns, with severity of retardation. In this latter regard a number of studies indicate that the more severe the retardation, the more detrimental will be the sibling's reaction (Farber, 1960; Adams, 1966; Kirk & Bekman, 1964). Grossman (1972) has proposed that the mildly retarded child is more stressful to his siblings. Some studies have concentrated upon reactions associated with the social roles of mother and father. Fathers have tended to be generally uncooperative with researchers and we have consequently less information about them than mothers. Culber (1967) suggested that fathers may experience career damage. Wolfensberger (1967) proposed that the father's acceptance of diagnosis may be problematic. Farber (1960) and Gorelick & Sandy (1967) all indicated that a father's reaction to a retarded *son* may be extremely negative. Mother studies have noted impairment of the nuturing role (Ricci, 1970; Cummings, Bayley & Nie, 1966; Dingman, Eyman & Windle, 1963). Others have argued that mothers of retardates when compared to normal mothers tend to be more rejecting and over-protective (ambivalent), more angry at the child, more depressed and received less enjoyment from the child (Erickson, 1968; Barsch, 1968; Routh, 1970; Stevenson, 1954; Burnett, Tymchuk & Smith, 1974).

Finally, a large literature on personality characteristics and personality changes in parents is available. Studies of normal vs. retardate mothers reveal no significant differences on standard personality inventories (PARI and MMPI) (Ricci, 1970; Dingman, Eyman & Windle, 1963; Garfield & Helper, 1962). Burnett, Tymchuk & Smith (1974) found a significant difference between self-concepts of normal mothers and mothers of retardates. Psychodynamic studies of parental reactions to retardates in the family have been characterized by Wikler as "subjective" (Wikler, 1976). All these studies agree that reactions to diagnosis are usually strongly negative. This is followed by a period of mixed feelings which can then be followed by various kinds of adjustment (ranging from acceptance to institutionalization). Saenger (1960) found that 43 percent of parents exhibited guilt. Solnit & Stark (1961) identify a mourning reaction and/or chronic sorrow as common patterns. Mannoni (1973) noted emotional scapegoating. Roos (1963) and Michaels & Schueman (1962) all noted the use of various defense mechanisms to avoid negative feelings toward the child. Cooke (1974) found a pattern of "magical expectation" in which parents search vainly for a "cure" to the retardedness of their offspring. All these results are exceptions to the overall characterization of these parents as basically normal but under high stress.

2. The orientation of this study—that is its concern with the everyday lives of family members—is largely a reflection of my association with Professors Garfinkel and Pollner. The only other work which professes a similar regard is Lynn Wikler's, *Delusions of Competence: A Socio-behavioral Study of the Maintenance of a Deviant Belief System in A Family With a Retarded Child* (Ph.D. dissertation, University of California at Los Anegeles, 1976). Her work was also heavily influenced by Professors Garfinkel and Pollner.

3. See, for example of the underlying reasoning. Aaron V. Cicourel, *Method and Measurement in Sociology* (New York: Free Press, 1964).

4. A walkette is a device consisting of a handle bar attached (in Breta's case) to the frame with four wheels. The device is designed to distribute weight away from the legs and feet during walking. It thereby makes ambulation an easier enterprise for persons whose legs cannot entirely support their weight.

5. The terms "emic" and "etic" are found in anthropology and refer to "the natives" or "the folk" perspective on events (the emic) and the outsider's or field worker's perspective (the etic).

6. Harold Garfinkel, Lectures in Ethnomethodological Methods, U.C.L.A., 1973.

7. Note the use of the term "alter-ego confusion." At the time I meant the term as a way to index confusion at trying to separate out the work and identities of mother and daughter. I do not use the term any more because it is highly solicitous of a fault-finding version of Betty and Breta's production. It was not intended as a way to locate what was wrong with these persons but rather to suggest a concrete feature of their relationship—that is, that there was no sensibleness to trying to understand who Breta was without considering Betty's sculpting work *and* that this self-same work became definitive, in part, of who I understood Betty to be. The fault of my naming this feature "confusion" owed to *my* own confusion at attempting to sort out what was a high degree of mutual, albeit asymmetrical, dependence in the relationship. The confusion was more mine than Betty or Breta's.

8. While I could not record many such examples see case (a) below. Normals "talking for" the retarded is quite common.

9. Lynn Wikler in her unpublished doctoral disseration, "Delusions of Competence" (Department of Sociology, U.C.L.A., 1976) documents in detail how this was accomplished in another family with a severely retarded daughter.

10. The idea of a "stock of practical" knowledge is taken from the writings of Alfred Schutz (see *Collected Papers I: The Problem of Social Reality*. The Hague: Martimes Nighoff, 1962). Schutz's writings were recommended to me by Professors Garfinkel and Pollner.

11. These remarks borrow heavily upon Garfinkel's comments about "normal appearances" made in his seminar on normal environments (Department of Sociology, U.C.L.A., 1976). Note I am not making an argument here which relies on a generally understood, normative set of motivations except insofar as "generally understood matters" were present to the specific interactions with the family.

12. A standing table is a device used in orthopedic medicine. It looks like a child's high chair without a seat and is used to keep a person's legs straight while he or she is standing. In Breta's case, her legs were normally contracted and even after her surgery the contracture set in again in a short time. The standing table device was suggested especially after surgery to prevent the return of the condition but, either because of Betty's failure to use the device regularly or the school's failure to do so, upon my entry into the picture Breta's legs were as bad as before surgery. In fact, there was an "issue" between Betty and Breta's school as to whose fault it was that Breta's legs had regressed to her preoperative state—i.e. who had been bothering to put her in the standing table for the required number of hours. She was supposed to spend at least four hours per day in it and it was my impression that Betty was not overjoyed by the idea that when Breta came home she would have to spend two hours in the standing table. Even though this was the proper procedure to follow there were a variety of reasons (to be discussed below) why Betty did not want to and often *did* not, put her in the standing table. For present purposes the reader should understand at least that the standing table is somewhat painful to Breta and thus it is *not* one of her preferred activities. But because it *is* painful to Breta the mother can use her dislike of the standing table as a "feature" of or a "way" of the "object" which she is sculpting. The jiggling of the slats of wood which keep Breta's body upright are then understood by her as action which will tempt Breta into displaying her disaffection.

13. Wolf Wolfensberger conceived of and popularized the term "normalization" in the fields of human services. Wolf Wolfensberger, *Normalization: The Principle of Normalization in Human Services* (National Institute on Mental Retardation. Toronto: Leonard Crainford, 1972).

14. See below on understanding Breta's communications as "indexical expressions."

15. An extremely deep and interesting phenomenon addressed by Garfinkel was the indexicality of expressions. No short characterization of the phenomenon would do it any justice. Yet the context of these remarks do not allow for an extended discussion. Perhaps a not misleading char-

acterization would be that indexicality refers to the essentially circum-
stantial, contexted character of any utterance. See: Garfinkel, *op. cit.*,
Garfinkel and Sacks, *op. cit.* The term here is used particularly with regard
to gestural expressions.

16. The utility of an analytic which explains interaction in terms of
"examined and unexamined resources" was suggested by Garfinkel in
seminars (Department of Sociology, U.C.L.A.). Ethnographic resource
refers more specifically to the practices of social analysis (also employed
by Garfinkel in seminar).

17. We *can* be said to "know it Praktognosically"—that is, a knowing
not necessarily available for saying—a knowing through praxis. This term
was first used by Grunbaum, *Aphasie and Motorik* (1930), who is cited
by Maurice Merleau-Ponty in his *Phenomenology of Perception* (London:
Routledge & Kegan Paul, 1962), P. 140 footnote 2. I encountered the term
while reading Merleau-Ponty for a Garfinkel seminar (1977). My thanks
also to Professor Melvin Pollner for directing me to that same Merleau-
Ponty reading in his seminar on pathological communication. Professor
Garfinkel characterizes the term as a "cognate version" of a praxiological
conception of action and interaction (personal communication, 1979).

18. Garfinkel, *op. cit.*, Chapter One and Two.

SECTION IV

EDUCATING THE RETARDED: RECOGNIZING INTELLIGENCE

CHAPTER 7

"EDUCATING" RETARDED ADULTS: AN ATTEMPT AT "NORMALIZATION"?

Sylvia Messina Bercovici

T HE FOLLOWING IS A participant observation study[1] of a group of retarded adults from board and care homes and a variety of other facilities, and the community's efforts at "educating" and "normalizing" them. Why such efforts are unlikely to succeed notwithstanding the good intentions of all concerned will be the central concern of this paper.

FORMAL SKILLS AS PASSPORT TO THE DOMINANT CULTURE

It has been observed that in a society like ours which values and stresses the acquisition of formal techniques of symbolization (reading, writing, arithmetic), these techniques can become ends in themselves and not necessarily related to the requirements of physical survival or cultural adaptation (Dexter, 1958). Assessments of retarded adults frequently reflect this cultural predisposition, and recommendations are frequently along the lines of the following example from a case study: "If a tutorial program was available, he could benefit from instruction in reading, writing—handling money." Many persons, like the mentally retarded adults in this study, who cannot perform these cognitive operations, not only lament their inability, but have a very clear understanding of the "passport" value of such skills.

---

[1] The research on which this paper was based was supported in part by the Neuropsychiatric Institute, UCLA, Center for the Health Sciences, and by DHEW/Office of Human Development, Grant #50-P45564/9-01. The author would like to acknowledge the invaluable contributions made by the project staff to this research with special appreciation to Gary Kielhofner and Nancy Takata.

Being able to read and write as a symbol of being "normal" may be valued more than its potential practical benefits. The following comments by retarded individuals were made in the context of a general dialogue on their lives:

Roger (a 37-year-old man who has spent most of his life in state hospitals and who now lives at board and care home #1):

> I figure it this way, it's not right to call a person a mentally retarded patient—mentally retarded. 'Cause I'm not. I can take care of a house and I can remember names pretty good. But I can't write no phone numbers down. If I could have help writing—writing numbers down and remembering them, that way I could prove to people that I could be on my own.

Arline (a 44-year-old woman who has lived at board and care home #2 for 5 years):

> I was retarded but I snapped out of it when I was 13 . . . I feel I can act just like the rest of you people in here . . . Do you feel I can talk just like all of you? . . . It's very mild, Dr. A said, very mild . . . A lot of people didn't want to have anything to do with us (referring to her sister) when we were that way. The other kids, they used to throw rocks at us, just because I didn't know what two and two was. But I know what it is now. Two and two is four. Ten and ten is five—I mean ten and ten is twenty. And five and five is ten.

Marie (a 23-year-old woman who has lived at board and care home #3 for the past 5 years):

> Researcher: Have you spoken to your parents about wanting to get married?
> Marie: I did talk to my mother about it once, but it didn't work out the way I wanted it to because she doesn't think I'm quite ready for the big step yet . . . She said she thinks I'd better wait.
> Researcher: Until when?
> Marie: Until the time comes—until it's time, when I'm good and ready.
> Researcher: What do you have to be able to do to get married?
> Marie: Cook, sew, read, count money, tell time, add, subtract, stuff like that . . . When I first came out of the hospital the doctor asked me if I could have three wishes what would I wish for. My first wish was that I could see Bobby Sherman (popular singing star) in person—and I wanted to learn how to read and

write—and I wanted there to be peace in the world . . . I was supposed to get a tutor to teach me how to read and write, but I haven't heard anything.

THE CLASSROOM AS AN HABILITATIVE SETTING

Given the emphasis in the society on the acquisition of formal skills and the general view that retarded persons suffer primarily from *cognitive* deficits, it is natural that the classroom and its pedagogical methods be recruited in the case of normalization. For those mentally retarded persons in residential placement who do receive regular outside habilitative services (many do not), these are likely to take the form of an instructional program in a classroom setting. There were four such settings that were attended by individuals in the research cohort. The statements made here are specifically based on observations in these settings but are applicable to other educational situations for developmentally disabled persons that have been observed by the researcher.

Just as schooling is used by society to socialize or acculturate its fledgling members and to provide them with the necessary knowledge for survival as adults, so the school, or class, is used analogously with mentally retarded adults to prepare them for participation in the larger society, although the nature of this contemplated cultural membership is undefined and its extent undetermined. Formal skills such as reading, writing and math are a major content area of such programs; it has been observed that clients of all levels of functioning engage in one kind or another of formal learning skills activity. However, it is important to take note that classroom education for these marginal cultural members is made to assume a responsibility it does not have with normal persons—that of providing the student with not only formal skills and academic knowledge, but also with the practical knowledge and skills of *everyday life*. In the normal course of events, members of the culture acquire these through an informal socialization process carried out by family and peers; this process begins in early childhood and is tried and tempered by repeated consequential interactions with the environment. For many reasons, e.g. stigmatization and institutionalization, most developmentally disabled persons have missed out on these normal and naturally occurring means of acquiring the requisites for adaptation to, and membership in, the larger culture. The current attempt to remediate this situation is the *formalization* and *prescription* of what are ordinarily *informal* and *naturally occurring* experiences.

Behind the widespread reliance of the classroom as habilitative setting is the premise that skills needed for adaptive functioning in the community are effectively learned in a formal educational setting and can be generalized to the daily life situations of the students. Instruction in such practical skills as preparing meals, using money, ordering in a restaurant, looking for a job, improving one's appearance, acquiring culturally appropriate responses and behaviors, getting along with others, budgeting and banking, etc., in a classroom context often employs many of the pedagogical methods and devices that are used in the traditional teaching of formal skills. In addition to group instruction from the teacher, such methods include manuals, guides, and workbooks. Such a formal approach to practical daily living skills may or may not be augmented by actual experience in natural situations. Regarding the population in this study, it was consistently the case that individuals were not provided with natural opportunities to learn and practice many daily living skills that were included in one form or another in the educational program.

One obstacle to normalization are the restrictions imposed by many residential facilities on their mentally retarded residents that prevent these individuals from acquiring practical experience in the community. Other barriers between developmentally disabled persons and community learning experiences can result from educational programs themselves. Programs in classroom settings could, theoretically, extend the teaching beyond the physical plant of the school and utilize natural contexts. It would also, theoretically, be possible for such programs to depart from formal, programmed, instructional methods and employ a model that more closely corresponds to the socialization mechanisms that the larger culture provides for its "normal" members. However, there are several things that seem to impede the changes for such transformations. First, the physical and organizational structures of school programs make it more convenient and managerially practical to keep the teaching in the classrooms. A physical plant which exists demands to be utilized. The administrative overseers of an educational program want to be able to have it visible and to be able to monitor it. Secondly, a program of given time limits is easier to plan within the walls of the classroom than it is if one has to take into account the unexpected events and difficulties of taking developmentally disabled students into community settings.

Other centripetal forces are the perceptions of the teaching role of the traditionally trained teacher and the technical and performance demands that are made by the educational system. Observations of classroom-oriented teachers of developmentally disabled persons while out in community settings revealed that they tend to experience some difficulty, since the teaching methods of the classroom are not the most effective ones in other situations. (Social control is one issue that crops up here.) In addition, a standard requirement of local school districts is that teachers who are assigned to special education settings *must* carry out their teaching duties *within* the classroom. There is regular monitoring of these teaching situations and the teacher may be withdrawn from an educational program if this regulation is not complied with. While this may be a reasonable requirement of the school district in more conventional educational situations—it is after all, providing teachers upon public demand—it is a condition which can thwart or even subvert the normalization goals of programs for the developmentally disabled.

A final reinforcement for the tendency of developmentally disabled training programs to stay in the classroom is a perception of risk on the parts of teachers and program administrators that comes from an unfamiliarity with working with developmentally disabled students in the community and from the adjunct fear of responsibility, legal and otherwise. The significance of the following discussion is to point out some of the broader consequences for mentally retarded persons of the current emphasis on academic curricula, the formalization of the teaching of everyday knowledge, and the neglect of natural settings in training for community adaptation.

NORMALIZATION AND NORMAL APPEARANCES

This section will attempt to describe how an application of a dominant culture model can prevent mentally retarded persons from being normalized.

The right to education has been a major cause for advocates for the mentally retarded. Many advocates strongly feel that not only are mentally retarded children entitled to an academic education, but that they should be integrated in traditional educational settings (Blatt, 1977). In this same vein, the rationale for including formal academic components in special programs for adults is the normalization principle. However, observations made of educational settings for mentally retarded adults show that what is frequently achieved in the place of, and at the expense of, normalization is the "production of normal appearances." Goffman (1971) uses this notion in describing how it is ordinary persons employ their implicit, member's knowledge of the culture in order to produce normal behavior even under non-normal circumstances. In this sense, a cultural member may be seen as producing a behavior for a particular effect. What is suggested here is that persons may use their own or others' behavior for its display value, knowing the meanings ordinarily attached to that behavior by other members of the culture. The term "normalization" is used by other sociologists (Berger & Luckman, 1966) to describe a related but somewhat different cultural phenomenon. They point out that members of a culture operate according to, and depend upon, certain cultural templates that define the real world. It is ordinarily disturbing and a cause for remedial action of one kind or another when objects, events, and persons deviate from the prescriptions of the cultural "Weltanschauung." One kind of cultural effort to reduce the dissonance between "real" and "ideal" phenomena is called "normalization" by these authors. An example of *this* use of the term "normalization" is the pressure that is exerted upon eyeless and limbless persons to wear prosthetic devices *whether or not* these are functional. The cultural definition of what is a human being includes an inventory of its constituent parts. An incomplete body is a source of discomfort and can even give rise to doubts on the parts of other cultural members whether, or to what extent, this being qualifies as *human.* As a result, attempts may be made to "normalize" this form, even if only cosmetically.

How do the concepts of "normal appearances" and "normalization" just discussed apply to the education of mentally retarded persons?

At first glance, there is something gratifying and reassuring about a classroom of substantially handicapped individuals busily working with pencil and paper at their desks or tables. Closer inspection and repeated observations may, however, reveal the "normal appearances" or cosmetic value of such activities. Some of the mentally retarded adults observed in classroom settings have spent years daily tracing and copying letters and numbers without having acquired any ability to understand or use these symbols. One 35-year-old man in this study, whom we will call Joe, was able to copy entire articles from magazines without making any errors at all. He could both print and write cursively. He was, however, unable to read at all or write anything on his own. Joe would carry around a sheaf of papers, a pencil and a magazine or two, and could be seen, when not otherwise occupied, busily "writing" away. Joe is, in many respects, much more competent and potentially independent than either his fellow residents at the board and care facility or his peers at the day care center. He is very aware of this and is particularly sensitive about being associated with people who appeared retarded or who are obviously handicapped. Any chance Joe gets, he separates himself from his house—or classmates—and does his "writing." He explains, "It gives me something to do." An unlit pipe that Joe constantly has with him, greatly enhances his production of normal appearance.

Another example of a symbolic, ritualistic, emulation of a "normal" activity was observed when a class for mentally retarded adults was taken on an outing to a local park. Several of the students brought their workbooks with them and two young women spent most of their time enacting the roles of teacher and pupil in an arithmetic "lesson." The researcher had come that day equipped with a portable video camera and "caught" this naturally occurring event. An inspection of the videotape revealed that while the movement, mannerisms, and verbiage of "teacher" were perfectly performed by one of the women (while the other went through the motions of a dutiful student) the *content* of the "lesson" was nonexistent—it obviously was not important to the participants. The "lesson" went on for 20 minutes. The casual observer might interpret a scene such as this in the same way as one would two children playing school or house. The implications of the two cases, however, are not the same. In the case of these retarded adults the progression from neophyte-emulator to bonafide cultural actor (teacher, housewife, etc.), will never come to pass.

Both of these instances are similar to the "Cloak of Competence" described by Edgerton (1967) in his study of dehospitalized individuals attempting to make an adjustment to life in the community. In all these cases there is a sense of status differential and relative deprivation on the part of this subdominant group vis-á-vis the dominant culture. The point here is that these retarded individuals demonstrate an awareness of the dominant culture's template. In the classroom situation and in other normalization efforts this template is frequently employed by "normals" on behalf of their "retarded" students, who may or may not themselves manufacture "normal appearances" as a strategy for eliciting more favorable responses from others. The teacher-imposed production of normal appearances may subtly become a goal in itself. In such educational programs, classroom and administrative personnel have to comply in one way or another with how the culture defines education and teacher and often lack an alternative educational approach. Various kinds of "lessons" were observed in this research to be carried out in a similar production-of-normal-appearances fashion.

The following are brief descriptions of three classroom programs observed in the course of the research.

THE SALTER SCHOOL FOR THE HANDICAPPED

This program is an evening class that is held in an elementary school for the handicapped. The school district provides the teacher for this class as part of its adult education responsibility.

The particular class observed is especially for mentally retarded persons and is held on a once-a-week basis. The evening adult program was described as being "more relaxed" than the day program for children, and that the highlights are really social events like the upcoming Halloween party. The teacher said that "socialization" (referring to social gatherings) was the "key to retardation."

The class itself is held in a large classroom and on the evenings visited consisted of approximately 22 adults (mostly women). Most of these individuals live in board and care facilities. Several women from Carver's Board and Care, one residential facility included in the study, attend this program. The observations were focused on two individuals the researcher was most familiar with, Marie and Lisa.*

The class normally runs from 6:30 to 8:30 or 9:00 PM. On the evenings observed, the program consisted entirely of "reading and writing" activities. The class was divided up into two groups of students who were seated at long tables. The smaller group consisted of six women, including Lisa and Carmen, another woman from Carver's board and care facility. This was the "high functioning" group. The other, larger, group that included Marie and several other women from Carver's was obviously the "lower functioning" one.

Lisa and the others at the high functioning table were given an assignment for the evening—to read the stories from an elementary school level "weekly reader" and then copy their favorite one. Five of these women, including Lisa, could read and understand the stories to some degree. Carmen, however, could not read a word of what she was copying. She is a very neat, compulsive person and prints her letters very well. The teacher came around to inspect the work and corrected Carmen's spacing—ignoring the issue of the meaningfulness of this activity

---

* These two women were studied over a two-year period during which time the researcher gained a first-hand knowledge of their life-circumstances, their capabilities, and their own views regarding these and other matters. During the course of this acquaintance, which included a dramatic change in their living situation, Marie and Lisa, when given the opportunity, eventually demonstrated the ability to independently manage many facets of their lives including shopping alone, using public transportation and preparing their own meals.

for her. Presumably, the rationale of such an exercise is that it will improve reading and spelling and give the student a chance to practice penmanship. In Carmen's case, and in the cases of many retarded persons observed in classroom settings, the copy work becomes an acceptable end in itself for both the classroom teacher and for the "student"; Carmen did not seem to mind doing this at all.

Lisa finished her writing chore for the evening very quickly and spent the rest of the time (perhaps an hour and a half or more) just sitting in her place. When questioned, Lisa admitted to sometimes getting bored because she was already able to read and write and there was not anything else for her to do; she reminded the researcher, however, that they sometimes do have parties at the school and it would seem that these occasions were worth the price of a few hours boredom.

The lower functioning group occupied the bulk of the teacher's attention. This group spent a portion of the evening coloring and practicing printing their names or initials. One woman, a resident of Carver's, is quite dyslexic and was capable of only copying her name backwards which she did, many times, over. (The teacher pointed this out, calling it a "case of perfect mirror writing.) Another woman from Carver's, who suffers from cretinism and is severely retarded, was capable of tracing her name if someone printed it for her. Her sister, also severely retarded for the same reason, was not able to form letters, but filled her page with "chicken scratches." The teacher called this to the researcher's attention explaining that this was an example of "perseveration." Another one of Carver's residents was capable of printing her name, which she did repeatedly in a scrawled, labored fashion. This woman also has difficulties with her eyesight. Juanita, a woman of 44, who is a resident of the Carver facility, did nothing but passively watch the others. When the researcher came over to the table to watch the work, she talked about her teeth, all of which had been recently extracted. Marie, who had been very concerned about learning to read, spent her time coloring geometric designs with crayons.

The only active instruction was given to the lower functioning women. The teacher pulled up a standing blackboard for a lesson in letter and word recognition. A few of the women could name some of the letters she wrote on the board but none recognized any of the words. The lesson consisted of the teacher's "feeding" to the class the sounds of the letters that made up the words and having them repeat these after her. It was very evident that no one would actually learn to read via this method even if cognitive capacity allowed, which, in the case of most of this group (with the possible exception of Marie) was quite improbable. Some of these women, including Marie and Lisa, had already spent several years in this educational program.

The next activity, again for the lower functioning group, consisted of showing the group pictures mounted on cardboard and asking them questions. The subjects of these pictures were clowns, monkeys, mother and baby animals, etc.—quite obviously kindergarten fare. The exercise consisted of getting the students to identify the subject, tell how many, and which one was the "mommy." Marie was praised when she answered these childish questions and the teacher occasionally made remarks to me like, "it's amazing how much they remember." Marie and some of the others, although capable of much more advanced, that is, adult activities, nevertheless readily adapted to these low expectations and even seemed to enjoy the interaction that issued therefrom. (Lisa remained aloof and mildly interested, but did not participate in this lesson which was not directed to her group anyway.)

The classroom management practices in this educational situation for adults was clearly patterned after a first or second grade. The students were not allowed to leave their seats and were discouraged from talking. When Mrs. Carver arrived to pick up her residents, some of them spotted her through the window and informed the teacher, expecting, then, to be allowed to put their things away and get ready to go. Their claim was not honored, however; the teacher paid no attention to what the women were trying to tell her. She insisted they sit down until Mrs. C. arrived. Her manner, in general, was sharp, authoritarian and humorless. There was the familiar role distance encountered in the residential facility setting. The impression conveyed by this situation was that the teacher felt her mentally retarded charges would not really benefit from the teaching but did not know what else to do but go through these motions. Furthermore, this seemed to generate some frustration and resentment; this teacher did not like her students.

It is understandable that these situations undermine the self-confidence of a teacher—there are so few, if any, results and what there are do not really make sense in the way that they do in traditional education with members of the mainstream culture. The researcher had the impression that this teacher had feelings of frustration and insecurity and, therefore, was quite self-conscious before a visitor—they do not seem to have too many people interested in observing such programs. After the class, she went to great lengths to display her professionalism in an apparent attempt to convince the observer that she knew what she was doing. She talked about doing a Ph.D. on "socialization" and sprinkled her dialogue with jargon from the special education lexicon. The formal educational model clearly had its hold upon her and in the face of its failure in this situation, it resulted in the teacher finding both herself and her students wanting.

THE HELPING HANDS ACTIVITY CENTER

This is another kind of educational setting for developmentally disabled adults that uses the classroom format exclusively. As contrasted to the Salter School evening program, this one is a daytime program that runs half a day (three hours), five days a week. Helping Hands is not an enterprise of the public school system (although the school district provides some teaching personnel on a part-time basis). The center was founded, and is operated, by an incorporated group of residential facility operators and is funded principally through four separate regional centers which pays for their clients' monthly tuitions. Helping Hands is licensed by the state as a day care center for 240 developmentally disabled adults. During the period of contact there were approximately 160 persons attending the center, most of these being regional center clients. Four of the seven facilities in the research sample sent their developmentally disabled residents to the Helping Hands center.

The physical set-up of Helping Hands is worth noting. Its plant is a former supermarket building located on a major boulevard in an economically depressed area. The main entrance is on the parking lot side of the building. The entire length of this side of the building is bounded by a chain-link fence which marks off a "yard" area. A barbed-wire strip runs along the top of the fence; the angle of the barbed-wire section is toward the building. While ample in its size, it has a somewhat improvised appearance. The interior of the building, which was formerly just one vast open space, is now divided up into "classrooms" by six-foot-high partitions. The overall effect of this partitioning is that of solid-walled carrels rather than separate rooms. Some of these "rooms" have doors; others just open doorways. One of the "problems" reported by center staff is very visible to the casual visitor: the clients tend to drift out of the doorless classes (actually they even leave the classes with doors) and wander about the labyrinthine corridors of the center. The lack of ceilings on the classroom areas allows noise to travel freely throughout the cavernous building; the strong odor of cleaning disinfectant pervades the air; and a casual visitor is usually besieged by center clients who not only gather about but grab, hug, kiss, and bombard the outsider with questions, tales and requests for charity. There is an overall institutional or ward-like atmosphere created by these features of the Helping Hands center. The following are excerpts from the field notes of three research assistants written after their initial visit to the center:

> The building is huge with a bright yellow interior and long fluorescent lights across the ceiling. It is divided into various lessons or activity areas by means of partial wooden walls that don't reach up to the ceiling . . . I noted the tremendous amount of noise generated in the building . . . the set-up allowed for every sound or noise from every partitioned area to be heard in every other area . . . One of the first emotions I felt was a sense of being overwhelmed by people wanting my attention.

> *   ✿   ✿   ✿   ✿

> Not much visual stimulation, but much auditory . . . The lights inside are glaring . . . so noisy. Rooms are "parceled" off by low walls. A number of clients started following us around, several trying to get attention by shaking hands, telling their names, pulling on my arms or touching my back. I felt like pulling away from these people as they invaded my space—my private, personal boundaries . . . I felt harrassed. I wanted to shake people off and

scream to reduce tension . . . After I left I was exhausted and the
last thing I wanted to do was write up field notes. It was too hard
to isolate clients in this situation, or to get a chance to talk to any
individual (there were multiple interruptions) . . . The building felt
like a bomb shelter, an artificial world. Like a zoo. I had the
feeling of imprisonment.

     ❁   ❁   ❁   ❁   ❁

Several of the clients in the study cohort complained about the
noise at H.H.; a few wore ear plugs or put cotton in their ears
when there.

     ❁   ❁   ❁   ❁   ❁

Helping Hands offers classes entitled ceramics, arts and
crafts, music, body dynamics, grooming, and basic education.
Most clients attend each of these classes except for ceramics and
arts and crafts. Specially chosen individuals who have shown
some aptitude spend their time in these two classes turning out
items for the center's "boutique."

The classroom model predominates at the Helping Hands
center. Due to funding difficulties that are commonly faced by
such programs, the center often did not have enough staff to
manage this large and heterogeneous group of developmentally
disabled adults. Even when staffing was maximum, however,
which meant that there were six teachers, merely controlling the
large numbers of clients was a principal concern. The classroom
structure provided a means by which this large group of persons
could be physically managed. It appeared that the content of
the classes and the ostensible educational goals were secondary
to the organizational needs of the center.

Like the Salter School, the Helping Hands center emphasized
formal skills such as reading and writing, but also included other
areas such as self-help skills (grooming), physical fitness (body
dynamics), and creative expression (music and dance therapy).
There were underlying similarities between the basic education
class at Helping Hands (two teachers were observed) and the
Salter School evening class.

First, there was the very obvious latent custodial function of
the class (consistent with the center itself) which resulted in
activities to "keep people busy." In both educational settings,
the custodial function allowed the inclusion of many individuals

in the classes who are required to merely "go through the motions" of academic activity. The meaningfulness of such activities, both from the perspective of the mentally retarded client and the perspective of educational philosophy, must be questioned. One teacher lamented that she did not have more time to spend with a very withdrawn "autistic" young man who was beginning to be able to "write" his initials by connecting dots she made; she feared he would lose this ability if efforts with him were not continuous.

Another commonality between these two educational programs is that, like any enterprise, much of the effort goes into self-affirmation and self-justification. So, it could be seen that even though it was a very difficult thing to accomplish, it was of paramount importance to classroom and center personnel that a given activity exhibit the appearances of a classroom and that anyone who might observe this situation would not mistake it for anything else but what it was supposed to be. As a result, what was observed over and over in these settings was the "doing" of "classroom" (as it is culturally defined), despite the inappropriateness of this model for many developmentally disabled persons.

A third feature shared by the educational programs observed is the unintended socialization experience they would seem to provide for these marginal members of the culture. The classroom model dictates that there be a teacher and that there be students. It also contains an inherent element of conflict. It has been noted that in every teaching situation the teacher, because he/she is knowledgeable, is superior, and that the pupil, because he/she does not have that knowledge, is inferior (Geer, 1968). Even in "normal" classroom teaching situations in the culture the teacher must control the interactional situation; in effect, the student's role is one of submission. In the mainstream society this subordinate/superordinate relationship has certain restrictions imposed upon it. It usually occurs during a particular period in a person's life. It is further limited by the fact that the role of submissive pupil takes place at most on a six-hour-a-day basis and that outside the framework of school, a child has the chance to meet others on an equal footing. In the case of this population of marginal adults, the classroom, because of its organizational needs, can only perpetuate and reinforce subordination. It thus unwittingly joins other social forces in the lives of these individuals in socializing them to be like children.

The basic education teachers at Helping Hands were not particularly authoritarian; in fact, they made a great effort to relate to their students in a friendly and humane way. Nevertheless, adults were put in a situation where they were having to guess the "right" answer in exchange for praise, stay in their seats, raise their hands to be recognized, and "line-up" in preparation for leaving the class. A project staff member made this comment after observing a class: "I felt the entire time that I was in a first grade class. The teacher was very gentle but somewhat condescending—like I am with my preschoolers."

A final common denominator in the educational programs for developmentally disabled adults that have been observed is testimony to the basic symbolic value of academic skills. The classroom teaching of cognitive operations like reading, writing, and arithmetic for developmentally disabled persons, tends to remain in the realm of the abstract. Little attempt has been observed to apply these to situations in daily life. In the Helping Hands basic education classes, for example, an ongoing content area was telling time. There were cardboard clocks with moveable hands that were used to teach students how to tell time. The intention was strictly academic, however, for at no time was a *real* clock used to help students mark off *real* immediate events like changing class, snack time, lunch time, or boarding the bus to go home. There was no actual clock anywhere in view. When it came down to it, the "knowledgeable" ones told the "knowledgeless" ones what to do and when to do it. Likewise the center's canteen, a potential instructional situation for teaching money values (real goods are being purchased with *real* money) is not used for instruction. Instead, currency recognition is approached through the use of workbooks and mimeoed sheets. At the canteen, the client just hands over his money and depends upon the "normal" behind the counter to give back the right change. The point being made here is that the teachers' structure of motives (to use a concept of Alfred Schutz) in the classroom is bound to the maintenance of classroom form (usually by means of certain pedagogical devices) and *not* to the normalization of developmentally disabled persons.

One effect of the classroom is that the demands for non-applied abstracted, cognitive performance makes people appear less competent than they are. The teachers themselves, in this situation, have little to foster a belief in the possibility of improved functioning. One gets the impression that these teachers do not believe that what they are doing is really helping the retarded person. What is referred to as "burn out" occurs when such helping professionals lose belief in what they are doing and see their charges as "hopeless."

Other classes at the Helping Hands center that were oriented towards habilitation similarly suffered from being confined to the classroom. For example, the "body dynamics" class presumably had physical fitness as its objective, but was restricted to an indoor area when a large outdoor space was available on the center's lot which could have been used to get clients into the sunshine and fresh air. A simple healthful activity like *walking,* which most residents of board and care facilities rarely get a chance to do, is bypassed because it cannot be accommodated by a classroom. As a consequence, clients are restricted to indoor activities and are cajoled and pressured into doing jumping jacks and touching their toes or are herded along in activities like forming a human train and shuffling around the room.

The grooming class could be seen as an opportunity to help reduce stigma for developmentally disabled persons by teaching them how to become physically more acceptable to the "normal" community. Without, however, the motivational element of actual social contacts with the larger community or special occasions to "dress up" for, a grooming class is an exercise in mere ritual. Such obeisance to the cosmetic norms of the larger culture without the opportunity to receive the benefits, would not appear to be a normalizing process. Furthermore, it seems unrealistic to expect classroom training to be at all effective without follow-up and incentives provided in the residential setting.

The perspective of the Helping Hands director regarding the value of the center's program is important to note. His assessment, of course, does not agree with the one presented here but is valid in the framework he invokes—that of a comparison with the board and care facilities. The researcher was told by the director of the Helping Hands center that the four residential facilities included in the study were some of the *better* ones. He offered examples of board and care facilities that were more repressive and neglectful, describing life in these homes as "terrible" for most clients. He said that the center's clients look forward to coming to the center because there is nothing else in their lives. One of the examples he provided was that the first things that clients do when they arrive at the center is to run to the drinking fountain for water and go to the bathroom. He explained that they do this because at many facilities they are not allowed to help themselves to food, to drink water freely, or to go to the bathroom without permission (all these restrictions had been observed by the researcher in various board and care homes).

As the researcher gained a better knowledge of the individuals in the study, partial substantiation was found for the director's claim that the center's clients looked forward to coming to the program. Some of the higher functioning individuals, however, expressed a dislike for the center and stated that they would rather do something else. To these individuals, the center was for "retarded" people and boring for persons like themselves. The following remarks were made by cohort members about the activity center:

Jerry G. (Board and Care Resident)

School is boring . . . Reading class, I don't get nothing out of it. Just sit around in a chair all day . . . I don't get nothin' out of reading, 'cause everybody would get in a crowd and talk. I would rather be in a workshop and make money.

Donna S. (Board and Care Resident)

. . . to me the center is boring. I wish we didn't have to go at all . . . People who want to go to the center, let 'em go. But people like me and Emmy who don't want to go to the center, let 'em do something else. 'Cause I don't like the center, it's so boring . . . I like to go places, do different things. For people who want to get out of there,

I think we should have a choice, don't you? I wish I had a choice. I would do something else, something different.

It should be added that Donna is very good at crochet work; she spends the entire time at Helping Hands in the arts and crafts class. Her work is in demand for the center's gift shop. She also crochets on order for some of the center's instructors and employees who pay her with snacks. Donna complains about the noise and confusion at the center (this was also experienced by the project staff) and admitted to stuffing her ears with cotton. Donna made the above remarks during a visit to the university with several other women from the board and care facility where she lives. Some of the women agreed with her comments. When the group was asked if those who did not want to go to the center could just stay home or do something else, they replied that they are "punished" if they do not go to "school" by having their allowances withheld.

This was not understood until information was gotten about the funding procedures for the center. The regional center pays on a daily basis for clients, providing they attend the program. If a client misses a day, the center receives less money. The caretakers, being the founders and proprietors of the center, have a greater stake in the enterprise than simply having somewhere to send their residents for half a day. It is easy to see, then, how it is that many clients attend this program whether or not it is the most suitable one for them or whether or not they wish to attend.

THE HARRISON FOUNDATION

This represents yet another type of educational enterprise for developmentally disabled adults. It differs from the Salter School and the Helping Hands center in that it operates on a full-day basis (Monday through Friday, from 9-3). Unlike the large Helping Hands clientele, the Harrison Foundation adult program serves only 25 persons and is carried out in a single classroom. (The foundation also has a program for retarded children). The physical and social environment is quite different from that of Helping Hands; the Harrison Foundation is located in a pleasant, middle-class, residential neighborhood. It is directly across the street from a city park and recreational center that boasts baseball fields, picnic grounds with barbeque pits, out-door gymnastic equipment, and a public swimming pool. The Foundation is within walking distance of restaurants and fast-food places, supermarkets, and a bowling alley.

Tuitions for the Foundation's clients are provided by the Regional Center at the rate of $156.00 per month. This pays for rent, office help, bus driver and expenses. The school district provides an adult education teacher who is the mainstay of the program. She is assisted by unpaid volunteers upon whom she heavily depends for the carrying out of this program and the management of the clients. A woodshop program is run by a retired engineer, himself handicapped; he is the one volunteer who is part of the regular staff. Some of the clients live with their families; others reside in board and care facilities or in residential dormitories run by other foundations for the handicapped. Several residents from a residential facility in the study attend the Harrison Foundation.

This daily, full-time, year-round program at the Harrison Foundation is called "Adult Effective Living." Unlike the Salter School and the Helping Hands center, the Harrison Foundation has an expresesd commitment to community adaptation, if one can interpret the phrase "adult effective living" in that way. In practice, however, it would appear that these adults are being taught how to live effectively mainly in a classroom despite occasional trips into the community.

The various activities at the Harrison Foundation both in the classroom and out were videotaped in some detail and so could be subjected to repeated observation and analysis. Two major activities that took place daily and which were videotaped were "basic education" and "physical fitness." These two activities recapitulated the situation at the Helping Hands center.

The education instruction at the Harrison Foundation does not differ from that of the Salter School or the Helping Hands center. This period is the longest one of the day, lasting approximately 1½ hours. The class is divided into ability groups: The high level group, which contains some persons who are quite adept at reading, writing, and basic math, is mostly occupied with workbooks. Such work can be done independently with only occasional checks by the teacher or assistant. Most of the attention is given to lower functioning individuals who require supervision, prompting, and even physical help to perform and sustain these activities. Videotapes of a "writing" exercise done by lower functioning persons at the Harrison Foundation class reveal in detail what was observed at both the Salter School and the Helping Hands center—the production of "normal appearances"—an imitation of life, so to speak. One of the videotapes shows a staff member physically guiding the hand of an individual who is not correctly following the outline of his initial. This scene has a benign appearance at first glance, but closer inspection reveals the coercive nature of the aide's "help," the boredom and resignation of the student, and the sheer, mechanical, ritualistic nature of the activity itself. One dutiful student, a Chicano man, is shown in this same tape copying pages of the same letter without any prompting from the classroom aides. He was, however, tracing over his own previous copy work instead of returning each time to the teacher's original and tracing *that*. The result was that with each generation of print, the letter deteriorated more and more in its form, which illustrated the nonsensical nature of this pursuit.

These adult students are similarly "helped" by mostly untrained aides in other activities as well. The videotape material clearly shows that physical manipulation is a common resort for such helpers of the retarded; we see classroom aides moving body parts for these adults during the "exercise" session; holding a woman's physically *capable* hand to guide it while she butters a piece of bread; pulling a physically disabled woman along during a ball game in which she (according to the "normal" form of the game) should be *running* from one base to another.

The application of formal skills to daily life are not part of this classroom paradigm. Even such a practical art as using a telephone is "academicized" and removed from its natural and *real* function. The teacher had gone to the trouble of borrowing "training" phones from the phone company for her class. Training in using the phone lasted for about a month when she had to return the equipment. The class did not, however, advance to making "real" telephone calls and when a university project, as part of its efforts to help these adults develop their adaptive skills, asked particular individuals to telephone the project offices (to confirm an activity arrangement, for example), the teacher actually made the call herself and then put the client on the phone. Despite the project's request, it was difficult for this teacher to allow clients to make their own telephone calls. It was as though it is all right for these individuals to "play house" but not actually engage in any of these things in the real world.

For the physical fitness activities adults were made to go through kindergarten-like calisthenics in the form of "Simon says . . ." type games. It is easy to see from the videotapes how irrelevant these exercises are to physical fitnes, and how perfunctorily they are performed by bored, captive students. For some, who are severely physically handicapped, this activity is sometimes too difficult for them to perform at all by themselves and requires the physical assistance of the aides. It is, however, an activity that can take place within the classroom, uses about forty minutes of time, can be done in a group where everyone is accounted for, and may appear to a casual visitor like a legitimate and beneficial activity. In short, it clearly fulfills the organizational requirements of a classroom. Now, there is an exceptional park directly across the street that is all but empty on weekdays during the school year. The classroom model, so dominant a force in this, as in other habilitative settings, apparently cannot adapt so as to take advantage of this naturally occurring resource. The university program, *could*, however, and did provide Harrison clients with the opportunity to do gymnastics, play baseball, and jog in this tranquil outdoor setting. After this project came to a close, the clients' physical fitness program was once again limited to the classroom. Manpower is but one element in the reluctance of programs like that at the Harrison Foundation to have activities take place in natural settings. The teacher, by requirement of the school district, has to stay in the classroom, which leaves any community excursions to the volunteer aides. Furthermore, there are school district requirements that not only the *teacher* be restricted to the classroom, but the students as well. To justify providing this teacher, a certain number of students have to minimally be in the classroom at any given time. However, this still leaves opportunity for the program to leave the confines of the classroom even with certain limitations. The program's community contacts consist of the following: Weekly bowling for all the clients, monthly trips to the laundromat and supermarket for a group of higher functioning individuals, an occasional lunch at a local pizzeria, and excursions to a miniature golf course or to amusement parks several times a year.

Almost all the clients in the class except the most severely handicapped are included in the weekly bowling session at a nearby alley they can walk to. The alleys are reserved by the Harrison staff who also arrange for shoes, payment for the games, etc. The staff members keep the score sheets, although several of the clients are skilled enough at math to learn to do this. In short, the bowling is utilized for its *amusement* value and is not an occasion for the clients to learn "effective living;" they could easily participate much more actively in this but the incompetent role that is required by the classroom model does not suddenly change when the teacher and student are out of the school building. The staff never seems to even *consider* allowing the clients to perform certain duties and routines that they see as appropriately being the responsibility of a "competent" or "knowledgeable" person. Although some of the clients who live at home walk freely alone about their own neighborhoods, they are never allowed, even in a group, to walk the block and a half from the Foundation to the bowling alley. This means that large groups of adult clients (some of whom are visibly handicapped or otherwise stigmatized) are required to walk together with a "normal" overseer on such excursions into the local community. This, in itself, attracts the attention of curious or fearful members of the normal community. To add to the stigma and "child" status of this group of adults, they are routinely required to have a partner and *hold hands* when in public. One videotape captures a group being told to line-up and take the hands of their partners before setting out for the shopping center. It focuses on two strapping men in their mid-twenties walking up the street holding each other's hands. It was the researcher's impression that these individuals were sensitive to the fact that they were drawing negative attention from the public and that they felt somehow demeaned by being required to go into the community under these circumstances. One of the hand-holding young men slipped his hand out of his partner's, and, in a gesture of recognition that he was disobeying orders, pretended to scratch his head (at least the semblance of an excuse); he did not resume the hand-holding when he was through. Other videotapes made of these individuals in some of the university project's activities shows these men in a local hamburger place, ordering and paying for their own food and appearing quite "normal."

When the Foundation class arranged a restaurant lunch, presumably to further "adult effective living," the clients remained completely *passive* recipients of this experience. Firstly, the pizzeria was alerted that the group was coming and it was arranged that they would go on an "off hour." They all went in the Foundation bus. Each individual was told where to sit, the pizza was ordered and picked up and the bill was paid by the staff. Many other similar instances could be presented. As a contrastive experience, a group of Foundation clients was taken by the university project to a restaurant. A videotape on that occasion shows each client deciding for him/herself what to order and giving the order directly to the waiter. Even clients with rather severe speech problems due to cerebral palsy and other conditions were able to make themselves understood without the help of the project staff. From this and other similar restaurant experiences, it was discovered that, by and large, serving persons made considerable efforts to understand and help handicapped persons who wish to be served. (This often seems to be as important an experience for these "normal" members of the community as it is for the developmentally disabled individual).

The following is another example of the form that community experience takes when it is guided by a managerially oriented classroom model and an underestimation of the competence and awareness of retarded persons: A group of higher functioning clients of the Foundation were to go to the local supermarket to buy the ingredients to make sandwiches for lunch. Since it was raining, they were unable to walk and the staff decided to take them in the Foundation van, which is equipped for wheelchair persons. While it was possible to enter and exit the van *without* using the motorized platform, although a bit awkward, the aide insisted that each of these persons get onto the platform while she lowered them from, and lifted them onto, the van in the supermarket parking lot. This episode was videotaped, and on reviewing it, one is reminded of the kind of "herding" process that one has seen in film clips of human prisoners of various kinds. What might have been a merely unusual experience for a "normal" person had a very stigmatizing effect on these persons since it was done in a public setting and alternatives were available.

As the foregoing material shows, the classroom model promotes a concern to produce activities that confirm the classroom structure and that solidify and differentiate the teacher and student roles. Out of this concern comes the particular content of the classroom activities and certain managerial actions on the part of the teacher, both of which are frequently nonnormalizing for the developmentally disabled adult subjected to them.

There is an additional element that combines with those already outlined to make "closed systems" of such habilitation environments. This is an underlying operating principle that does not allow normal risks to be taken in these settings, with this population. For example, while even the youngest "normal" school children are allowed to exit the school alone and even cross the street by themselves without the school necessarily assuming responsibility for their welfare, organized services for the handicapped assume a much more protective, even custodial position. At the Harrison Foundation, for example, at no time could a client, regardless of higher level of physical or intellectual capacity, be sent on an errand to the corner shopping center, cross the street alone to get to the park, or even leave the school building to wait in the parking lot without being accompanied by a "normal" adult. This was a source of minor conflict between the Harrison Foundation staff and the university project's occupational therapists who, in their efforts to give individuals the opportunity to exericse their competence and independence, tried to arrange to meet particular small groups at a certain destination rather than always going to the classroom and fetching them. The classroom teacher, however, did not want even very competent clients to wait in the Foundation parking lot for the university staff.

Another example of this conservative position regarding risks involves one very capable and very normal looking mildly retarded woman from a nearby board and care facility who ordinarily takes buses by herself to get to various destinations all over the city. She asked permission to come by herself to the Harrison Foundation from the facility instead of being picked up by the Foundation bus. But she was not permitted this much independence, despite the claim of the Foundation that its goal is "adult effective living," and consequently must submit to the stigmatizing experience of being passively transported together with seriously handicapped persons. A client from another activity center not in this study was in a similar situation. He, however, lived at home and did not yet know how to use the bus, but expressed to an interviewer his great desire to do so. The reason? "Well, how would you like it if a bus of laughing idiots pulled up at your door every morning?"

To summarize, the combination of classroom model and fear of risk lead to an underestimation of client competence. Within the classroom, the constant monitoring and controlling of clients amounts to an environment which may be seen as institutional due to these custodial practices. Most importantly, the lack of opportunity for such mentally retarded persons to learn from experience in natural contexts in the community may prove to be a major deterrent to their development.

REFERENCES

Berger, Peter L., and Luckman, Thomas. *The social construction of reality: A treatise in the sociology of knowledge.* Garden City: Doubleday & Co., 1966.

Blatt, Burton. The integration-segregation issue: Some questions, assumptions and facts. In Burton Blatt, Douglas Biklen, and Robert Rogdan (Eds.), *An alternative textbook in special education.* Denver: Love Publishing Co., 1977. 127-134.

Dexter, Lewis A. A social theory of mental deficiency. *American Journal of Mental Deficiency, 62*(5), March, 1958.

Edgerton, Robert B. *The cloak of competence.* Berkeley and Los Angeles: University of California Press, 1967.

Geer, Blanche. Teaching. In *International encyclopedia of the social sciences, Vol. 15.* New York: Macmillan & Free Press, 1968, pp. 560-565.

Goffman, Erving. *Relations in public: Microstudies of the public order.* New York: Harper's Colophon, 1971.

CHAPTER 8

EVERYDAY MEMORY TASKS IN A CLASSROOM FOR THE TMR LEARNERS

Harold G. Levine
Andrea G. Zetlin
L. L. Langness

INTRODUCTION

It is now relatively common to find critiques of the strict, laboratory-based experimental approach to the study of learning, problem-solving, and memory. The two major sources of concern are that the structure of laboratory tasks are not representative of the everyday tasks with which people in real-life settings must contend, and that with few exceptions laboratory studies seldom control for setting or experimenter effects.

One solution to the dilemma posed by basing our laboratory studies of learning on tasks and procedures which are not "ecologically valid" is to undertake fine-grained, environmentally-based observational work e.g. Brown, 1975; Brown & Campione, 1978; Butterfield, 1978; see also Cole & Scribner, 1975; Cole, Hood, & McDermott, 1978. Unfortunately this is far more easily called for than accomplished. One reason is that we lack an accumulated body of descriptive accounts of such behavior which would make comparison and contrast possible (though the work of Charlesworth, 1978, is promising in this regard) and which would thereby allow us to test our conceptual notions about what distinguishes one kind of task, performance or behavior

The research of the second author was partially supported by an NICHD Post-doctoral Traineeship. The authors would like to thank Ronald Gallimore, Kazuo Nihira, and Ray Perez for their helpful comments.

From, *Quarterly Newsletter of the Laboratory of Human Cognition* (forthcoming). Reprinted by permission.

from another. As a result we cannot yet answer the question of whether a laboratory task is "representative" of real-life tasks because (a) we do not have any systematic knowledge of what real-life tasks exist "out there," and (b) we do not know what demands, cognitive or otherwise, such tasks make on individuals and therefore have no conceptual scheme for gauging degree of "representativeness." In addition, while we appreciate that everyday tasks, by their nature, are embedded in an on-going "stream of behavior" we are not yet able to reliably predict in what way(s) the environment actually impinges on the person or on the task itself. Thus while observational researchers typically include setting and participant effects in their studies they have yet, in this area of research at least, to systematically analyze these effects. As in laboratory settings they remain ill-understood confounding variables.

The present paper provides descriptive material of everyday memory tasks collected from observations of public school classrooms for trainable mentally retarded (TMR) students[1]. In addition it proposes a multidimensional classificational scheme for understanding these tasks which includes aspects of the task and of the task environment as well. We believe that school-related tasks *cannot* be defined or categorized through the exclusive use of unitary "objective" criteria; and that any classificatory scheme ultimately has value only insofar as it mirrors how the culture structures, and the student perceives, such tasks.

DESIGN AND PROCEDURE

Our research was conducted in three age-graded classrooms of a special day school for trainable mentally retarded learners. The students ranged in age from 6 to 14.9 years and had IQ scores spanning 25 to 55. Most of the children and adolescents were from middle-class families and lived at home.

We used naturalistic observation techniques—the observation and recording of verbal and nonverbal behaviors in their natural settings (Bogdan & Taylor, 1975)—carried out over a three-year period. During that time the researchers were able to develop an extensive data base and to become familiar with their subjects so that their presence was no longer obtrusive (Pelto, 1970).

Our initial guiding strategy in these observations was to focus on a wide variety of everyday tasks. We used two criteria for regarding a behavioral episode as a task: (1) the student must recognize a behavioral demand (whether self- or other-imposed) which we could also recognize through the student's subsequent verbalizations and/or other behaviors; and (2) we must be able to define two separately identifiable states which are functionally linked to each other through the student's behavior. The actual functional behavior we define as performance. These definitions are purposely broad so as not to ignore any situation properly considered a task for the child or any behavior regarded in some sense as performative.

Observers spent hundreds of hours in the classrooms observing all major periods of classroom activity such as reading lessons, workshop simulation activities, recess, lunchtime, music periods, etc. They maintained field notes of the behaviors they observed, noting with care any aspect of the situation, the participants, their actions, the task or any materials in use which could conceivably have been noticed and hence evaluated and/or acted upon by the student learner.

From the total record of everyday tasks which we are now in the process of assembling and ordering, we selected the representative sub-sample of "memory task" items listed in Table 8-I. We decided a task had a memory component if (1) a teacher (or other adult) keyed a student's task-related performance with some verbal instruction to remember or with some reference to a past skill, project, event, etc. (or the student him/herself did so); and/or (2) we were able to identify the skill or experience undertaken by the student as something already encountered by him/her in the past—that is, we used our long-term involvement with and knowledge of these students and their learning environment to build up a "file" of items of which students should have memory.

Insofar as possible, our description of task items in Table 8-I reflects how the task was originally presented to the student. Although our methods do not permit us to know whether the student defined the task in the same way we did, we can at least make some judgement as to the task with which the student was initially confronted. Some of these tasks are ones which teachers

TABLE 8-I

MEMORY TASKS AT A SCHOOL FOR TMR CHILDREN

1. In a typical "Going-on-a-trip" game teacher asked W. to repeat the five items other children before him have mentioned.
2. C. wrote his name on his completed art project when not specifically told to do so.
3. The teacher asked M. to say his telephone number.
4. In a verbal response game the teacher varied the order and combination of "address category" questions—e.g. "What is your street?" "What is your state?"
5. B. had to repeatedly respond in the refrain section of the song "This Land Is Your Land" . . . (see Item #6)
6. (From Item #5) With the lyrics: "This land is your land; this land is my land . . . (etc.)"
7. The speech teacher told M.: "When you see D . . ." (see Item #8)
8. (From Item #7) ". . . tell D. to come see me." (Continued in Item #9)
9. (Continued from Item #8) When M. saw D . . . (see Item #10)
10. (From Item #9) M. said: "D., go see Mrs. G. [the speech teacher]."
11. The teacher asked the class if they recalled a previous lesson.
12. M. had to set up the school phonograph so that he and others could dance to music during free time.
13. Class had to recite the Pledge of Allegiance.
14. Teacher asked K. if she remembered the names of her siblings who would be attending "Sibling Day" at the school.
15. Teacher asked J. to remember a list of food items which J. had "written" on a sheet of paper (child can neither read nor write) when teacher was absent.
16. J. passed through cafeteria line getting all items (food, utensils, napkins) he needed for lunch.
17. During daily graduation rehearsal S. had to attend to the musical cue which would indicate it was time for her performance, and . . . (see Item #18).
18. (From Item #17) S. had to remember the actual dance steps which she was to do during the song "Did You Ever See a Lassie?"
19. F. wished to neatly tear a page from a magazine as he had been shown the day before.
20. F. tried to find recipes in a magazine for a self-generated project.
21. At the end of the school day M. had to remember to do his weekly assigned classroom "chores," which included . . . (see Item #22)
22. (From Item #21) Inverting the chairs and placing them seat-side down on the tables.
23. Teacher told L. to put classroom objects away where they belong.
24. N. decided to put a classroom object which was out of place on the floor onto an empty shelf.
25. In the math bingo game M. was designated the "called" and had to remember the name of a number and geometric shape.
26. In the math bingo game M. (and the other players) had to remember how to both play and win.

27. In the math bingo game M. had to remember to turn over the numbered cards after announcing them (as the teacher had shown him so that he wouldn't get confused).
28. In doing her math workbook problems L. had to remember the meaning and use of "+" and "—" symbols.
29. In doing her math workbook problems L. had to remember the steps necessary to solve the following math problem:
$$N(\Phi T\text{\S}) - N(\Omega) = \underline{\hspace{1cm}}.$$
30. The teacher told D. to use her "arithmestick" (a plastic, abacus-like counting device) to solve the addition problem.
31. M. began to count on his fingers when he saw the math problem on his worksheet. (See Item #32)
32. (From Item #31) In counting on his fingers M. had to remember how to use his fingers to count and manipulate the numbers from the math problem before him.
33. During the morning calendar exercise J. had to identify the numbers which the teacher had removed from the calendar while J. followed instructions and kept his eyes closed.
34. W. had to identify functioning words, e.g. "poison," "stop," "danger," from flashcards presented by the teacher.

would define as "memory development" tasks, while others seem to involve memory as only one component of a larger task. Some items are highly routinized and are probably overlearned by the students; others involve novelty in some way. Our operating assumption is that all memory tasks, no matter how different from each other or how intractable to a standard universal definition, bear a "family resemblance" to one another which make them amenable to conceptual analysis.

DIMENSIONS OF EVERYDAY TASKS

We have examined the variety of tasks listed in Table 8-I as well as the classroom situations in which these specific tasks were actually embedded. Our intention has been to develop as many dimensions of contrast as possible to describe these tasks. By doing so we hope to discover new ways of thinking about everyday tasks, to isolate features of tasks or task-environments which elicit learning success or failure by students, and to provide direction in a future probe of those dimensions which actually are salient for student learners. To date we have identified five dimensions which describe our data. These are listed in Table 8-II.

TABLE 8-II

DIMENSIONS OF EVERYDAY MEMORY TASKS

a. Problem presenting environment:
   a_1—teacher or other familiar adult structured problematic situation
   a_2—child-structured problematic situation
b. Task demands calling for memory of or awareness of:
   b_1—unconnected words, numbers, symbols
   b_2—semantically connected words, e.g. messages, song lyrics
   b_3—location
   b_4—an indication that some action, verbal or nonverbal, is required
   b_5—events to be remembered as whole
   b_6—number of steps sequentially arranged
c. Frequency of task occurrence:
   c_1—daily occurrence
   c_2—frequent occurrence but not daily
   c_3—irregular occurrence
d. Predictability of response set:
   d_1—type of response and task content are always the same
   d_2—type of response and task content always vary
   d_3—type of response is the same; task content varies
e. Feedback system:
   e_1—teacher and child come to "agreement" as to what counts as correct or
   acceptable response
   e_2—child is left on his/her own to decide what "counts" as acceptable
   response
   e_3—child is "informed" by the situation that his/her response is acceptable
   or unacceptable

Dimension *a* represents the way in which tasks come into the learner's awareness. Tasks are either structured by the teacher or another familiar adult (a_1) as in having the learner state her address (Item #4 of Table 8-I) and telephone number (Item #3), or by the individual student (a_2) as in writing his name on a finished art project (Item #2) and in recalling the steps to operate the record player (Item #12). With some of these student-structured tasks, although the teacher may be the one to initiate the action, as when she takes the class to the cafeteria line (Item #16) or assigns them a number of math workbook problems (Items #28 and 29), it is then left to the individual students to proceed with the task demands on their own.

Dimensions *b* through *d* document aspects of the task itself. Category *b* refers to the kinds of memory demands which this school culture places on its students. Unconnected words, numbers, and symbols (b_1) are stressed to be remembered as a child's name (Item #2), a telephone number (Item #3), a list of foods (Item #15), or when confronting the + and − symbols in math workbook problems (Item #28). The students are also called upon to remember semantically connected words (b_2) as in delivering a verbal message (Item #8) or reciting the Pledge of Allegiance (Item 13); places where objects are located (b_3—e.g. Items #20 and 23); an indication that some action, verbal or nonverbal, is required (b_4, e.g. Items #5 and 17); and certain events which are meant to be remembered as a whole (b_5, e.g. Item #11). Finally, the students are called upon to remember how to do something which involves a finite number of steps sequentially arranged (b_6), as the steps required in setting up a phonograph (Item #12).

We have also been able to meaningfully group tasks on the basis of the frequency of their occurrence in the classroom. Some tasks (c_1) occur daily such as the Pledge of Allegiance (Item #13) or on a daily basis for a short period of time while the class is engaged in a particular project such as the graduation rehearsals (Items #17 and 18). Other tasks, such as the "Going-on-a-Trip" game (Item #1), are frequent but not daily occurrences (c_2). Finally, a third group of tasks (c_3) occur very irregularly, and therefore are not as likely to have a patterned response set available to the student (Items #15 and 20).[2]

Dimension d groups tasks on the basis of how predictable the response is to the student. We distinguish tasks in which (1) both the type of response and its actual content are always the same (d_1), such as the Pledge of Allegiance (Item #13); (2) both the type of response and the actual content vary with each new problem-presenting instance (d_2), such as the placement of an object which was found on the floor onto an available empty shelf (Item #24); and (3) the type of response is typical but the actual content varies (d_3), such as a student having to do a daily classroom chore while the chore itself changes from week to week (Item #21).

Category e reflects the type of feedback (if any) the student receives on his/her task performance. We have found that feedback to the student comes about in one of three ways: (1) the teacher and student come to an agreement as to what counts as an acceptable response (e_1); (2) the student is left to him/herself to judge whether the demands of the memory tasks have been fulfilled (e_2); and finally (3) something intrinsic to the task provides feedback, such as a phonograph which will not work if the steps necessary to start it were not followed (e_3).

RESULTS AND DISCUSSION

Each of the 34 memory items in Table 8-I were scored by two independent raters according to the dimensions of contrast listed in Table 8-II. Overall interrater reliability was .96. Agreement indices for each dimension are as follows: .97 for dimension a; .97 for b; 1.00 for c; .94 for d; and 1.00 for e. A list of these dimensional sets is given in Table 8-III.

TABLE 8-III

DIMENSIONAL SETS FOR 34 MEMORY TASKS AT A SCHOOL
FOR TMR LEARNERS

1. $a_1 b_1 c_2 d_3 e_1$	18. $a_1 b_6 c_1 d_1 e_1$
2. $a_2 b_1 c_1 d_1 e_2$	19. $a_2 b_6 c_3 d_1 e_3$
3. $a_1 b_1 c_2 d_1 e_1$	20. $a_2 b_3 c_3 d_3 e_3$
4. $a_1 b_1 c_2 d_3 e_1$	21. $a_2 b_4 c_1 d_3 e_1$
5. $a_1 b_4 c_2 d_1 e_2$	22. $a_2 b_6 c_2 d_1 e_1$
6. $a_1 b_2 c_2 d_1 e_2$	23. $a_1 b_3 c_2 d_3 e_2$
7. $a_1 b_4 c_3 d_2 e_2$	24. $a_2 b_3 c_2 d_3 e_2$
8. $a_1 b_2 c_3 d_2 e_2$	25. $a_1 b_1 c_2 d_3 e_1$
9. $a_2 b_4 c_3 d_2 e_2$	26. $a_2 b_6 c_2 d_1 e_1$
10. $a_2 b_2 c_3 d_2 e_2$	27. $a_2 b_6 c_2 d_1 e_1$
11. $a_1 b_5 c_3 d_2 e_2$	28. $a_2 b_1 c_2 d_1 e_1$
12. $a_2 b_6 c_2 d_1 e_3$	29. $a_2 b_6 c_2 d_3 e_1$
13. $a_1 b_2 c_1 d_1 e_2$	30. $a_1 b_6 c_3 d_3 e_1$
14. $a_1 b_1 c_3 d_3 e_2$	31. $a_2 b_4 c_2 d_1 e_2$
15. $a_1 b_1 c_3 d_2 e_2$	32. $a_2 b_6 c_2 d_3 e_1$
16. $a_2 b_6 c_1 d_3 e_1$	33. $a_1 b_1 c_1 d_3 e_1$
17. $a_1 b_4 c_1 d_1 e_1$	34. $a_1 b_1 c_2 d_3 e_1$

The 34 items selected for analysis here were intended to be representative of the range of tasks and task environments in these classrooms. Although we probably have not exhausted the variability to be found in tasks and task environments we feel that these do offer a useful guide to understanding everyday tasks. In addition, even though it was not our specific intention to examine the levels of demand placed on students in TMR classrooms we can use these 34 dimensional sets as basic data for understanding how memory demands are actually structured there. In this context, a number of noteworthy findings emerged.

First, the most obvious finding was the high degree of routinization in this setting for teacher and student alike. Of the 34 tasks, twenty-five (.74) have values of either c_1 or c_2 and d_1 or d_3, indicating that the vast majority of tasks occur daily or "frequently" and require the same type of response (from the teacher's point of view) while the actual content of the response may vary. In contrast only six of the 34 items appear to be truly "unfamiliar"—occurring infrequently (c_3) and requiring a novel response (d_2).

The second interesting finding was that three values of dimension b account for an extremely large share of the variability, 24 of the 34 items (.71). In other words, the greatest memory demand (in terms of frequency of occurrence) involves the recollection of words, numbers, and symbols remembered individually (b_1) or in some longer, semantically meaningful sequence (b_2), or of procedures for doing things (b_6). Clustering b_1, b_2, and b_6 values with values of other dimensions provides limited but additionally suggestive evidence bearing on the nature of this task environment. Of 14 b_1/b_2 tasks, 11 (.79) are a_1 tasks and 10 (.71) are c_1 or c_2 tasks as well. That is, the majority of verbal memory demands are teacher-initiated and occur on a daily or frequent basis. Much the same pattern emerges with b_6 tasks. While b_6 tasks tend to be student-initiated (8 out of 10, or .80), they also tend to be daily or frequent in occurrence (9 out of 10, or .90). In addition all b_6 tasks (10 of 10) are either d_1 or d_3 tasks (that is, the type of response is always the same though the actual content of the response sometimes varies). Combining all 24 b_1, b_2, and b_6 tasks we see that 19 of them (.79) have values of either c_1 or c_2 and d_1 or d_3, further highlighting a very "familiar" environment.

Third, an unexpected outcome of our observations of the task environment was an inability to consistently divide task responses into categories of "right" or "wrong." Of greater salience within the classroom setting was the question of whether a response was acceptable and who decided that it was so. Whether a response was "actually" correct or incorrect (such as the answer to a mathematics problem) seemed to be less important to the teacher than the fact that a response was called for and given.

In making a distinction between correct responses and acceptable ones it is interesting to note that our sample of 34 items contains no example of "acceptability" as solely determined by the teacher. When it is not situation-dependent (dimension e_3) or student-dependent (e_2), acceptability comes about through an interactive process between teacher and student (e_1). We have come to think of this process as a dance-like "pas-de-deux" (see also Cicourel, 1974; Mehan, 1979). In this process the teacher typically makes a demand, the student further adjusts the demand, the teacher responds, and so forth until the two reach an agreement on what is to count as acceptable performance. The final task for the student is therefore two or more steps removed from the original demand.

Though we are still documenting the frequency with which this pas-de-deux occurs, initial indications are that it is relatively high (17 of the 34 tasks in Table 8-I have an e_1 value). If this does indeed prove to be the case we feel justified in arguing that the seemingly poor classroom performance (from an "objective" point of view) of TMR learners even on highly routinized tasks is partially a result of the greater value attached to "acceptableness" over "correctness." For example, neither teacher nor student seems to care that the Pledge of Allegiance be learned "by heart." Apparently each is mainly concerned that an acceptable level of sound be produced which, in its modulation and with a few "correct," audibly distinct words here and there, follows the recording of the Pledge which is playing in the background. It is fair to say, we feel, that these TMR students find few classroom situations in which they are expected to remember "correctly." The implications of this observational finding for various kinds of memory testing with their emphases on correct answers should be obvious. It should be equally clear that any cognitive analysis, even if methodologically feasible with everyday tasks, may be directed to the wrong task—one with which neither the student nor the teacher is concerned.

Finally, our microlevel approach to everyday memory demands reveals additional complexity with the cognitive analysis of everyday tasks. We believe that although many everyday demands involve a kind of "set" problem for the student, many others involve attention to shifting values of the dimensions which define the task and its environment and which become part of the cognitive "load" on the student. Items #5-6 of Table 8-I, for example, define two components of what might otherwise be mistakenly regarded as one single task. This is true for Items #17-18 as well. While values for the a, c, d, and e dimensions remain constant, the b values change from memory for a "cue" (b_4) to (1) memory for semantically connected words (b_2) in Item #6 and (2) memory for a number of sequentially arranged steps (b_6) in Item #18.

A more complex "translation" process may be found in Items #7 through 10. In this case only three dimensions (c, d, and e) remain constant; the actual memory demand alternates between a cue (b_4) and a sequence of words (b_2) and the initiator of the action changes from the teacher (a_1 in Items #7 and 8) to the student (a_2 in Items #9 and 10). We believe that these sometimes subtle shifts in task definition are relatively common in everyday settings and produce meta-level cognitive demands, e.g. the student's "recognition" that s/he is the initiator of an action when originally it was the teacher, which transcend the "simple" demands of the task itself.

CONCLUSION

The goal of our analysis has been to develop a scheme for categorizing everyday memory tasks and discovering any underlying patterns in these tasks. We also feel that our data directly bear on the more general issue of the relationship between "everyday" and "laboratory" tasks.

To date, we believe researchers have been concerned with four basic types of studies of tasks. These are represented by the four cells in the 2 x 2 matrix in Figure 8-1. We compare

Original Location of Task

	Laboratory Setting	Non-Laboratory Setting
Laboratory	A	C
"Real World"	B	D

Place
Where
Studied

Figure 8-1. Different approaches to the study of tasks.

the kinds of tasks, i.e. whether they were developed for use in the laboratory or in other settings, with where the tasks are actually studied, i.e. in the laboratory or in nonlaboratory settings. In Cell A we place typical memory tasks such as serial recall, problem-solving tasks such as the Tower of Hanoi puzzle, and the like. These evolved in the laboratory and are used to study cognitive processes. In Cell D we place the kind of tasks studied here, and represented by Table 8-I. These are tasks created by teachers and students for each other and themselves. The tasks in Cell B are adaptations of laboratory-based tasks for use in other settings. This strategy is common in cross-cultural studies, and usually involves manipulating the content and materials of the task so that they are "culturally appropriate" (for one example of such an approach see Cole, Gay, Glick, & Sharp, 1971). Often, such studies explicitly examine performance on these tasks over time in order to make comparisons across settings. The strategy for studying Cell C tasks involves assessing how certain tasks are formatted and contextualized in a given "natural" setting and then modeling one's experiments on this pattern (see, e.g. Lave, 1977).

Since our initial interest was the interrelationship of Type A and D tasks we analyzed three typical Type A memory tasks in terms of the conceptual scheme developed here. Interestingly the three tasks—free recall, serial recall, and paired-associate learning—all have similar dimensional sets. Thus we found that all three laboratory tasks emphasize recollection of isolated words (b_1) and initially occur quite irregularly (c_3). Two of the tasks (serial recall and paired-associate learning) have the same response type, i.e. the verbalization of a single word with variable content, i.e. different words on each of the trials (d_3). The third task (free recall) requires that the type of response and task content are always the same (d_1). In terms of the memory demand, the novelty of the task, and the type of response called for, these laboratory tasks have counterparts in the classroom environment. Indeed we found one task (Item #4 in Table 8-III) which has a pattern identical to these laboratory tasks—$b_1c_3d_3$.

Type A and D tasks differ in the *a* and *e* dimensions. All Type A tasks involve an outsider who is responsible for presenting the task, and we created a new value (a_3) to represent this dimension. We do not feel, however, that this difference is a significant one as students in classrooms frequently encounter new persons—substitute teachers or aides, new volunteers, administrators—who assign them tasks. Dimension *e* represents a more important difference. Laboratory tasks require a single person to make a unilateral judgment on the correctness of a response. Not only is the emphasis on correctness, but also there is no feedback to or negotiation with the subject on the satisfactoriness of the latter's response. As we have seen this is quite unlike the classroom setting. As a result no classroom task we observed has a structure identical with these three laboratory memory tasks, and none of these laboratory tasks taps the wide range of different task types (28 in even our limited sample) actually confronted by student learners.

Although studies of tasks as represented by Cells A and D are not without their problems, they seem to be "pure" forms of a method of analysis and type of task. The approaches represented by Cells B and C on the other hand seem to be "compromises" desirable on methodological grounds—Cell B studies achieve the generalizability that conventional laboratory tasks are said to lack and Cell C studies provide more control over and reliability of task performance in which nonlaboratory tasks are said to be wanting. Thus both Type B and C tasks attempt to bridge the "gap" between laboratory and nonlaboratory settings. Our limited goal in this paper has been to suggest one classificational framework within which all tasks can be grouped. We feel that further research needs to be done to fully understand "tasks," regardless of the setting in which they were originally developed or actually studied. This is a critical first step in our eventual understanding of the demands we place on youngsters and the nature of their task-related competencies.

FOOTNOTES

1. For the purposes of this discussion we consider "everyday" tasks to include both school- (or curriculum-) related tasks and "daily living" tasks as well. In reality there may be some overlap between laboratory and school-related tasks which is not shared with living tasks in that many laboratory tasks are often derived from or considered parallel to formal schooling experiences (see Cole, Sharp, & Lave, 1976). However, the curriculum in these TMR classrooms tends to emphasize pragmatic, everyday skills, and a large percentage of classroom time is undirected time which seems to allow the students to engage in self-initiated activities. In this sense the classroom and the tasks found there share characteristics with "everyday" settings and tasks.

2. Additionally we feel that the difference between a learner's first encounter with a task and subsequent encounters may prove to be important. Our intention is to examine this distinction more systematically when we look at actual performance.

REFERENCES

Bogdan, R., & Taylor, S. J. *Introduction to qualitative research methods.* New York: Wiley, 1975.

Brown, A. L. The development of memory: Knowing, knowing about knowing, and knowing how to know. In H. W. Reese (Ed.), *Advances in child development and behavior.* New York: Academic Press, 1975.

Brown, A. L. & Campione, J. C. Permissible inference from the outcome of training studies in cognitive development research. *Quarterly News-*

letter for the Institute for Comparative Human Development, 1978, *2*(3), 46-53.

Butterfield, E. C. On studying cognitive development. In G. P. Sackett (Ed.), *Observing behavior: Theory and applications in mental retardation* (Vol. I). Baltimore: University Park Press, 1978.

Charlesworth, W. R. Ethology: Its relevance for observational studies of human adaptation. In G. P. Sackett (Ed.). *Observing behavior: Theory and applications in mental retardation* (Vol. I). Baltimore: University Park Press, 1978.

Cicourel, A. V. Some basic theoretical issues in the assessment of the child's performance in testing and classroom settings. In A. V. Cicourel, K. H. Jennigs, S. H. M. Jennings, K. C. W. Leiter, R. MacKay, H. Mehan, & D. R. Roth, (Eds.). *Language use and school performance.* New York: Academic Press, 1974.

Cole, M., Gay, J., Glick, J. A., & Sharp, D. W. *The cultural context of learning and thinking.* New York: Basic Books, 1971.

Cole, M., Hood, L., & McDermott, R. P. Concepts of ecological validity: Their differing implications for comparative cognitive research. *The Quarterly Newsletter of the Institute for Comparative Human Development,* 1978, *2* (2), 34-37.

Cole, M. & Scribner, S. Theorizing about socialization in cognition. *Ethos,* 1975, *3,* 248-268.

Cole, M., Sharp, D. W., & Lave, C. The cognitive consequences of education: Some empirical evidence and theoretical misgivings. *The Urban Review,* 1976, *9*(4), 218-233.

Lave, J. Tailor-made experiments and evaluating the intellectual consequences of apprenticeship training. *The Quarterly Newsletter of the Institute for Comparative Human Development,* 1977, *1*(2), 1-3.

Mehan, H. *Learning lessons: Social organization in the classroom.* Cambridge, Mass.: Harvard University Press, 1979.

Pelto, P. J. *Anthropological research: The structure of inquiry.* New York: Harper & Row, 1970.

CHAPTER 9

A COGNITIVE SKILLS TRAINING PROGRAM
FOR MODERATELY RETARDED LEARNERS

Andrea G. Zetlin and Ronald Gallimore

Abstract

Moderately retarded adolescents from a special day school for TMR learners received cognitive training through a program which emphasized the direct teaching of comprehension. The methodology was adapted from a reading comprehension program developed for use with Hawaiian children at risk for school failure. Question and answer sessions were used to permit the students to be systematically guided through the cognitive processes related to understanding a story. The leader's strategy was to be a skillful questioner, adept at leading the students to the correct answers rather than telling them the answers directly. The questions focused on Experience—Text—Relationship information as well as different levels of comprehension so as to provide the students with opportunities to explore many dimensions of the story and to integrate features of it with their existing knowledge and ideas. Pre- and post-standardized test results, criterion referenced test results, and analysis of the training sessions' transcripts indicated an increase in listening comprehension for all the students. These results are discussed in terms of recent developments in cognitive theory and research.

Problems Inherent in TMR Curricula

Most TMR curricula emphasize the development of independent living skills. These include habits of self-care, communication, work, ability to follow directions, and the rudiments of

Support for this research was provided by NICHD Post-doctoral Traineeship awarded to the first author. Statistical analysis was suggested by Donald Guthrie and performed by the Computing Resources Group, MRRC, UCLA. We acknowledge Harold Levine, Kathy Hu-pei Au, and Roland Tharp for helpful comments.

From *Education and Training of the Mentally Retarded* (forthcoming). Reprinted by permission.

163

social participation. Academic instruction is ordinarily minimized since these skills are "unlikely to be functionally useful to the TMR adult." (Robinson & Robinson, 1975).

These emphases in TMR curricula are the subject of some criticism. For example, Haywood (1977) has argued that limiting instruction to personal and social development is pessimistic, focused on limitations, and does not provide opportunities for cognitive growth. It has also been suggested that typical TMR curricula feature lower level tasks and do not develop or promote use of higher order cognitive processes (Winschel & Enscher, 1978).

These criticisms of TMR curricula find support in contemporary research developments, for example the studies of strategic memory processes, e.g. Butterfield, Wambold, & Belmont, 1973; Brown, 1974. Investigators have shown that retarded children are often capable of higher order cognitive processing provided sufficient instructional supports are available. More recently, it has been suggested that the processing capabilities of retarded youngsters are underestimated by reliance on assessments in artificial laboratory settings with tasks that lack ecological validity (Brooks & Baumeister, 1977). In addition, Goodstein (cited in Milgram, 1973) has suggested that the limited reasoning and discovery abilities of retarded children may be partly an artifact of the curricula to which they are exposed; it would not be surprising to find limited use of higher order processing if the retarded children who become subjects in experiments are ordinarily instructed by imitation and drill strategies while their nonretarded counterparts are exposed to more varied classroom experiences and teaching styles.

Studies using a wider variety of tasks and settings suggest that the mentally retarded may have available more higher order processing and may use it more often in daily life than performance on common laboratory tasks indicated. Friedman, Krupski, Dawson, and Rosenberg (1978) found TMR youngsters capable of generating many different functional memory strategies within the context of their daily lives. Naturalistic observations of TMR classrooms suggest a variety of competencies with which students confront spontaneous as well as teacher-presented problems (Levine, 1978).

Observations of classrooms in a suburban school for TMR students identified several elements of the instructional program which seemed to discourage development and use of higher order processing, and encourage reliance on less efficient learning strategies (Levine, Zetlin, & Langness, 1979). Within these classrooms most tasks and activities were presented in the absence of a familiar context, or in what is sometimes called an episodic style (Brown, 1974). As a result, the tasks may have appeared to the students to be unrelated to existing knowledge and experience derived in the course of daily life. Although teachers demonstrated awareness that training of daily skills such as brushing teeth and handwashing could be best accomplished by integration into school routine, academic skills were not embedded in meaningful contexts. For example, functional vocabulary words were taught by flashcard drill with picture and/or verbal associations accompanying presentation of the words to aid the student's comprehension. During review sessions students were asked to identify words and associated meanings: to the word poison, it was not uncommon for students to respond, "Poison, don't eat the bones." (a response which seemed to focus specifically on the skull and bone picture association). This instructional approach assumes the best strategy to be memorization of an appropriate verbal response to the "poison" stimulus, achieved by repeated presentations and reinforced responses. Whatever familiarity the students had with poisonous materials, or exposure to such dangers, was not exploited or integrated with the new knowledge being taught. Such a teaching procedure is contrary to Goldstein's (1972) contention that the ideas and concepts to be learned be related to an overall structure rather than be acquired as isolated and fragmented bits of information.

To summarize, two related concerns are apparent in the literature reviewed so far: (1) the emphasis on lower level tasks, and corresponding lower order cognitive processing in the TMR curricula to the exclusion of higher order tasks and processing, which may result in a self-fulfilling special education prophesy; (2) the importance of providing meaningful contexts and tasks for school instruction, in order to maximize comprehension and achievement, and to exploit existing student knowledge and skills.

APPROACHES TO COGNITIVE TRAINING

Two general strategies have emerged for training cognitive skills of the retarded learner. One approach involves training cognitive strategies independent of content areas such as reading (Feuerstein, Rand, Hoffman, Hoffman, & Miller, 1979; Ross & Ross, 1978; 1973, Haywood, 1977). Such training programs require transfer and generalization of these cognitive strategies which research has indicated is difficult to achieve in mentally retarded children who tend to acquire information "welded" to the form in which it was learned (Shif, 1969; Brown, 1974). Some cognitive training researchers have thus concluded that "decontextualized" strategy training is not a promising avenue (Brown, 1978).

An alternate approach addresses the issue of context as well and attempts to embed or integrate cognitive training into regular academic content area. Programs employing this approach include the Social Learning Curriculum (Goldstein, 1972; Heiss & Mischio, 1972) and the Kamehameha Early Education Program (KEEP: Tharp & Gallimore, 1979).

The Social Learning Curriculum is a comprehensive socially-oriented education program for retarded learners to develop skills, critical thinking and independent action, presumed necessary for adjustment at maturity. A task analysis was used to build a problem-solving strategy into the curriculum content: students learn to learn by using the analytical steps of labeling, detailing, inferring, predicting, and generalizing. Aside from task analysis of problem-solving into its subcomponent skills, no further instructional modifications were made to assist the retarded learner in acquiring these cognitive skills. KEEP on the other hand, has developed teaching strategies that include but go beyond a task analysis of cognitive skills.

KEEP implemented a multi-strand reading program for Hawaiian Island children at risk for severe academic underachievement, which after several full years' formative and summative evaluation proved successful in instructing these minority pupils to read near national average. On-going analysis suggests a key feature of the KEEP program is the direct instruction of comprehension which is conducted daily by a teacher who seeks through questioning, to help students relate material being learned to existing knowledge (Tharp, in preparation). All teacher-directed lessons are begun with a Socratic dialogue in which the students are prompted to describe personal experiences related to the story to be read. Later, after reading portions of the story the teacher uses an empirically validated question pattern which seeks to promote understanding from literal comprehension to the higher levels of inferential comprehension.

On several accounts, the KEEP comprehension lessons match emerging criteria for effective cognitive training, including strategic behavior (Brown, 1978). First, the teacher functions as a skillful questioner, a role which Brown specifically identifies as important in promoting cognitive strategy development and use. Second, comprehension activities meet the criteria which Brown also proposed to be used to select tasks for cognitive training: they can be readily seen by the child to work and to relate to real-life activities and the component processes are well understood in the sense that elaborate curricula are available in the form of instructional objectives. In addition, the KEEP program includes teaching strategies which are sufficiently operational in that they may be taught to teachers and used to assess program implementation. These include a task analyzed "levels of comprehension" hierarchy (Crowell & Au, 1979), and an operationally defined question pattern (Au, 1979).

SIMILARITIES AMONG MENTALLY RETARDED AND MINORITY SCHOOL PROBLEMS

Continuing research suggests the KEEP program is effective because it assists the minority children in making the transition from home/community learning to school learning (Gallimore & Au, in press). Brown (1978) has suggested there is a similarity in transition problems for both retarded and cultural minority students. Prior to school most of their learning is context bound and experientially based (what is sometimes called semantic learning). Confronted with the episodic learning for learning's sake nature of most school instruction, both minority and retarded students seem to make little progress, display consistent use of

existing skills and knowledge, and suffer the alienating consequence of repeated failure.

Gallimore and Au (in press) have suggested that the KEEP
comprehension lessons help minority children recognize the
relevance of existing knowledge and skills to episodic, or school
learning tasks. The comprehension lessons help promote generalization of processing strategies from semantic or experiential
learning to school learning. If taught with an approach in which
stored memories and ideas are not tapped, they seem to rely
more consistently on rote memory, guessing and other lower
learning strategies. In effect, some curricula tend to suppress the
development and use of higher order strategies, and to promote
an already strong inclination to approach school-type tasks with
the least efficient strategies; for example, an over-reliance on
decoding written text word-by-word with little attention to context or sentence environment (Gallimore & Au, in press).

A similar pattern may be occurring with the retarded learner.
A TMR curriculum that features lower order, episodic processing
to the exclusion of higher order processing, might serve to
further encourage least efficient learning and discourage or suppress complex processing. The work of Butterfield and Belmont
(1979), among others, suggests that retarded persons continue
to need encouragement to use higher order processing even when
they have demonstrated such capacity on previous occasions:
for reasons not yet fully understood, reliable use of higher order
strategies by retarded individuals is not readily achieved.

The study reported here adapted features of the KEEP
comprehension program for use with a small group of TMR
students. Because of the limited reading skills of the group
selected, the systematic development of listening comprehension
became the focus of the training program. The major goal was
to encourage the students to become active processors of story
information while providing them with a bridging experience
so that the content of the material presented was meaningful to
them. The central question was: can TMR students use or learn
the necessary variety of cognitive skills from literal to inferential
comprehension which would allow them to benefit from a
curriculum that requires higher order processing.

METHOD

Subjects

The training group consisted of three students, two boys and one girl, classified as trainable mentally retarded by the Los Angeles City Unified School District. The students attended a special school for trainable mentally retarded learners in suburban Los Angeles. They came from white, middle class families and lived at home with their parents. They were all from the same class which covered an age range of 12 to 14.9 years and was considered by the school administration to be as a whole, a high functioning class. At the start of the training sessions one child was 13.10 years, another was 14.2 years, and the third was 14.7 years. All had IQ's within the 40 to 50 range. One child was diagnosed as Down's Syndrome; the etiology of the other two was unspecified. In terms of their reading skills, two of the students had basic sight vocabularies of approximately 30 words, and the third was essentially a nonreader.

Procedure

The group of three students and leader met three times a week unless otherwise prevented by the school schedule or a holiday. A total of 23 sessions, each session lasting 20 to 30 minutes, took place in an auxiliary room, adjacent to the main classroom. All sessions were tape recorded.

The format for each session was a page by page presentation of a story selected from the first or second preprimer of the Bank Street Basal Reading Series. Depending on the length of the story, either the whole story or half the story was covered during a session. The leader directed the student's attention, and through her questions provided opportunities to explore many levels of the story and to integrate features of it with existing knowledge.

There were two dimensions by which to describe the form questions took: the information focus and the level of comprehension of the questions.

1. *Information Focus.* The information focus of questions provided for eliciting Experience, Text, or Relationship informa-

tion (Au, 1979). The experience (E) questions permitted the students to discuss their store of experience or knowledge (cumulative information from daily life experiences) which was related in some way to the story that was to be read. These questions were meant to show the students that they had informaion which could be brought to bear in reading the story. For example, prior to reading a story about people going shopping, a series of questions which tapped the students (G, M, C) own experiences in going shopping were asked by the leader (A):

Session 3

    A: G, tell me some different stores that you go to?
    G: I go to the store
    A: What kind of store?
    G: K-mart
    A: What do you buy in K-mart?
    G: Food
    A: M, tell me some stores that you go to?
    M: Shoe store
    A: What do you get in a shoe store?
    M: Shoe
    A: What other kind of stores?
    M: Shirt store
    A: What's the name of the shirt store?
    M: Penney's
    A: What store do you go to C?
    C: Penney's
    A: What do you buy there?
    C: New underwear and new socks and new shoes
    A: Why do people go to stores?
    C: I buy puzzles to do
    A: Why else do people go to stores M?
    M: Food
    A: C, why else do people go to stores?
    C: Because, buy Taco Bells

Text (T) questions required the students to respond to questions directly related to the literal content of the story. These questions focused on either picture details or the written text as in:

Session 13

A: Who is the man M?
M: Workman
A: The workman. What kind of clothes does he wear?
M: Pajamas (referring to the man's flannel shirt)
G: Workclothes
A: He wears workclothes. What does he wear on his head?
M, G: Hat
A: And what does he wear on his hands?
M, G: Gloves

These literal comprehension questions were followed by relationship questions which were designed to extend the students' level of thinking about the details of the story questions and their own outside experience and knowledge. Relationship questions were intended to help the students realize that they need to apply their stored information to the story in order to arrive at a more complete interpretation. The text comprehension passage of the previous example from session 13 continued with relationship questions such as:

A: Why does he wear a hat and gloves M?
G: So he has splinters
A: Good G, so he doesn't get splinters. M, why do you think he wears a hat?
M: When he work
A: When he's working. What's the hat for?
M: Wear house (referring to the house under construction in the picture)
G: So he don't get hurt on the head

The E-T-R information focus of questions represents a readily identifiable pattern to structure the instructional sequence (Au, 1979).

2. *Level of Comprehension.* The second dimension referred to the level of comprehension tapped by the questions. Comprehension was operationally defined as the ability to answer different types of questions falling along a hypothetical continuum from various levels of literal comprehension to the highest levels of inferential comprehension; the first three levels were literal while those at the last two levels were inferential (Crowell & Au,

1979). The leader was able to guide the students' thinking through these levels of comprehension by the sequence of questions asked. Questions at the lowest level were designed to elicit any details of the story that could be recalled. At level 2 simple interpretations were required, usually at the feeling level. At level 3 questions dealt with the interrelationships among details or the sequence of events. The fourth level required the integration of the various elements in the story into a structure not necessarily presented in the story, as in summarizing events, predicting the story's outcome and justifying that prediction. At the highest level the questions were intended to reveal the students' understanding of the story and events and in changing their ideas on the basis of new information. This hierarchical model of listening comprehension skill was previously validated with nonretarded, primary age children (Crowell & Au, 1979).

RESULTS

Changes in the students' listening comprehension skill were evaluated by analysis of the transcripts from the tape-recorded sessions and pre- and post-test results.

Transcript Analysis

Informal observations suggest that at the onset of the study the students' participation was not as flexible and fluent as in later sessions. As the training proceeded and students became more familiar with the structure of the session and the type of involvement that was expected of them, changes in their performance were noted:

1. Initially the leader had to restate and restructure questions which called for information that went beyond the details of the story. In later sessions the students showed greater flexibility in responding to inferential comprehension questions.

Session 4

    A: How can you tell from their clothes what kind of weather it is?
    G: Dirty.
    A: What kind of clothes are they wearing?

G: Dress and shirt.

A: Are they wearing coats?

G: No.

A: What kind of weather would it be if they were wearing coats?

G: Cold   M: Winter.

A: And if they were wearing raincoats what kind of weather would it be?

M: Rain.

A: Are they wearing coats or raincoats?

C: No.

A: So we can say it's not raining and it's not cold out, so what kind of weather it is?

C: Hot.

After the unsuccessful attempt to have the students infer ideas from the details depicted in the picture text, the leader restructured subsequent questions to have a narrower, more specific focus. Thus she reduced the amount of inference the students would have to make in determining the correct response. The effects of the adjusted "inferential" load are apparent in the following excerpt:

Session 6

A: What are the children doing?

G: Running out.

A: Why do you think they're running C?

C: Cause they're late for school.

A: They're late for school, so they've got to run. Why do you think they're late for school?

C: Cause the teacher got mad.

A: Because the teacher's going to get mad if they're late. But where did they go that made them late for school?

M: School.

A: Remember where they stopped?

C: I know, candystore?

A: They stopped at the candystore. That made them late for school. And because they stopped, what happened?

G: They get in trouble by the teacher.

A: They're going to get in trouble. Why are they going to get in trouble?

G: Cause they're late from the candystore

During session 6, the students began to make inferences about the story events and to see the relationship of those events to each other.

By session 20 when presented with an inferential question which probed beyond the literal details presented in the story, the students were able to integrate related ideas which they generated from their own information store with the story concepts.

Session 20

A: Who comes to visit the birds?
G: Ben.
A: Why do you think Ben visits the birds?
M: They kiss his hand?
M: Yeah.
A: G, why do you think Ben goes to visit the birds?
G: Wants to buy a bird.
A: Maybe he wants to buy one. C, what do you think?
C: Because.
A: Because what?
C: Uh, Ben loves birds.

2. Students initially responded to literal detail questions with the same vocabulary as was presented in the written text. In later sessions they occasionally rephrased the vocabulary and responded in their own words, as illustrated in excerpts from sessions 4 and 19.

Session 4

A: G, would you read this for me
G: "Many boys are in the city. Many girls are in the city. The boys and girls go to school. They work in school."
A: Where do the boys and girls go?
G: To school.
A: What do they do in school?
M: Work.

Session 19

A: What does this girl want to do when she grows up?
C: Be a teacher.
A: This girl?
C: No, other girl.

A: Yeah. What does this girl want to be? Listen again, she says "Someday I will have three boys." What does that mean? What does she want to do when she grows up?

C: Have a baby.

A: That's right, have a baby. What will that make her? If she has three boys, what will they call her?

C: Mother   M: Mother.

Being able to rephrase the ideas presented in the written text into their own words contributes further evidence of the students' comprehension of the concepts implied in the story.

3. In the beginning, students responded to questions independently of other students' responses.

Session 2

A: Show me somebody in the picture; what are they doing?

G: She's washing the clothes.

A: Where's she putting the clothes?

G: On the hanger (referring to the clothesline).

A: What happens to the clothes when they stay outside?

G: They dry.

A: If it were raining would the lady hang her clothes outside?

G, M: No.

A: Why not?

M: It off.

A: She'd take them off. If she left them outside, what would happen to them?

M: Rain, wet.   C: Get wet.

A: So do you think it's raining outside.

G, M: No.   C: No, it's sunny out.

A: And what does the sun do to the clothes?

G: Dry them.

In Session 2 each student waited for the leader's question to be directed at them and responded specifically to that question. There appeared to be little reaction to each other's responses. In Session 16 a different pattern emerged:

Session 16

A: Where is the firetruck going when it makes that sound M?

M: Fire.

G: To a store. Stores on fire.

A: Okay, the stores on fire. What else might be on fire besides a store?

C: A house. G: A house.

A: A house, good.

C: A roof.

A: A roof, good.

M: A body.

A: What?

M: A body.

C: A body.

M: Yeah.

A: A body might be on fire?

M: Yeah.

C: No. Get a car out, and the car blow up.

A: A car might be on fire?

C: And the other people.

A: The people might be on fire from being in the car?

M: Yeah burn.

C: No, no, in the car.

A: They might be on fire in the car?

C: No out of the car, and the and the . . .

M: They burn.

C: And "Emergency" come and—

A: Oh "Emergency" the TV show.

C: Yeah.

A: They come and save the people.

G: It's on tonight.

C: In the morning.

G: Tonight.

C: Morning.

G: Night.

C: Morning.

During session 16 the students seemed to attend to each others responses and interacted and collaborated with each other as well as the leader; the students began to support, augment, and challenge each other as part of their processing of story ideas.

4. As time passed the students demonstrated an ability to alter and change their own responses when confronted with contradictory evidence.

Session 14

A: Why do you think Ann and her mother are saying goodby to each other?
C: Because have a good day.
A: Where's her mother going?
C: Going to school.
A: And where's Ann going?
C: Ann going? To work with her mother.
A: Why are they saying good-by to each other then?
C: They're gonna go to school.
A: Where is Ann going in the school building?
C: Of work, work. G: She gonna read.
A: Where do you think Ann's going in the school building?
G: She gonna study.
C: In the classroom.
A: Ann is going into the classroom. Is her mother going into the classroom too?
C: Yeah.
A: You think so?
C: You know why, mother is, mother is teacher.
G: Lunchhelper.
A: If her mother was a lunchhelper would she go into the classroom with Ann?
C: No.
A: Where would she go?
G: Cafeteria.
C: In the lunch.
A: In the lunchroom. Yes, Ann would go to her classroom and her mother would go to the lunchroom, so they say good-by to each other because they're not going to see each other.

C was unable to grasp the concept implicit in Ann and her mother's saying good-by to each other until the leader presented the evidence which C finally seemed to accept and comprehend. However, by Session 21 more fluent processing of information was observed:

Session 21

A: How's the man feeling now?
M: Happy.
A: You think he's still happy.
M: Yeah.

C: Sad.
A: Why is he sad?
C: Cause the monkey ran away.
A: Yeah, do you think he's happy or sad, M?
M: No sad.
A: Why is he sad?
M: He run away.

During session 21, M willingfully switched his initial response to A's question when C disagreed with his response and presented M with a justification for his response. In contrast to the earlier sessions, new ideas and conflicting interpretations were more readily integrated and reconciled.

5. At first, students exhibited difficulty describing what the story was about. Their summarizing responses consisted of isolated details of the story which generally occurred on the last page or two. As time passed, their review of the stories tended to focus more on the story as a whole and details were sequenced rather than presented in isolation. The change is reflected in the contrasts across sessions 4, 6, and 21.

Session 4

A: What do you think this story was all about?
G: About them running.
A: Who was running?
G: The boy and girl.

Session 6

A: What was the story all about?
G: A policeman, a car stops, and people go across the street.

Session 21

A: What was the story about?
C: I know, M: Ben's house.
C: Ben's house.
A: Ben's house?
M: Fly.
C: Fly away.
A: The birds fly away from Ben's house and . . .
C: And the sun going down and the sun go up, the birds, the birds go away.

M: Down.
A: What do they do?
G: They fly back.

In session 4, in response to the summary request, one isolated detail which occurred on the last page of a four-page story was recalled. The response appeared to show a lack of grasp of the relatedness of events occurring throughout the story, and perhaps a "recency" effect. A few sessions later, although the recency effect was again exhibited, this time a number of details were recalled and stated in the order they appeared on the last page of the story. By session 21, after a question "prompt" by the leader, there was a minimally assisted sequential recall of details spanning the whole story.

Analysis of the discourse sequences which occurred during these sessions provides evidence that given an opportunity and some encouragement to engage in higher order processing, these students were capable of such processing. They indicated an inclination to respond to different levels of questions concerning the ideas presented in the stories and they showed an increase in performance efficiency over time.

Formal Test Results

An additional source of data was obtained from pre- and post-test results. Prior to the first session, the Gates-MacGinites Reading Readiness Test and a criterion referenced listening comprehension test were administered to three of the students. The listening comprehension test consisted of four short stories which were read aloud to the students, each followed by five questions which focused on various levels of comprehension, i.e. literal details, cause and effect relationships, idea sequencing and prediction. A similar listening comprehension test was administered after every six training sessions. At the completion of the training sessions some three months later, the Gates-MacGinite Reading Readiness Test was readministered.

The Gates-MacGinite test results indicated that over a period of ten weeks, the most substantial gains were made in the listening comprehension subtest. Since only three students were included in the program, these data should be considered as further support rather than convincing evidence that these students seemed to deal more effectively with listening comprehension tasks.

TABLE 9-I

STANINE GAINS FROM PRE- AND POST-TESTING OF
GATES-MacGINITE READING READINESS TEST*

	M		Student C		G		Total Stanine Gains
Word recognition	8	(8)	5	(7)	8	(7)	+1
Listening comprehension	3	(4)	4	(6)	4	(6)	+5
Auditory discrimination	6	(6)	4	(5)	3	(5)	+3
Visual discrimination	3	(3)	5	(4)	4	(4)	—1
Following directions	2	(3)	2	(2)	1	(1)	+1
Letter recognition	7	(7)	6	(6)	8	(8)	0
Visual motor coordination	9	(9)	9	(9)	8	(9)	+1
Auditory blending	3	(3)	4	(5)	5	(5)	+1
Readiness percentile	34	(42)	34	(46)	31	(38)	27

* Post-test scores in parentheses.

Results from the listening comprehension test also indicate an increase in performance across the five tests by each student. The scoring system for questions involved a three-point scale. No points were awarded for completely incorrect responses, one point was counted for incorrect responses that either had some relationship to the storyline, or appeared to be logical given the question asked, and two points were assigned for completely correct answers. A score of 40 was the highest score that could have been attained on the test. One student's total score increased from 27 to 31, another student's score increased from 31 to 37, and the third student's score increased from 21 to 33. The improvement over weeks represented a statistically significant change ($F(1,8=16.61$ $p<.0005$). A follow-up listening comprehension test was administered six weeks after the sessions had been terminated; results indicated that all three students maintained the level of comprehension attained at the completion of the program.

Table 9-II

Results from Listening Comprehension Tests*

		M				G				C			
test week	score	2	1	0	TOT	2	1	0	TOT	2	1	0	TOT
	2	6	13	1	27	12	7	1	31	8	5	7	21
	4	9	8	3	26	10	8	2	28	11	6	3	28
	6	8	9	3	25	17	2	1	36	11	8	1	30
	8	10	9	1	29	17	3	0	37	15	4	1	34
	10	12	7	1	31	17	3	0	37	13	7	0	33
Follow-up		13	5	2	31	16	4	0	36	14	6	0	34

* 2 = correct response
1 = incorrect response but shows some relationship to story
0 = completely incorrect
TOT = Total score

DISCUSSION

In many cases a training study can be viewed as a procedure for uncovering a capacity as opposed to establishing a capacity from scratch (Gelman, 1978). It may be that participation in this program provided the students with the opportunity to demonstrate skills previously presumed absent and therefore left untapped by the curriculum. These students seem to have skills and knowledge and appear capable, if provided with guidance and direction, of responding to a program that depends upon the availability of higher order skills. When actively involved in the sessions they appeared capable of responding to literal comprehension questions which focused on identifying story details and sequencing events, and inferential comprehension questions which required inferring cause and effect relationships and making predictions. Furthermore their responses to these inferential questions indicated that they were using information from their existing store to make inferences about ideas and events in the story.

Traditionally such skills were considered beyond the abilities of the TMR child. This presumption was derived from characterization of the TMR child's cognitive structure in terms of what it lacks. In most cases, this was based on very limited experimental investigation of particular abilities. The results of our study are another indication that TMR youngsters may possess capacities beyond what often is expected of them and what is emphasized in typical TMR curricula.

Classroom teachers can readily employ these instructional strategies with their TMR students when presenting new material to be read or discussed. As implied in the introduction of this paper, the provision of comprehension lessons has value beyond developing reading skills. The lessons may be conceived of as cognitive training in the sense that students are taught in a face-to-face social situation, how to integrate new information with existing knowledge to arrive at new understandings. The skills tapped include: extracting information from what is read or heard, bringing to bear a large quantity of formal and informal information to the story ideas, using linguistic cues to under-stand the intention of the speaker or writer, and making infer-ences. Providing a context in which all of these skills are practiced, a context that includes a leader and peers, may itself yield benefits beyond those to be achieved in isolated cognitive training situations. It is not difficult to imagine that TMR students might better adapt in several settings if they could comprehend better. All of this seems to argue that embedded cognitive training is likely to be a more satisfactory solution in the long run than programs that seek to identify and train separate skills in isolation.

REFERENCES

Au, K. H. Using the experience-text-relationship method with minority children. *Reading Teacher,* 1979, 32 (6), 677-679.

Brown, A. L. Knowing when, where, and how to remember: A problem of metacognition. In R. Glaser (Ed.), *Advances in instructional psychology.* Hillsdale, N.J.: Lawrence Erlbaum Assoc., 1978.

Brown, A. L. The role of strategic behavior in retardate memory. In N. R. Ellis (Ed.), *International review of research in mental retardation.* Vol. 7, 1974, 55-111.

Brooks, P. H. & Baumeister, A. A. A plea for consideration of ecological validity in the experimental psychology of mental retardation: A guest editorial. *American Journal of Mental Deficiency,* 1977, 81, 407-416.

Butterfield, E. C. & Belmont, J. M. Instructional techniques that produce generalized improvement in cognition. Paper presented at the 12th

Annual Gatlinburg Conference on Research in Mental Retardation and Developmental Disabilities, Gulf Shores, Alabama, April, 1979.

Butterfield, E. C., Wambold, C. & Belmont, J. M. On the theory and practice of improving short-term memory. *American Journal of Mental Deficiency*, 1973, 77, 654-669.

Crowell, D. C. & Au, K. H. Using a scale of questions to improve listening comprehension. *Language Arts*, 1979, 56 (1), 38-43.

Friedman, M., Krupski, A., Dawson, E. T., and Rosenberg, P. Metamemory and mental retardation: Implications for research and practice. In P. Mittler (Ed.), *Research to practice in mental retardation: Education and training*, Vol. II. Baltimore: University Park Press, 1977.

Feuerstein, R., Rand, Y., Hoffman, M., Hoffman, M., & Miller, R. Cognitive modifiability in retarded adolescents: Effects on instructional enrichment. *American Journal of Mental Deficiency*, 1979, 83 (6), 539-550.

Gallimore, R., & Au, K. H. The competence/incompetence paradox in the education of minority culture children. *Comparative Human Cognition Quarterly*, in press.

Gelman, R. Cognitive development. In M. Rosenzweig and L. W. Porter (Eds.), *Annual review of psychology*, (Vol. 29). Palo Alto: Annual Reviews, Inc., 1978.

Goldstein, H. Construction of a social learning curriculum. In E. L. Meyen, G. A. Vergason, and R. J. Whelan (Eds.), *Strategies for teaching exceptional children*. Denver: Love Publishing Co., 1972, 94-114.

Haywood, H. C. A cognitive approach to the education of retarded children. *Peabody Journal of Education*, 1977, 54, 110-116.

Heiss, W. E. & Mischio, G. S. Designing curriculum for the educable mentally retarded. In E. L. Meyen, G. A. Vergason, and R. J. Whelan (Eds.). *Strategies for teaching exceptional children*. Denver: Love Publishing Co., 1972, 115-135.

Levine, H. G. Everyday problem-solving in a school for children with moderate retardation. Paper presented at the Annual Meeting of the American Anthropological Association, Los Angeles, November, 1978.

Levine, H., Zetlin, A. G., & Langness, L. L. Everyday memory tasks in a school for the TMR learner. Paper presented at the 103rd Annual Conference of the American Association on Mental Deficiency, Miami, Florida, May, 1979.

Milgram, N. Cognition and language in D. K. Routh (Ed.), *The experimental psychology of mental retardation*. Chicago: Aldine Publishing, 1973.

Robinson, H. B. & Robinson, N. M. *The mentally retarded child* (2nd Ed.). New York: McGraw-Hill, 1975.

Ross, D. M. & Ross, S. A. Cognitive training for EMR children: Choosing the best alternative. *American Journal of Mental Deficiency*, 1978, 82, 598-601.

Ross, D. M. & Ross, S. A. Cognitive training for the EMR child: Situational problem-solving and planning. *American Journal of Mental Deficiency,* 1973, *78,* 20-26.

Shif, Z. I. Development of children in schools for the mentally retarded. In M. Cole and I. Maltzman (Eds.). *A handbook of contemporary Soviet* psychology. New York: Basic Books, 1969, 326-353.

Tharp, R. Kamehameha reading objective system. KEEP Technical Report. Honolulu: The Kamehameha Early Education Project, in preparation.

Tharp, R. G., and Gallimore, R. The ecology of program research and development: A model of evaluation succession. In L. B. Sechrest (Ed.), *Evaluation studies review annual,* (Vol. 4). Beverly Hills: Sage Publications, 1979.

Winschel, J. F. and Ensher, G. L. Curricular implications for the mentally retarded. *Education and Training of the Mentally Retarded,* 1978, *13,* 131-138.

SECTION V

THE INSTITUTIONALIZED RETARDED

CHAPTER 10

THE WORLD OF THE CONGENITALLY DEAF-BLIND: TOWARD THE GROUNDS FOR ACHIEVING HUMAN UNDERSTANDING

DAVID A. GOODE

FOR A YEAR and a half I conducted an ethnography of a state hospital ward for congenitally deaf-blind, retarded (rubella syndrome) children. I entered this research enterprise as a social scientist but with no particular theoretical or methodological issues in mind. Rather, I let these concerns emerge during the course of the research. I did not know what my involvement with ward personnel or residents would come to in the long run but was motivated by a genuine interest in the interaction of the congenitally deaf-blind with normally seeing-hearing persons. This paper represents one extremely important part of this ethnography.[1]

Ordinarily we take it for granted that we live in an intersubjective world, a world whose physical, social, and psychological aspects are communicated and shared with reasonable accuracy. Yet on this ward there were in a sense two "worlds," one shared by myself and the staff (normal perceivers) and another inhabited by the residents. Indeed, by the very differences in our sense organs, the residents were living and acting in a different perceptual place than I—one in which the reception of audiovisual stimuli had been degraded as a result of a prenatal viral infection. It was decided that only intimate and persistent

This research was supported by PSH Grant No. HD04612 NICHD, The Mental Retardation Research Center, UCLA, and No. HD-05540-02, Patterns of Care and the Development of the Retarded. My special thanks for their assistance in guiding my enterprise to Robert B. Edgerton, Harold Garfinkel, Melvin Pollner, and Michael Gaddy. My thanks to Harold Levine for his editorial assistance.

From Howard Schwartz & Jerry Jacobs, *Qualitative sociology: A method to the madness,* New York: The Free Press, 1979. Reprinted by permission.

interactional contact with the residents would be likely to enable me to enter into their world. A major obstacle to such a task stemmed from the variation in perceptual abilities displayed by particular residents; it was not the case that they inhabited a deaf-blind world at large; rather, each exhibited a specific configuration of perceptual/cognitive skills and deficiencies. Consequently, I decided to concentrate on a nine-year-old female resident, Christina (Chris), and spend a number of daily cycles (24-hour periods or longer) with her, sharing "average days" in her "ordinary life." In addition to naturalistic observation of her behavior, I employed videotaping and viewing of normal ward routines and other interactional procedures ("mimicking" and "passive obedience").

My relatively long-term involvement with Chris gave me access to observational data unavailable to medical practitioners, who would see her during relatively short, structured, and "nonordinary" medical examinations. From our interactions and my observations over a period of a few months, I gathered the following information about her perceptual, motor, behavior, and language abilities (see also Goode, 1974a, 1974b, 1975b).

MEDICAL AND BEHAVIORAL PROFILE

Medical examination records, developmental assessments, and interviews with the child's mother were used to construct a medical/behavioral profile.

During Chris's prenatal existence, she (the fetus) was subject to an "attack" of a virulent and destructive cyclical virus (rubella). During the second or third week of pregnancy, the rubella virus entered her mother's bloodstream and attacked the sensitive, rapidly multiplying cells of the embryo (rubella embryopathy), causing damage in the forms of hemorrhage, brain lesions, lysis damage to the cochlea, cataract, and so on. As a result, Chris was born with a severe syndrome of multihandicaps (the rubella syndrome) whose sequelae included bilateral cataracts, congenital heart disease (patent ductus and stenosis), functional deafness (the "intactness" of Chris's hearing mechanism has never been established), clinical microcephaly, central nervous system damage (a low-grade diffuse encephalopathy), abnormal behavior patterns, and severe developmental retardation. The degree and nature of Chris's multihandicaps have been difficult to assess since medical procedures for making such determinations are usually designed for normally perceiving and communicating persons (see Goode, 1974a). At the age of five Chris was diagnosed as legally blind, legally deaf, and mentally retarded and was placed in a state hospital for the retarded.[2]

Vision

Chris was able to orient visually to large objects in her path and would normally "fend" against these by using her right arm. She was also able to inspect objects at a very close range and was observed to eat by bringing the spoon to her right ("good") eye to a distance of perhaps one to two inches, for the apparent purpose of inspecting the food's color and consistency. Chris's visual acuity varied considerably depending on such factors as setting, emotional state, motivation, and quality of visual stimulus. In close face-to-face presentation, she sometimes seemed to be studying my physiognomy.

Hearing

Chris's auditory acuity also seemed to vary considerably. When motivated, she seemed to be able to orient to the sound of my guitar being played at a considerable distance from her, and in a number of "natural experiments" she was observed to "home in" on this sound from distances of more than twenty feet. She loved sound stimulation of all types—especially music, with its regular rhythms and variety of frequencies. She attended to my singing to her or speaking to her in her ear (she used her right ear more than her left and would maneuver herself so that she could turn this ear toward the sound stimulus). It was difficult to assess the amount or quality of sound she was receiving, but several clinicians concurred with my belief that she *received* a variety of sounds but had problems in "processing" the sound as normal hearers do.

Touch

Chris was extremely touch oriented. She used her tongue as her primary organ for perception whenever possible and would lick anything within her reach. I learned to conceive of this activity as Chris's way of asking, "What is it?" although repetitive licking of smooth surfaces (apparently for purposes of sensory gratification) was also observed. Chris was a "ticklish" person and usually responded to being touched all over her body by laughter (sometimes, as her teacher noted, this laughter may have been defensive—that is, an effort to curtail interaction rather than to fully participate in it). While she could easily distinguish between textures by touching objects with her hands, her sense of heat and cold seemed depressed relative to mine.

Autostimulatory Behaviors

Light and sound for Chris were often a matter of self-gratification and self-stimulation, that is, compared with normal youngsters of her age. She exhibited many autostimulatory behaviors, including "finger-flicking" (autophotic behavior), repetitive licking of smooth surfaces (autotactual behavior), rocking, and head swinging (autokinesthetic behaviors). We developed a number of games (described below) based upon her pursuit of perceptual gratification. It is important to note that Chris's use of her senses was not purely autostimulatory. She also used them in goal-directed activities (for example, finding a toy, building up some objects so that she could climb on them and get her ear closer to the radio in the day room, looking for the ward door, fending against objects, finding the guitar sound). The autostimulatory use of her senses was, however, a characteristic and conspicuous feature of her behavior.

Gross Motor Behavior

Chris enjoyed gross body activities of all kinds and was in this regard a fairly active deaf-blind child. She loved to interact with me by having me pull her up while she simultaneously grasped my neck with her arms and my waist with her legs. From this rather common position between parent and child, she would engage in a variety of head-swinging and head-rocking movements. Often I would bounce her and throw her into the air, and she seemed to enjoy her helplessness—abandoning herself to the sensations these activities provided for her. Common to most of these activities was genital contact and rubbing. Chris also characteristically rocked her body to music and in autophotic reactions to strong light sources (such as an overhead fluorescent) light). In a life described as one of "scattered achievements," Chris's most significant ones were in the areas of gross body interaction and in her use of the sensation of touch.

Self-Help Skills

At the time of my study Chris was almost totally untrained in all areas of self-maintenance other than eating. Urination and defecation "accidents" often occurred during the course of data collection (and in a gesture of good faith vis-à-vis the staff, I took care of these). Chris was unable to dress, wash, bathe or walk without assistance. Teaching such skills to the congenitally deaf-blind-retarded is a very time-consuming and difficult enterprise, and given the paucity of staff in general and trained staff in particular, Chris had never mastered these skills.) Of course, she could engage in elaborate behavior schemes in order to gratify herself (she could get up without any cue, go to the music room, and let herself in), but she could not master the skills and rationale behind toileting and dressing. By hospital regulations these matters were usually taken care of as a matter of routine. Chris was cleaned and dressed whether she participated voluntarily or resisted violently.

Communication Skills

Chris did not seem to share any awareness of what a linguistic symbol was. However, this is not to say that she did not regularly communicate with me and with staff. To communicate her wishes, she used gross physical actions which relied heavily on "background expectancies" (Garfinkel, 1967)—for example, walking into the dining area and sitting at her table ("I'm hungry") or going to the ward door and waiting ("I want to go out"). She also used gross body movements to indicate that I should continue or cease some of our activities (for example, grabbing my arm and simulating a strumming movement apparently to indicate her desire that I continue playing, or pushing me away to indicate her wish to terminate interaction). At one point her language teacher claimed to have gotten her to say the word "more," and

I have seen her use the gestural symbol (Signing Exact English symbol) for "more" when I rigorously structured the activity and coaxed her by reward/punishment conditioning. It is doubtful that Chris had any grasp of the symbolic character of these actions. At the time of this writing Chris can receive a modified version of the "food" sign but has not been seen to use the sign expressively.

General Behavior Summary

When I was present in the research setting and interacting with her, Chris appeared to possess an inquisitive and active intelligence, housed in an extremely flawed body. She was oriented toward getting physical and perceptual satisfaction in any way she could. She displayed her dissatisfaction and liked to have things "her own way." She actively pursued contact with adults and was socially sophisticated relative to other areas. At an educational conference at the hospital, one administrator commented on her ability to "wrap me around her little finger" and, in some sense, this observation was true. Granting all the difficulties in making a determination of this kind, I felt that Chris's primary difficulties stemmed from her lack of intact audiovisual perceptual fields, upon which we build our systems of symbolic communication and organize our practical interactional activities. She had never had an intact behavior model and did not understand our "recipes," "motivational relevancies" (Schutz, 1970), and courses of rational activity. This is not to say that Chris was an acultural being, only that in many areas of her life the skills we find manifested by normal cultural members were not evident.

MEETING CHRIS ON HER "OWN GROUNDS"

The staff's institutional rationale and its concomitant "purposes at hand" (maintenance and teaching) were directly related to the particular features they formulated about the residents. I came to understand that I could take advantage of my institutional position (my not being charged with maintenance and teaching) to pursue a particularly interesting line of research. I could examine the staff's construction of certain of the residents' behaviors as retarded (that is, as faulted) to discover the logical underpinnings behind their system of practical reasoning—a system which produced behavior-displays-as-faulted. By doing this I hoped that I might also be able to unmask some of the skills the children exhibited—skills which the remedial stance of the staff was "hiding." This enterprise would entail establishing intersubjectivity with the residents on a somewhat different basis from that of the staff. I wanted to avoid—as Jean Itard failed to do with the "Wild Boy," Victoire of Aveyron[3]—seeing the children as tabulae rasae, as deficient cultural beings who needed cultural repair work done on them. While they were culturally deficient, to make them seeable and describable in only those terms was to ignore a whole storehouse of skills which they had developed but which were not specifically cultural achievements. Mannoni (1972) rightly noted that if Itard had accompanied Victoire to live in the Caune Woods (where Victoire had survived for eight or nine years as a youngster), Itard's storehouse of cultural knowledge would have been quite beside the point. Stripped naked, battling the elements, *he would have had to learn from Victoire in order to survive* (the woods creatures' "purpose at hand"). In that setting an understanding of Victoire's world, using only the stock of knowledge at hand in eighteenth-century French culture, would have been maladaptive. Metaphorically speaking, I decided to "go to the woods." To make this journey I had to locate where I was.

I saw my task as an attempt to establish intersubjectivity with Chris in more or less her "own terms." The problem was how to recognize what her "own terms" were. First I attempted to approximate her perceptual environment by the simultaneous use of ear stops and blindfolds. I discovered that I was quick to make the necessary adaptations to the features of the visual/auditory world I already took for granted. This is not to say that the blindfolds and ear plugs did not cause me a lot of trouble, that they did not render me essentially helpless without the aid of a sighted and/or hearing person. Rather, the cognitive categories I already possessed allowed me to be deaf and blind in a fashion which bore little resemblance to the *congenital* deaf-blindness of the residents. There was no simple technology by which I could accomplish my purpose—any procedures would have to be accompanied by a "willing suspension of belief." It seemed impossible to bridge this gap between our worlds and the consciousness interior to each. My "world" was thrust into relief by Chris's, and I started to perceive it as perceptual biological mechanisms accompanied by rules for their use—that is, a relatively coherent gestalt of seeing-hearing beliefs and practices which allowed me to produce a stock of practical knowledge about my life-world. This body of knowledge had taken on a *sui generis* character, since the activities I had been taught to realize were the same activities by which the knowledge was "validated." The knowledge was Castaneda's "description"; it was a perceptual "bubble" (von Uexkull, 1934) in which I was trapped. On the level of discourse, I had been experiencing a natural language version of my phenomenology, reified but kept alive by the activities which comprised *doing* my phenomenology. It was a bubble I had to burst in order to discover Chris's "own terms."

Obviously Chris did not share the staff's evaluation of her behaviors. The construal of these behaviors as deficient was clearly an interpretation of our seeing-hearing world view. I thought I could begin my task of willing suspension of belief by attempting to separate the evaluative from the descriptive components in my accounts of Chris's actions. This pursuit was manifested in the following field notes:

Watching Chris walk it was clear that her arm movements were spastic, her gait wide, and her movements and balance awkward. She also did not seem to walk purposively—that is, she would walk a few steps, stop, bend over or stare into the sun, run, twist around, laugh, sit down, get up, walk, etc. *She seemed to enjoy the physical sensations involved in her admittedly "abnormal" techniques for ambulation.* While it is clear that she does not walk correctly, it is equally clear that it is only incorrect with respect to the dominant seer-hearer culture's version of walking—a version, by virtue of her impaired sensors, almost inaccessible to her. Most importantly, while watching her we were occasioned to ask ourselves, "Who is getting more from the activity of walking, Chris or us?" It is no great cognitive accomplishment, no mystery, no great analytic task to watch Chris walk (eat, play, excrete, and so on) and to find her actions "faulted," "wrong," "abnormal," and so forth. Any competent cultural member (Garfinkel and Sacks, 1970)—that is, anyone who understands the rational and socially sanctioned set of activities for which walking (eating, playing, excreting) is an appropriate name could and would find Chris walking abnormally. The question is, how *should* we evaluate what we see? Is it "wrong" to act abnormally, and does one's detection of "abnormal" or "faulted" behavior require that remedial work be done upon the child to correct the observed flaws? These questions seem particularly important when asked with regard to persons who, in very obvious ways, do not share the perceptual cognitive world that occasions "normal" walking.

Evaluations ("fault finding"—see note 5) seemed inextricably involved in my simple descriptions, my direct experience of Chris's behavior. To find a "way out" of these evaluations-embedded-in-experience, I had to turn not to a cognitive re-shuffling of categories, but to a change in my practical activities with the resident. In other words, a suspension of belief could emerge only if I reorganized the material, concrete interaction which Chris and I produced.

I felt I could use certain interactional procedures (changes in my purposes at hand) in order to provide myself with an experiential basis for the kind of understanding I sought. Achieving this understanding was to be my new purpose at hand. I stopped trying to remedy the obvious faults I perceived in Chris and tried instead to intuit, while interacting with her, what purposiveness or rationality her activities might have from her perspective. My first major change in interactional strategy was to allow Chris to organize activities for both of us by *"remaining obediently passive."* On the first occasion I did this, she organized the following activity for us:

Activity No. 1, or "MMmmm . . . mmm . . . K . . . h"
Chris maneuvered me in such a way that she was lying on my lap face up and had me place my hand over her face. By holding my hand she eventually maneuvered it in such a way that my palm was on her mouth and my index finger was on her right ("good") eye. She then indicated to me that she wanted me to tap on her eyelid, by picking my finger up and letting it fall on her eye repeatedly, smiling and laughing when I voluntarily took over this work as my own. (She has also "shown me," by moving my body, that she wanted me to speak in her ear and flick my fingers across her good eye.) While I tapped Chris's eye, she licked and sniffed

my palm occasionally and softly hummed seemingly melodic sounds. *We did this* for about ten or fifteen minutes.

I named this activity by the sound Chris produced while doing it, in order to remind myself, even in the reading of my own material, that my purpose was to burst the "bubble." To do this consistently I could not *properly* code my sensory experience of the activity into a natural language (as Chris apparently cannot do) because the "bubble" and the "language" were so intimately related that to sort one from the other would have been a practical impossibility. Thus, in my first encounter with Chris's desired form of interactional activity, I became aware that in my writing about the activity I necessarily transformed what it was she could possibly intend in organizing it as she did. The description I sought to suspend belief in was itself imbedded in the very language I used to formulate my attempt. I realized that *my enterprise was a standing contradiction,* but I was willing to let this be, since to do otherwise would have meant to abandon all attempts to communicate to others what I was discovering. I was in much the same position as the anthropologist trying to code the native's language into his (the anthropologist's) own tongue. I was like Castaneda trying to speak of the world of the sorcerer by employing the language of the layman—admittedly the "old" language left much to be desired in terms of its descriptive power in the "new" world, but it was for him, as it was for me, the only language available.

An interesting example of the use of natural language categories in "making sense" of the residents was the staff's use of the category "play." Resident-initiated activities were considered by staff "play" activities and not particularly relevant to their purposes at hand. Usually these activities merited a smile from the staff or an utterance such as "Cute." There was an interesting parallel between the staff's approach to these and Itard's approach to his walks in the woods with Victoire (seen by Itard as play periods and not relevant to his teaching of the boy except insofar as the walks provided Victoire with relief from the stress of the pedagogical situation). It was not as if Chris hadn't played with ward staff before I arrived on the ward. It was a question of how they, normal seer-hearers, interpreted and categorized her actions and what consequences these interpretations had in formulating the resident as social objects.

Chris quickly expanded our repertoire of activities to include many varieties of bodily exchange and perceptual play. Patterns of the activities were constantly being refined and varied, sometimes in very subtle ways. These activities consisted of *gross body interaction* — swinging, jumping, rocking, running — and generally long-term and repetitive *perceptual playing*. They also included volitional participation in the activities of perception in order to achieve gratification—for example, including such things as having me play with her light reception (as above), singing and jumping from a baritone to falsetto range (which delighted her), or putting my fingers in her ears to rhythmically "stop" sound. When I began to cooperate with her in such pursuits, these activities often culminated in Chris's reaching peak periods of excitement. Sometimes these peaks would result in her urinating and defecating.

I introduced Chris to a small toy electric organ and observed the following:

> Chris would place her left hand on the keys of the organ which produced the lower frequency sounds. She would then engage in two related sets of body movements. One was to move her head and body in a rhythmic rocking motion which brought her right (good) ear closer and farther from the organ sound source. The other set of movements involved her leaning her head back so as to face the overhead light, and swiveling it back and forth, from side to side, accompanying these actions with vibrating her lips (something like the way little children imitate motorcycle sounds but without the vocal component). In both sets of body movements there was an obvious rhythmic quality—such as to suggest the kind of thing seer-hearers do when they are engrossed in the activity of keeping beat to music. In Chris's case, however, there was no clearly available beat to the droning sounds she was producing by holding the organ keys down.

As with Chris's brand of walking, my initial encounter with these behaviors was characterized by my engaging in the "vulgarly available."[4] I "naturally" saw that these behaviors were obstacles which I would have to overcome in my pedagogical enterprise (my initial purpose at hand)—a pedagogy designed to make

Chris attend to sound in the "right" way. Once I gave up this remedial stance toward Chris, her alternative treatment of light, sound, and tactile stimulation took on a rational and even intelligent quality.

I decided to *mimic her actions* in order to gain more direct access to what such activities were providing her. I utilized wax ear stops (placed more securely in the left ear, i.e. Chris has "better" right ear than left ear) and gauzed my left eye with a single layer of lightweight gauze to simulate the scar tissue which covers Chris's left eye. I proceeded to imitate Chris's behaviors at the organ. While the procedure had its obvious inadequacies, with respect to my gaining access to Chris's experience of these activities, I did learn a number of interesting things in this way.

In both sets of body movements *the motion of the head itself gave the experienced sound a beatlike quality, and this was uniquely present by virtue of performing those movements.* In adapting to deficient eyes and ears and their resultant degraded perceptual fields, Chris had developed a way of "doing" hearing, so as to make any long-term and reliable sound source available as a source of music. For example, when Chris was wearing her hearing aid, I would sometimes find her engaging in similar kinds of body movements even though there was no hearable sound source in the room. This became a clue for me that Chris was probably getting "white sound" (feedback) from her hearing aid. I knew that Chris was able, when presented with appropriately amplified music, to keep "accurate" beat to that music in the fashion described above. I had also found Chris keeping completely inappropriate beat to music while listening to a small transistor radio with low amplification and a small speaker, which was unable to emit bass notes. Put simply, when beat was not a "hearable" feature of the mechanically given sound stimulus, Chris had learned to endow her experience of that sound with that quality.

Rolling the head on the shoulders (the other set of body movements Chris engaged in) was a difficult practice for me to mimic in that Chris's neck muscles were supple and loose in comparison with my own. Her muscles allowed for apparently painless and easy rolling movements, while my own head rolling was somewhat less comfortable. Nevertheless, I discovered that Chris's head rolling provided not only for a beat to the music (which in its performance it does), but also for what one observer called a "light show." By "light show" I mean that the head rolling, which Chris performed with her head leaned back and her eyes facing the overhead fluorescent light, provided an overall effect something like the following:

Alternative musical beats, occurring when the head was accelerating from one extreme position to the other, were culminated, when the head came to rest, in either light stimulation (when the head rested on the left shoulder, thus directing her good eye toward the light) or a lack of light stimulation (*when the head rested on the right shoulder, thus interposing her nose between the light source and her good right eye*). Chris was providing her otherwise impoverished perceptual field with a richness her eyes and ears could not give her. She accomplished this by the use of her available and intact bodily resources—her good eye, her nose, her muscles, and her skeletal frame, which provided for the possibility of making such movements. I was, and still am, struck by a certain inventiveness in this activity.

Another excerpt from my field notes is relevant to the present discussion. This was written after a particularly interesting teaching session with Chris (Goode, 1974a). I was trying to demonstrate the use of various music-making toys vis-à-vis the "familiarizing" procedures described by Robbins (1963).

Chris demonstrated skill in *"alternative object readings."* By this I mean that Chris's inability to grasp the intentional meaning and activities for which "triangle" or "rattle" are appropriate glosses— that is, "rattle" or "triangle," as members' glosses for the practices entailed in recognizing, picking up, and shaking a rattle to make rattle sounds or banging a metal triangle with a metal bar so as to produce triangle sounds, allowed her to constitute a rattle as an object which could provide for her a number of alternative experiences. Initially, our play sessions consisted in precisely my attempting to provide for her the "proper" cultural formula—that object X is a rattle and is to be used (in satisfaction of the criteria of a rational course of action) in such and such ways. I would hand her the rattle after demonstrating its use to her by placing the rattle in her hand and placing her hand within my own, then engaging in the appropriate shaking motion. While such demonstrations were successful in that Chris would hold and shake the rattle appropriately and unassisted (for ten seconds or so), she invariably brought the rattle to her right (good) eye or mouthed it. She would bring it within two inches of her eye with the apparent purpose of determining what it could visually supply for her (parts of the rattle were metal and reflected the fluorescent light in the room). This visual examination would be of short duration (less than fifteen seconds). Of the longest duration, often lasting till I would interrupt her somewhat intense involvement, was her use of the rattle as an object with which she could obtain various forms of stimulation in and about the mouth. Parts of the rattle were employed as tongue thumper or lip thumper, licked inside and outside the mouth, rubbed against the front teeth, banged against the front teeth, pushed against the cheek, and so on. Characteristically, when Chris was through with or had exhausted the immediately present and interesting possibilities of the rattle, she would drop it with no concern as to where it fell, its breakability, or its future uses. While such actions were easily accessible as "problems" with regard to teaching Chris to use objects appropriately (similar behavior was observed with regard to many objects), I was occasioned to ask myself: Who is getting maximum mileage out of the rattle? Is it we, who use it singularly and for specific purposes, or Chris, who uses it in a variety of ways? Let's put it another way. What Chris's not knowing how to use a rattle might mean is problematic. Her not knowing disqualifies her from membership in the category of persons who know how to use a rattle. However, it also *qualifies* her as a member of a category of persons who, by virtue of their not knowing how to use a rattle, do things with it which are inaccessible to persons who "know" its proper use. *The superordinate ranking of our use of the rattle, on the basis that we realize its intended purpose by our actions, constitutes the "ground" for the pejorative figure "Chris does not use the rattle appropriately."*

It is quite reasonable, given Chris's deficient eyes and ears, that she should place rattles or triangles or paper or fingers in her mouth. The tactility of the relatively sensitive tissue of the lips and tongue, as well as the ability of the teeth to conduct vibration, make her mouth the organ around which she can successfully organize reliable perceptual activities. Her adaptations to her perceptual handicaps have allowed her to become an "expert" in the use of the mouth as as organ of primary perception (something like the use of the mouth by young infants). From this perspective, her behavior is available to normal seer-hearers as an alternative set of mouth perceptual practices against which our mouth perceptions are deficient versions of her more active pursuits. Yet most of her mouthings are inaccessible to the competent cultural member. Chris will put almost anything into her mouth which does not frighten her. For example, she will not mouth a lit match, does not like toothpaste or a toothbrush, but would undoubtedly try to lick a broken piece of glass or the procelain parts of toilets if given an opportunity to do so. The researcher was not able to adopt this stance toward objects—I was unable to overcome the culturally engrained notion that "something bad" would happen to me were I to lick a window, the floor, and so on.

My initial reading of these observations provided me with two general categories of findings. One concerned the reasoning embedded in my (and the staff's) "fault-finding procedures"[5] with the residents, and one concerned the rationality or purposiveness (from Chris's point of view) behind these same behaviors. It was not as if Chris's behaviors, or the meaning ascribed to them, existed apart from the procedures and circumstances by and in which she was apprehended. Her behaviors were "rational" to *me*, "faulted" *to the staff*, and this multifacetedness of Chris was an important finding. As a material object, Chris's "horizons" were open. Like her rattle, she could be seen as multifaceted, or she could be discovered to be singularly "dumb."

With regard to Chris's purposiveness, she was basically self-seeking, hedonistic, and amoral in her interactions. She would often rub her genitals against me or pantomime her (our?) recognized "behavior display" to denote a rocking or swinging activity. She did not seem to care whether I was getting pleasure from the activity. Instead she focused on structuring the interaction so that she could get as much of what she inwardly recognized as "good feelings," though I really don't "know" what these words index in terms of her experience. This seemed quite understandable to me since, in terms of her life on the ward, Chris did not live a life particularly filled with gratification— especially when she was interacting with others. However, left to herself, she was quick to provide herself, through varieties of autostimulatory behaviors, with experiences which she apparently enjoyed. Generally she occupied a powerless and frustrating position in many of her interactions and did not have the cognitive equipment (concepts, language, logic) through which she could rationalize (understand). She could only accept or reject, and on rare occasions "puzzle." She did not have the physical capability to aggress or, for that matter, to even defend herself against "attack." Compliance with sometimes not understood pulls and pushes from staff was characteristic. When staff could not force compliance (for example, when her language teacher could not get her to make the sound "Mmmm"), she seemed to sit in a sort of dull passivity. Other times she seemed

to be puzzling—that is, trying to "code" what it was I was trying
to do into some understanding or feeling she could deal with—
what a program administrator called her interior "language"
system. Generally when she initiated interaction it was to seek
as much pleasure as she could, however she could. We often
index such a behavior pattern by the term "infantile," but Chris
was no infant. She was nine years old and had lived long enough
to have gained some sophistication in achieving her pleasure-
seeking activities.

Within the limits of hospital routine, I cooperated with her
in achieving her goals. I became a sort of "superplaymate"—
perhaps (with the possible exception of her father) the only one
in her life she had ever had. While there were a number of
sympathetic and loving custodians and teachers in her life, the
institutional definition of their relationships to Chris prevented
them from simply cooperating with her. From time to time I
did observe activities in which the staff's role was precisely to
be Chris's playmate (for example when it was hot out and they
would sprinkle the residents with a hose, or when they took the
residents to the pool to "swim"), and on these occasions the staff
and residents seemed to enjoy themselves immensely. By the end
of my stay on the ward I had become a little sad about the way
in which the institutional and medical "contexting" of the children seemed to victimize the staff as well as the children.[6] An
even sadder thought was the impossibility of ever changing this
situation under the present approach in the fields of human
servicing.

By employing the kind of procedures I have described above,
I felt as if I had discovered in Chris the "internal contradictions"
by which she was propelled into relation with others and by
which she could be particularly distinguished from other social
beings (Mao, 1971). This was evident in my concluding remarks
on Chris's rattle activities.

> Perhaps the most interesting feature of Chris's mouth perceptual
> practices is the way in which they can be seen as illustrating how
> *she is both wise and deficient in how she constitutes objects and
> experiences the world.* I described her alternative object reading of
> the rattle and I noted how Chris used the rattle for three general
> purposes: what she could make seeable with it; what she could

make hearable with it; and what she could provide tactually with it. I claimed that her not grasping the intentional meaning of the object allowed her to get, in some sense, more out of the rattle than *members* who attend to the rattle singularly and employ it in satisfaction of a set of rational guides for use. The "kicker" here is that, seemingly, the very thing which allows her to get more mileage out of the rattle (her visually and auditorally deficient body and her development of perceptual practices appropriate to such a body) is that very same thing which delimits her experience of the world as it is composed for us and by us—as a world of intentional meanings. For Chris, *objects can only be sources of perceptual stimulation of the sorts outlined above.* When I watched her "do her thing," it was with both joy and sorrow that I appreciated what I was seeing. *Her blindness and her deafness constituted her strongest asset as well as her greatest deficiency.* They sometimes provided her with incredibly intense enjoyment of the simplest things. At other times they were a source of "troubles" as equally intense.

My abilities to see and hear allowed me to engage in the practices by which the culturally defined objects and activities of my world were realized. These abilities allowed me to experience certain pleasure as well as pains. Obviously, Chris did not comply with culturally prescribed courses of rational activity. Yet in a most generic sense, she seemed to conduct herself quite rationally. Perhaps she could not give her hedonistic pursuits names like "self-realization," "the pursuit of personal power," or "transcendence," but that she was a pleasure-seeking creature made her quite understandable to me. In this most basic enterprise, we were in basic agreement. We just used different technologies to accomplish our goal.

CONCLUDING REMARKS

All creatures, that is, all subjectivities, seek, in their own terms, to fulfill needs and to gratify themselves. They do not do this in any haphazard fashion. Certain needs must be met before others (this is Maslow's insight), and in Chris's case survival-related needs were almost exclusively taken care of for her by others. Next in her "motivational" hierarchy were emotional and perceptual gratification, and in this regard she was not dissimilar to other humans. She differed primarily in the forms in which these needs would be met. Many of the rational activities of our culture are built upon these very motivational projects. But the specification of these enterprises into culturally acceptable forms is not what defines our humanity to ourselves or to others. If we learn to believe this, then we have stopped one of our basic self-deceptions and have moved away from a view of man which raises us above other creatures—which affirms our presence here as an "emergent" phenomenon. We are not "better" than other creatures. We are "different." I was not "better" than Chris, I was, in many ways, "different."

Given this view, what is to be made of my personal attempt to share a world with a very different human being? What can we learn from this attempt, and what is its future use? In this regard there are several positions to take. One can "believe in" the phenomenon of intersubjectivity; one can take it as possible that human beings "really" or "in fact" can, and do, share their worlds. Starting from there, my experiences can be seen as providing technical resources and interactional methods for accomplishing this goal—for "starting with two worlds and (to a greater or less extent) making them into one." Insofar as the methods and their results are taken to be valid, the further question can be asked: How is it possible for two worlds to become one in the course of intimate human interaction? That is, are there species-specific characteristics, activities, or aspects of our common "habitats" which make this accomplishment possible? If so, what are they?

Another kind of lesson that might be drawn from my experiences with Chris proceeds from a different perspective. In this approach to the text, either one does not accept the "real" possibility of intersubjectivity or one is not interested in discovering whether what we take to be a common world *is* a common world in actual fact. Instead the question is "How do people start out with the feeling of being cut off from each other and together achieve the mutual feeling of being in touch with each other in the same world?" For example, Schutz, among others, has described some of the working assumptions that constitute people's sense of being in touch with each other. The previous ethnographic field notes can be read as my attempts (and those of Chris) to find ways of being, such that our interaction could be characterized in part, by the kinds of working assumptions about which Schutz has written. That is, we progressively developed common schemes of communication, congruent practical relevancies, mutually defined things to do in the world, and so forth. But even if it is the *sense* of a shared world we achieved, the question can still be asked: How is it possible for human beings to accomplish this?

These perspectives are not necessarily mutually exclusive, but from either of them intersubjectivity becomes a *practical and empirical issue*—an issue for which, it is hoped, this paper has provided some initial technical resources. By utilizing procedures appropriate to the particular setting in which ethnography is conducted, field researchers can collect data from which the procedures for constituting intersubjectivity can be made objects for analysis.

NOTES

1. In the spirit of this text, designed to deal with issues of field method and procedure, this article focuses almost exclusively upon the interactional strategies used in collecting ethnographic *data*. Conspicuously absent are analyses of these procedures—that is, conclusions about how my involvement with the deaf-blind allowed me to produce findings about the nature of human intersubjectivity. At least two modes of analysis are suggested in my concluding remarks. I plan to publish analyses of the data along these lines as well as with regard to more ethnological concerns.

2. If the reader finds that this writing is "very scientific," he should bear in mind that the work was motivated by very human concerns. Foremost among these was my desire to improve the life situation of both deaf-blind resident and normally perceiving staff. The staff regarded their charges as prospective cultural converts. Much like the religious missionaries of the eighteenth and nineteenth centuries, they attempted conversion without any true appreciation of the "natives' culture," and this had the consequence of creating confusion and frustration for both residents and staff. While there was no easy solution to this problem, clearly attempts had to be made to understand the deaf-blind "in their own terms." This present writing tells of such an attempt with a particular resident. In some sense I have to discover Chris as a creature whose existence is comparable to my own. This was a strong motive for the work. But it must be made clear that very human interests often lead to problems which must be dealt with technically and rigorously. This can be true whether the objects of analysis are atoms or persons. Readers concerned with the application of my approach in actual programming for the deaf-blind are referred to Goode and Gaddy (1976).

3. The work of Jean Itard (an eighteenth-century teacher of deaf-

mutes) with Victoire of Aveyron (a "wolf boy," or child raised in the woods) was, in various ways, quite instructive during the course of my research, even though Chris was a product of a humanly ordered world (home, schools, and hospital), while Victoire was not.

4. Harold Garfinkel, personal communication, 1974.

5. "Fault-finding procedures" is a phrase suggested by Dr. Harold Garfinkel (personal communication, 1974). I have adopted the phrase (not Dr. Garfinkel's sense of it) to refer to a structure of practical reasoning in which the deaf-blind retarded are found to be faulted with respect to some setting occasioned normative criterion of action. While the specific flaws located will vary from setting to setting (for example, a child can be found to be an incompetent eater at lunch, or an incompetent test subject for normal audiometric examination procedures, or an incompetent ambulator in walking from the ward to the classroom, and so on), the *form* of the reasoning—that is, the judging of the child as deficient with respect to a normative criterion of behavior or action—is invariant from setting to setting. The ethnography of the ward indicated that staff (and other normals) also engaged in "asset-finding procedures" which, in similar fashion to the faulting practices, find the child as competent with respect to some "normal" behavioral capacity. Both asset and fault finding are suggested as possibly basic structures of practical reasoning in that all settings are seen to produce "their cast of local heroes and villains" (Dr. Melvin Pollner, personal communication, 1975). For a more detailed discussion of these matters, see Goode, 1975*b*.

6. Toward the end of my stay on the ward the staff began to resent my presence and complained that my playing with Chris was interfering with her programming. I feel that at least part of this resentment stemmed from my relatively enviable position—that is, I could play with Chris and not be responsible for her training and maintenance. I began to notice that when staff were allowed to simply play with the residents (for examples, when they took them to the pool or to the trampoline), both staff and residents seemed to enjoy themselves a great deal. "Play" was that time in hospital routine when the normative rules and goals for interacting with the children could be suspended and the staff were afforded the opportunity to experience the residents in nonideologically defined activity. Play activity, for the sake of itself, transcended the institutional goals of remedialization and provided for the staff a time when they could "meet the residents on their own grounds."

REFERENCES

Garfinkel, H. *Studies in ethnomethodolgy.* Englewood Cliffs: Prentice-Hall, 1967.

Garfinkel, H., and H. Sacks. On the Formal Structures of Practical Actions. In J. C. McKinney and E. A. Tiryakian (Eds.). *Theoretical sociology*:

Perspectives and development. New York: Appleton-Century-Crofts, 1970.

Goode, D. Some Aspects of Interaction Among Congenitally Deaf-Blind and Normal Persons. Working Paper No. 1. Unpublished paper. Mental Retardation Research Center, UCLA Medical Center, 1974a.

————. What Shall We Do with the Rubella Children? Unpublished paper. Mental Retardation Research Center, UCLA Medical Center, 1974b.

————. Some Aspects of Embodied Activity on a Deaf-Blind Ward in a State Hospital. Unpublished paper. Mental Retardation Research Center, UCLA Medical Center, 1975a.

————. *Towards the grounds for achieving intersubjectivity: an initial report from a ward for the congenitally deaf-blind. retarded.* Department of Sociology and Mental Retardation Research Center, UCLA, 1975b.

Goode, D., and M. P. Gaddy. Ascertaining Choice with Alingual, Deaf-Blind and Retarded Clients. *Mental Retardation* 14, no. 6, 1976.

Mannoni, O. Itard and His Savage. *New Left Review* 74 (July/August), 1972.

Mao Tse-tung. On Contradiction (originally written 1937). In *Selected Readings from the Works of Mao Tse-tung.* Peking: Foreign Language Press, 1971.

Robbins, N. *Auditory training in the Perkins deaf-blind department.* Perkins School Publication no. 23, 1963.

Schutz, A. *On phenomenology and social relations.* Chicago: University of Chicago Press, 1970.

von Uexkull, J. A Stroll Through the Worlds of Animals and Men. In C. Schiller and K. Lashley (Eds.). *Instinctive behavior.* New York: International Universities Press, 1934.

CHAPTER 11

WAR IS HELL AND HELL IS WAR: THE AUTOBIOGRAPHY OF A RETARDED ADULT

Lois M. Easterday

INTRODUCTION

T HIS IS THE autobiography of Al Lansing, a retarded adult, as told to me in a series of four tape-recorded interviews. Rather than merely present the typed transcripts in their entirety (some 100 pages), I have edited Al's story for brevity and in order to put events he recounted into proper chronological order. In doing so I have retained Al's words and grammatical form. I want this to be his story, his autobiography.

While it might be argued that one case does not a theory make, it is also true that "even though the life history does not in itself provide definitive proof of a proposition, it can be a negative case that forces us to decide a proposed theory is inadequate" (Becker, 1966:x-xi). If we are searching for an understanding of the world and not merely proof of our own ideas, then the life history approach can be a very valuable research tool. It allows us to both experience and get to know people in a way that only autobiographical studies provide for.

The purpose of this work is not to attest to the value of autobiographical case studies for social science. This has been well demonstrated by others (See, for example: Becker, 1966; Bogdan, 1974; Bogdan and Taylor, 1975; Allport, 1942; and Jacobs, 1971). Rather this is the story of a man who has been labeled by society and lives with a spoiled identity (Goffman,

---

Edited and abridged by Jerry Jacobs. The original study was done in consultation with Robert Bogdan. The names of all persons and places have been changed to insure anonymity.

1963). This is his reflection on his life and how he sees all he has done and all that has been done to him.

There are contradictions in Al's story and some might say that it does not reflect reality. I would argue that it honestly reflects Al's reality, and given that "things perceived as real are real in their consequences," it is this reality that we seek to understand. I will also include excerpts from Al's case record, i.e. the "official version" of Al's life. I will then conclude with a discussion of the goodness of fit between the two.

AL'S AUTOBIOGRAPHY

I was probably born in about 1909 or 1910, but I never checked it up. Hell with it. It's just another day to me. I was born in Germany but my family moved to the United States when I was about five or six years, something like that, seven years. I guess there were seventeen in the family, seventeen kids and I was the youngest. Well, there was sixteen in the family; seventeen, one died.

My parents were both German. My father worked for a steel works in Germany and made good money there, too. Then he changed his mind. He had a big idea that he was gonna make millions over in this country. He comes over there I guess he threw over a million dollar business over his head because the family and him couldn't agree. He was head strong up here, in the head. Not enough sense in there. If he'd a kept it he'd a been a millionaire today, but he's dead and gone and he don't need any money. My grandfather was in the laboratories, scientist, engineer, government engineer. Oh, Jesus, he had a lot of money, I guess so! Practically owned half of Germany. My father worked all his life. He was gonna take things easy. I guess he did all right. In two weeks' time, kaboom, that's it, dead. He was a great man to save money, a great man to invest money, you know, to make money takes money to make money always. And he could do it, boy. He had in the neighborhood of five hundred thousand dollars, property, one thing another. I guess he was a nice guy. He stuck to his guns and he was all right to me.

My mother was about five feet five, stocky build. She'd give you the shirt right off her back, only kind she was. She worked pretty hard, day in and day out. Too bad. I was close to my parents, we used to live in the same building with 'em. I got along pretty good with my brothers and sisters, they had ups and downs but that's what life is made of. They was a lot older than I was. They all passed away years ago. I'm the last dog in the mud puddle, the last man in the boat. One of my parents had a heart attack, the other one had a stroke. One after another of my family passd away of heart attacks, pneumonia, kidney disorder, stomach ailments . . . strokes, shock, that's the way it went.

My childhood was OK, what you could expect. You get what you get, not what you want. We worked hard, but it didn't bother us any, we were brought up into it. We worked a farm down to Smithtown and most generally raised grain, corn, beans, and potatoes. There's a farm about 190 acres, 200, about 200 acres. I did regular farm work. Worked—Sunday was a Monday and a Friday was a Wednesday—around the clock it went, year in and year out. We started out in the fields, three o'clock in the morning until 11:30 at night.

We didn't have no school whatsoever because you had to have the money and you had to go out and work. I did different kinds of work back then. I had a hell of a good job in a machine shop before we left Germany. I was about 15, I think it was. Work was my middle name. I'd rather work than I would set around. Something to break the ice, you know. I did some construction work. I was in electrical engineering, then the military came and drafted us.

My life was practically always military. I was about 25 when I was drafted. I was drafted, sent right to the German lines. That was close to Normandy; that was '41, '45. Along came the military and swept us off our feet. Shoved us to Germany and from there to Japan, then Japan back to North Africa, then back to Japan again. They put you where they want you. Then after that was over I went to Korea and from Korea to Viet Nam. I was at Pearl Harbor, Guadalcanal, Iwo Jima, all over the world. They just push you here they push you there, they do any God damn thing they want.

Christ, I must of been in the military Goddamn near fifteen years, twenty years—about twenty—rough estimate. No, I was in 35 (he was 39 when first institutionalized at Stone State, a facility for the retarded). I've been out, oh, I don't know, ten or twelve years. I got shell shocked in Korea but I didn't get out then. When you get shell shocked why you don't remember half what you done or where you was, don't make any difference. One day's like the other day all the way through. Affects your nerves, that's what it does. Then I got shot up in Viet Nam. After I got out of service I was in the military hospital. They check you over. Then it's gotta go on the card, just what's what. Then they release you. And if they got room, they keep you, if not, why you say goodbye and go on. They most generally release you, because there's always some comin' in, all the time. Boy, some rough cases. I would of stayed in the military hospital, but they was overloaded. They didn't have no place in the military hospitals so we shifted to Stone State and then I had epilepsy. I didn't tell them I had it. I had it before then but it didn't show up too much, see, 'till I got in service and went through it and I really cracked up. The military hospital said, "We can't handle this case. We'll have to send you to Stone State. That came from shell shocked.

I've had epilepsy since I was knee high to a grasshopper. You go in on the job, by Jesus, just one seizure, and the foreman goes around there and he spots you. Right away he calls the shop doctor and the doctor says, "Well, he's an epileptic, don't hire him." He tells you to go to the office and get your check and we'll let you know if we need you. That's a goodbye callin' card. I had seizures years ago, but when I was drafted in the service, well I got by with that, you know, and they were short of pilots in the military outfit. And it didn't bother me, see. We hit the booze up in the service and after that they died right down. Went for years in the service and when I came back out of there and no drinks, you know, and kaboom, one hit me one day and then the next day another one hit me, and that's the way it was, back in the same channels again. You can't never tell when that takes place, you know, when or where it'll happen. It just comes and that's it.

Jeez, I forget the names of places, yet I know them. Shows

the mind ain't all there . . . sometimes I slip. I have epilepsy, a mental disorder they call it, see. Fractured nerve. Them nerves is just like little threads, you know, tiny threads. It don't take much to break them. When they're broke, you're all done. Your aviating days are over.

Stone State is an epileptic institution up there, supposed to be. There's more of 'em died up there, by Jesus, than lived. They give 'em a lot of drugs and dope, hell knows what they didn't give 'em. But they just passed on. So many seizures and zing, you're gone. They gave me about a handful of drugs a day. If you didn't want to take them, they'd send you to locked ward for six months or two years, or they didn't care how long. That's all there was to it. They kept you doped up all the time. That's all they know is drugs in this country. Not a Goddamned thing beyond that they don't know. Medicine, they don't know that, they only know it by name. Medicine you can smell before you see it, but drugs there's no odor to that at all. If you died of a heart attack or anything, why they'd mark something down there and the doctor signs his John Henry on it. That's all there is to it. Could be their fault, yet they clear themselves, just sign their name, that's it.

You can guess pretty close to what Stone is like. If places like that have to be, guess they have to be. More of the same old story. You get the rough end of the stick. They tell you what a wonderful place institutions are but you know different than that if you had a grain of sense in your head. When the state controls anything they give you the rough end of it. They don't give you somethin' good. If it was any good, they'd keep it themselves. Anything comes in there, from outlaws to killers and from rapists and firebugs and everything else.

It's all right. Rough game. What the hell are you gonna do? What they don't want at Stone they shove down to River State. That's the way they always did. Number of buildings up there and what they didn't want in one building they pushed in another and what they didn't want there they pushed in the next and that's the way it went. They don't ask you about it at all. They're the boss, you know, because they're big shots of Stone State, you know. Supervisors and head engineers and the whole damn thing, and they just shove you where they want you. I

didn't give a damn. I've been around the world so God damn
many times it ain't funny. Life to me means nothin' but the
wind blowin'. But one place is like another when you're shell
shocked. You don't care where you live or how you live or anything, you know. Life is blasted. That's it, it explodes your
nerves, shell shocked does.

I was in Pine cottage. The bottom two floors is a day ward,
and up is where the beds are. Then you got your sink, bathroom
and stairways go down. It was men about my age, oh, they'd
put anything in there. They didn't care who the hell went in
there, as long as they went in. What they didn't want in one
cottage they threw in the next. And what they didn't want in
the next, they threw in the next. That's how it worked. I was
over to Elm and then I was over 'cross the way, what the hell's
the name of that other house? That other cottage, wasn't in
there. Oh, Jesus, the one that guy killed himself up there.

At Stone State they kept the men and women separated.
Police patroled the roads all the time. You didn't dare to talk
to a woman or look at one. If you did they locked you up in the
locked ward for six months to a year. That didn't ever happen
to me. Hell, I didn't never bother any women. A guy'd go over
to the girls and the police'd catch up to him and back to the
locked ward they come.

Everybody at Stone State has to dance to their music. They
hire any employee, it doesn't make any difference. They draw
their check and set in their office and drink their coffee, that's
what happens. You done the work and they give the orders.
They told you what to do. You didn't have what all you wanted,
not that was the orders. You think you was back in the military
again. That place you could call a POW camp. They all work
under the same branch, you know what I mean. Christ Almighty,
freedom's gone. They bought and sold that years ago. Dictatorship.

I did different work at Stone. I did garden work. I worked
there for a long time and I worked on the ward, and I worked
in the laundry for a long time. That about winds the clock up
right there. That's all. I did odds and ends now and then. We
used to work on the ground crew, laundry, wards, you know.
All that work. They kept you going, don't worry about that.

They always found another job in case you ran short. If you didn't want to work they'd throw you in the locked ward, that's all. And then you worked in there. They didn't teach you anything at Stone. You worked. Don't have to worry about sitting around. They put you on a job, you do it or else they'd send you back to the cottage, then from the cottage they'd send you back to the locked ward and you'd be there maybe a year, six months or so, and then they'd send you back on another job. That's the way it worked.

We worked on a farm crew, what I mean is, we worked around the buildings, but we didn't go outside beyond that. We weren't allowed out there. They kept us guarded pretty close. They's afraid you was gonna run away, and you might start a lawsuit and the county didn't want to lose a lot of money, and get yourself killed and they'd be responsible and all them things. That's what they was afraid of. A number run away. Brought 'em back, shoved 'em in the locked ward for about two years. Stone State was just like an old hen coop, a chicken coop. You were watched like a cat and mouse.

The locked ward had bars around it. That's all there was to it, a building. I was in the locked wards a number of times. The locked wards and before I got out of the military, was in prison camps and concentration camps. The locked ward was only kid's play. When they get you in a concentration camp, that's where they give you the works. In the locked ward they beat you up once in a while, that's about it. You had to stay in the ward, or else they'd tie you down in a restraining sheet or some God damn thing. Rope you down. I got sent to the locked ward usually because I said somethin' out of the way to one of the employees. They figure they was a big deal, you know, and they figured they oughta walk on silk all the time. And bing, up the God damn locked ward. Jeez, big deal. You didn't talk just right, you know, to the employees, they figured they was God Almighty himself. Oh, up the locked ward you go. I said, "Big deal. You're doin' me a good turn, I won't have to look at that mush of yours all the time." Told 'em. What the hell? I don't give a God damn about that.

Up at Stone they had a school for little kids. That's about it.

Poor souls. Shoved in a place like that. Jesus. Boy, that takes guts. Little tots stand about that high, you know. Hardly could walk. Jesus, man. I couldn't do it. How a family could put 'em there is more than I know. They must be made of steel or they're creatures, one of the two. I couldn't do it. Jeez, I hate to see little kids put in a place like that. Jesus Christ, man. That tore my guts right there. Must be creatures, you know. Guy socked 'em around and hurt the kid pretty bad and he lost his job up there. He should of lost his life, not his job. Job don't mean nothing. That's a position. Them creatures up there. If they was any good, they'd be on the outside makin' the real stuff. But they wasn't no good for anything only trouble. Easy life they wanted and that's the place they pick. Yeah, an attendant socked the kid around. Guess the kid up and passed away shortly after. He was a foreigner anyway.

There's a hell of a lot of things they don't like to let people know about Stone. There's abuse, one thing and another. Our money was missin' and nobody could know where the hell it went to. But I think it went in their pocket. They got one hellava racket about it and nobody, nothin' was done about it. I don't know, they cover up everything.

They never changed Stone at all, they never made any improvements. Same old buildings there was years ago. They condemned the whole thing and they was gonna tear it down and build a new one. And that fell through. They were condemned for a long time and yet they kept on running it. Then they started moving them to different institutions and a lot of 'em went home, and that's the way it went. A lot of 'em went to the graveyard, the marble orchard.

Somebody said they closed Stone. I wouldn't be surprised if they did. Why anything comes in there, what the hell. Like it? Well, what else can you do, you know, in the case of nick and tuck. Oh, He'll tear it down above. That's the last time they build it, no more. Did you ever hear 'em say, and to dust one day shall return? This is the day. They think they're gonna be sanctified, they're gonna be eternal, they're gonna be reincarnation, and all that crazy stuff, ho! Jesus, man, that's one for the books. Piece of dust and that's it. Sure. You better believe it.

Wound 'em up like a clock. They think they're comin' back to earth again in the form of a different type of life and all that crazy lunatic stuff. They're comin' back in a heap of dust, the whole damn shootin' match.

The big shots at Stone State, they figured they were big dogs, because they wore the white collar. Big deal! They'd send you to the doctor and check you over once a month, I think it was, and that was it. "Nothing wrong with you." Well if there wasn't nothin' wrong, what the hell did they come for anyway? Christ, they ship 'em in there by the hundreds. That was just like a receiving center, that's what it was.

The staff people had the regular headquarters. They didn't stay in the cottage, just the attendants, took care of the building. There were four or six, sometimes three attendants in each cottage. All depends on how much help they had. They didn't pay 'em too much money, and a lot of 'em quit. If you was the right hand man, you was all right. If you was the wrong hand, then why that's it. You gotta be the right type of guy to be right hand man—well, rat on everybody and stuff like that. Carry the information. I wasn't no guy to do that. They ain't all gold that shines in them institutions, don't ever guess wrong. They're makin' the real stuff. You think they're runnin' 'em for the patients? Oh, Jesus, that's a laugh. You wanna find out a lot of things, you go in there as a patient, then you find out the real stuff. You can't tell them guys anything. They wear the white collars. They're the big brass. The best thing to do is to stay out of the institution. But probably there's no way somebody could do it. Because the judge and the jury and the whole outfit and the society get together and say, "We don't want this man in the neighborhood," and up to the institution you go. Society is one of the worst God damn things was ever built. That's where all the trouble starts. Politicians and religious along with it. You just clean the slate once and you'd have livin' after that. Not hell and misery all the time. Sure that's how a lot of these fellas get in these institutions is through society. They don't want 'em, they don't fit their colors. They want that flashy appearance and that smart talk and that wise accent and so on, and so on, and so on. You don't fit their colors, up you go. Get rid of 'em. You don't think they'd send 'em for their own benefit? Huh. That'd make anybody laugh, that had a brain. The institutions don't help anybody at all. They're just the dumping grounds of the human race.

There were about six or eight doctors at Stone. They would talk to you once in a while, just to find out a few things and that was it. They never talked to you about why you were there; they already knew, long before. They wouldn't take your word, Christ, they wouldn't take no patients' word, because you was a patient, you was mentally afflicted.

The doctors called you in for an interview to see what you knew and what you liked and what you didn't like and a secretary would type it all down. Make a big circus, the whole job, that's all there was to working. They made a good impression, you know, on the big shots. That's what they do at work, see. But a day's work'd kill 'em. They'd be dead forever. Christ. They tell us what they like. Now it's gettin' so everybody likes it.

Christ, these fellas been around home and then shove 'em out in a place like Stone State, well, you might better shoot 'em. Because they don't know people, they don't know what to say or what to do, or nothing.

We didn't wear uniforms at Stone, just wore regular clothes. You wasn't allowed a uniform, but the attendants wore uniforms, all dressed in white always. Dollied up, you know, Jesus, fit to kill. Thought they was the brass of the outfit. Who the hell cares about that? Clothes never made a man, they usually wrecked 'em. Went to his head, like money does. If it ain't money, it's women, and if it ain't women, it's booze. That's the way it works out. If he ain't got one habit, he's probably got four more. That's what life is made of. But what the hell they ever built Stone for, I never knew. I don't think I want to know, either.

You couldn't leave Stone if you wanted to, at any time. The big shots had to sign the OK and they wouldn't sign it. Oh, "the reason's unknown," they'd say. And, "We don't explain our circumstances. We have no time to discuss that matter," and so on, and so on, and so on, see. If you're a good man to work around, oh, Jesus, they'll hang on to you. But if you ain't no damn good, there's the door. I went down and seen 'em about twenty or thirty times about getting out and that was it. The hell with it, I says. It was the same old racket, over and over.

They shipped me to Stone State, like I said, and then they was gonna rebuild it and they had too much to do and this had to be done and they had to have room for newcomers comin' in, and oh, Jesus, then they shipped me down to River State. I was at Stone State for about six to eight, nine years. About eight years, I guess. I was up to River State about a couple years. River State is all right. Of course they was overcrowded. They had to have room for newcomers, same old stuff as it was at Stone State and same as anyplace. They didn't ask me what I wanted to do before I came here. They just up and said, "Well, you're goin' to such and such a place." I never knew, been here in all my life.

Up at River State I swept floors, dusted and polished, and one thing and another, stuff like that. It helped break down the day anyway. There are no locked wards at River State that I know of. Up there, if you talk back to the employees they probably transfer you to some other institution or somethin' like that. River State is like it always was, trouble one day to the next. Squabbles and arguments and brawls and one damn thing another.

You couldn't get out of there anytime you wanted. No, big shots, they had their way of doin' business. All the top guns there, they have the right to do anything, you have the right to do nothing. Dictatorship, see. It was a free country once, but it ain't no more. They bought and sold it, for the mighty ten dollar bill. That dictatorship they got in the United States. They don't have to go to foreign countries. Only they control it by the dollar bill. White slavery.

I don't know how they decided I should leave River State. (Al was moved to a family care home.) They come in and says, "Oh, you gotta go down. We gotta have room for a new resident comin' in. You go down with the fella by the name of Jones." Oh, Jesus, I didn't know him from a bag of apples. "Well, come on, come on, come on, let's go, let's go, let's go." That's the way they are. They didn't ask me if I wanted to go. They gotta do the talking. Didn't make any difference to me. One door is another door and another and another. That's it. That's the way it works.

This place (the family care home) is all right. You've got things to yourself, you know what I mean. And you ain't got a lot of ruckus to contend with, fights and squabbles and one thing and another. Thefts, Jesus, you name it, it's all there (at the institution). I don't know if I'll stay here very long. Oh, I might and I might not. Can't never tell. I like it better here than River State. Change of pasture they say makes fat calves. I'm glad I moved down here, hell anybody'd know that. We don't give a God damn, we've been around so many years. Another place is another place, you know. Of course the place is nice, you can't say nothin' against that, never. But what I mean is, you been around so God damn many years, you know, around people, Jesus Christ, that nothin' ain't new anymore, see. Just a goin' in one door and out the next, see, that's what he's doin'. Goddamn. The edge of life is gone, see, that's what I mean.

I'm working at a workshop now, in the mornings. I'm sewin' some cloth. That's what I'm doing. It's all right. It's a job. To me a job is another job. Just something to kill time, that's the idea of it. You don't get any money for working over there. Get a slip of paper, that's tokens. You can get a certain amount of things from the cabinet they got there, like shaving cream or cigarettes or watches; ash trays and stuff like that. Every week you get paid. I'm making quilts. Then they sell 'em anyplace they can find a buyer. It takes about twenty of 'em to build one, and it takes oh, Jesus Christ, a couple of weeks to make one. They're made damn good. Do I like sewin'? Well, it's something to break up the time, you know. Somethin' to kill the day, that's all mainly. Sewin' from the time you get in 'til you go out. Ain't a bad job. Oh, one job is another job, what difference does it make? God damn, there ain't any difference. You get just about a standard measurement of tokens. It depends how many hours you spend.

Them tokens are just like money, you can spend 'em there. The gravity of money is powerful, money's what talks and the rest walks. When a piece of paper controls life, a one dollar bill, a ten dollar bill, they make slavery out of you. You go downtown and you ain't got a ten dollar bill or a twenty in your pocket, goodbye, they don't know you. That's the idea of it. The more money you got, the more friends you'll have. We tried too many times. Money does funny things. Turns a man's conscience this or that way.

I don't know what I'll be doing. I don't know. Haven't really made up my mind yet. Oh, Jesus Christ, I don't know if I'd ever go back to Germany. I'm getting pretty old for to do anything. God damn, go back, you'd probably be nothing but a flower on the wall. One thing I do know, though, is that when you're dead, you have peace. Otherwise you never have it. That's impossible.

INFORMATION FROM AL'S CASE RECORD

Al's case record was not made directly available to me in its entirety. In order to receive the information cited here, I called River State and spoke with an administrative worker. I explained to her the kind of information I was looking for. She then consulted Al's records and relayed the information to me. This severely limited the kind and amount of information I was able to obtain.

I was told the following: according to the record, Al was born on October 11, 1912. His parents were both born in Germany. Al had thirteen siblings, two sisters and eleven brothers.

Al's father was a farmer and Al's life was spent on a farm. The family continued on the farm after the father's death in 1929. Al's father was 68 years old when he died of heart trouble. His mother died of heart trouble or a stroke, but the record does not show when she died or how old she was. After his parents' death, Al lived with his brothers up until the time that he was admitted to Stone State early in 1951. He was then 39 years old.

The record shows that Al was admitted to Stone because of epilepsy, which started when he was approximately 31 years of age. However, at another point the record states that he finished the eighth grade and was expelled from school because of seizures. Therefore, the officials are not certain when his epilepsy started.

In 1964 Al was moved from Stone State to River State, where he remained until 1976, when he was moved into a family care facility. The officials state that Al has no military background but that they believe that he got the military ideas from reading and/or watching movies. The person I spoke with at River State did not know Al's IQ, but her impression was that he was probably currently retarded because of his extensive institutionalization. However, she doubts that he had been retarded prior to being institutionalized. Al will probably live in a family care home setting for the rest of his life. He is currently working at a workshop at River State, but it is hoped that in the near future he will begin working at a sheltered workshop in the community. There are at the present no plans to move him farther in his work career.

DISCUSSION AND CONCLUSION

One might read Al's story and case record and conclude that he was suffering from delusions. There are after all many "reality disjunctures" (Pollner, 1975) between the official records and Al's story. However, it must be remembered that "in reading the autobiography, the reality of the world is not at issue. What we are concerned with is how the world is seen by the author" (Bogdan, 1977:4). I believe that the above account accurately portrays how Al sees his world.

Al's story of his life shows some confusions, but I think that most of us would have to say the same about our own. I propose that Al's life story, including his military career, is based on his life, on his observation and upon things which happened to him.

I do not propose that Al "really" was in the military. Rather, that he was in the military as he saw it. It is true that much of his information about the military probably comes from the media. In describing wars and battles he often uses phrases that are "pure media," such as "the skies were black with aircraft," "the ocean was red with bodies and blood," "the sands of Iwo Jima," and "the bloody road to Tokyo."

I think it is not too much of a leap of faith to suppose that at some point in Al's life Stone State went from "being *like* a POW camp" to *being* a POW camp. At the time Al was institutionalized there were a great many war pictures and many lively discussions of war. Even though war is seen as terrible, it is also viewed by many as glamorous. I propose that Al's war stories were a way for him to "manage his spoiled identity" (Goffman, 1963). They are also consistent with the accounts stigmatized persons tend to offer others in an effort to "pass" (Edgerton, 1967).

In looking back over the autobiography, it can be seen that Al discusses the military experiences and the institution experiences in the same way, often in the same terms. He talks about the "big brass" at the institutions and how they give all the orders and how you must take orders. He says that you can't get out of the military when and if you want to, and that the same is true for institutions. He talks about people in the military and people in institutions being creatures. I think it very plausible to argue that Al has substituted a more acceptable total institution (the military) for a less acceptable one (a state institution for the retarded) (Goffman, 1961). In taking most of the sentences or paragraphs out of context, one could not be sure whether he was talking about one of the state institutions or the military. I think that in his mind they were one and the same. Often when I asked him questions about the institution, he would answer "yes" or "no" and launch into a long discussion about some battle or other military fact.

I don't think that Al's story can, or should, be written off as a mere delusion. Many of the things he says he experienced or saw in the military might have happened to him in the institution. He discusses being given shock treatments and powerful serums or drugs in concentration camps. It is well known that both of these things happen at institutions, but one would have to see Al's record to know if this was part of his "treatment."

Even if not taken as "truth," I think that Al's story can give us some food for thought about institutions. "The way we imagine our lives is the way we are going to go on living our lives" (Hillman, 1975:146). We might question what it is about institutions or being institutionalized in a home for the retarded that makes the horrors of war a preferable alternative.

REFERENCES

Allport, Gordon. *The use of personal documents in psychological science.* New York: Social Science Research Council, Bulletin 49, 1942.

Becker, Howard. "Introduction," in Clifford Shaw, *The jack-roller.* Chicago: University of Chicago Press, 1966.

Bogdan, Robert. *Being different.* New York: John Wiley & Sons, 1974.

————. "Autobiographies as an Approach to Understanding Clients," Unpublished Paper, 1977.

Bogdan, Robert and Taylor, Steven J. *Introduction to qualitative methodology.* New York: John Wiley & Sons, 1975.

Edgerton, Robert B. *The cloak of competence: stigma in the lives of the mentally retarded.* Berkeley, Calif.: University of California Press, 1967.

Goffman, Erving. *Asylums.* Garden City, New York: Doubleday & Company, Inc., 1961.

————. *Stigma.* Englewood Cliffs, New Jersey: Prentice-Hall, 1963.

Hillman, James. "The Fiction of Case History: A Round," in James B. Wiggins, *Religion as story.* New York: Harper & Row, 1975.

Jacobs, Jerry. *Adolescent suicide.* New York: John Wiley & Sons, 1971.

Pollner, Melvin. "The Very Coinage of Your Brain: The Resolution of Reality Disjunctures," *The philosophy of the social sciences* 5:411-430, 1975.